A STUDENT'S GUIDE TO THE INTERNAL REVENUE CODE

FIFTH EDITION

LexisNexis Law School Publishing Advisory Board

A STUDENT'S GUIDE TO THE INTERNAL REVENUE CODE

FIFTH EDITION

I. Richard Gershon
Dean and Professor of Law
Charleston School of Law

Jeffrey A. Maine
Professor of Law
University of Maine School of Law

Library of Congress Cataloging-in-Publication Data

Gershon, Richard.
    A student's guide to the Internal Revenue Code / I. Richard Gershon, Jeffrey A. Maine. — 5th ed.
    p. cm.
    Includes index.
    ISBN 978-1-4224-1168-1 (softbound)
    1. Income tax—Law and legislation—United States—Outlines, syllabi, etc.
    2. Taxation—Law and Legislation—United States—Outlines, syllabi, etc. I. Maine, Jeffrey A. II. Title.
KF6369.3.G35 2007
343.7304—dc22   2007035921

Editorial Offices
744 Broad Street, Newark, NJ 07102 (973) 820-2000
201 Mission St., San Francisco, CA 94105-1831 (415) 908-3200
701 East Water Street, Charlottesville, VA 22902-7587 (434) 972-7600
www.lexis.com

For Donna:

You taught me that love cannot exist without truth,
and that truth cannot exist without love.
— IRG

For John, Richard, and Jack:

My deepest appreciation for all your support and
guidance.
— JAM

PREFACE

Taxation is a very scary subject to many law students and attorneys. One of the primary reasons for "tax phobia" is that the substantive tax laws constantly change. Thus, tax students, and tax professionals for that matter, are frustrated by the feeling that everything they learn is subject to repeal. Since much of the substantive tax law learned by a modern law student or attorney will indeed change, it is futile for students, attorneys, or accountants to memorize substantive tax law.

On the other hand, while the tax laws themselves change, the language of the Internal Revenue Code (hereinafter "the Code"), which is the source of the tax law, remains constant. Thus, a student who learns how to read the Code effectively will be able to understand each new tax reform.

The purpose of this *Student's Guide* is to help you teach yourself the language of taxation. To that end, the first part of this book (Chapters 1-3) is dedicated to a discussion of statutory organization and language. The second part of the book (Chapters 4-7) serves as an introduction to some very basic tax constants, which will affect any future legislation, and will give you a frame of reference from which to view tax law, no matter what future tax reform might bring. The third part of the *Student's Guide* (Chapter 8) teaches you how to use and research the cases, regulations and Internal Revenue proclamations that have an effect on the formation of tax law and policy. Finally, and maybe most important, the fourth part of the manual (Chapters 9 and 10) involves problems and sample exams that will test your ability to apply the language of the Internal Revenue Code. Included in this section is a suggested approach to taking an exam on Federal Income Taxation.

Appendix III and Appendix IV are new to the Fifth Edition. Appendix III contains answers to ALL sixteen problem sets included in Chapter 9. Appendix IV contains sample answers to Practice Exams #1, #2 and #3 in Chapter 10. **If you have questions about these answers, please feel free to email us at rgershon@charlestonlaw.org or jmaine@usm.maine.edu. Also, we will be happy to supply you with the sample answers to Practice Exams #4 and #5 in Chapter 10 if you email us your solutions first!** Although the Fifth Edition provides answers to many problems and practice examinations, we encourage you to work through the problems on your own before looking at our answers.

Some additional thoughts as you begin to explore the tax law: relax and enjoy! Many students make tax law more complicated than it needs to be by expecting the worst. Generally, the Code's solution to a problem is the most logical. Ask yourself what would be the common sense solution to the problem you are attacking. As you become more comfortable with the Code, you will find that the Code's solution often will be exactly the same as your common sense solution. Finally, you do not need to be a mathematical or accounting genius to excel as a tax student. If you can understand the methodology of tax, you can easily "crunch" the numbers on your pocket calculator, or your personal computer, because numbers in tax are merely placeholders. We hope that you are as pleasantly surprised by the study of this fascinating body of the law as we were.

I. Richard Gershon
Charleston School of Law
Charleston, South Carolina
March 2007

Jeffrey A. Maine
University of Maine School of Law
Portland, Maine
March 2007

ACKNOWLEDGMENTS

We wish to thank the students whom we have had the pleasure of teaching use these materials. We are particularly indebted to Professors John Cooper, Bruce Jacob, and Jason Demetris for their input and advice on earlier versions of this book. We could not have completed the Fifth Edition of *A Guide to the Internal Revenue Code* without the contribution from Julie Welch, Christine Hepler, Maureen Quinlan, and Corinne Gagnon, whose research and editorial assistance was invaluable.

Professor Gershon would like to thank his wife, Donna, and his children, Michelle, Benjamin, Claire, and Eve, for helping him understand that tax is not even close to being the most important thing in life.

Professor Maine would like to thank his co-author Richard Gershon for including him in this book. Professor Maine is indebted to John Cooper, Richard Gershon, and Jack Miller for all they have taught him about taxation, including how to make tax fun.

TABLE OF CONTENTS

Chapter 1

INTRODUCTION
(Just What Is This Thing Called the Internal Revenue Code?)

§ 1.01 THE CODE IS THE LAW

The Sixteenth Amendment to the Constitution of the United States provides that "Congress shall have power to lay and collect taxes on incomes, from whatever source derived, without apportionment among the several States, and without regard to any census or enumeration."[1] Even though the Sixteenth Amendment faces periodic challenges from tax protesters concerning the propriety of its ratification,[2] there can be no *reasonable* question about its validity.[3] Consequently, there can be no *reasonable* question about Congress's authority to tax income from whatever source derived.

On the other hand, there is nothing in the Constitution that grants the judiciary, the Treasury Department, the Internal Revenue Service, or even tax professors the power to tax income from whatever source derived. Therefore, the primary focus of your study of the law of federal income taxation must be the federal statutes adopted by Congress. You can find the federal statutes pertaining to income taxation in Title 26 of the United States Code, which is affectionately known as the Internal Revenue Code. In a very real sense, the Internal Revenue Code (hereinafter "the Code") is the law of federal income taxation.

§ 1.02 A BRIEF HISTORY OF THE CODE

The Income Tax of 1913, which was adopted shortly after the ratification of the Sixteenth Amendment, encompassed only fourteen pages[4] of statutes. Now, that was true tax simplicity! As you must realize from looking through your copy of the Internal Revenue Code of 1986, there has been a tremendous amount of tax legislation since 1913. In fact, Congress added so much to the body of tax law between 1913 and 1939 that it was necessary to assemble all of the revenue statutes, including the income tax statutes, into one body known as the Internal Revenue Code of 1939.[5]

The 1939 Code sufficed for about fifteen years, until it was replaced with a new, improved, and no doubt simplified version known as the Internal Revenue Code of 1954.[6] The 1954

---

[1] U.S. Const. amend. XVI. The Sixteenth Amendment was ratified in 1913. While Article I, section 8, clause 1 of the United States Constitution grants Congress the power to levy taxes, the Sixteenth Amendment allows Congress to levy a direct tax without apportionment. In *Pollock v. Farmer's Loan & Trust Co.,* 157 U.S. 429 (1895), the United States Supreme Court had held that the Income Tax of 1894 was unconstitutional, because it was a direct tax without apportionment among the states. The Sixteenth Amendment rectified that problem.

[2] *See, e.g.,* U.S. v. Thomas, 788 F.2d 1250 (7th Cir. 1986); Sisk v. Commissioner, 791 F.2d 58 (6th Cir. 1986). The tax protesters in both *Thomas* and *Sisk* argued that the ratification of the Sixteenth Amendment was invalid, because there were spelling or typographical errors in the instruments of ratification of several of the states adopting the amendment. It is amazing that taxpayers have persisted in making such ridiculous challenges for more than ninety years. In fact, there have been several recent memoranda decisions rendered by the United States Tax Court on this issue, including the 1993 case of *Zyglis v. CIR,* 66 T.C.M (CCH) 296, T.C.M (P-H) 93-341.

[3] *See, e.g.,* U.S. v. Burton, 575 F. Supp. 1320 (E.D. Tex. 1983), *rev'd on other grounds,* 737 F.2d 439 (5th Cir. 1984).

[4] 38 Stat. 166-180 (1913).

[5] The Code was officially adopted on February 10, 1939.

[6] P.L. 591, enacted August 16, 1954, during the Second Session of the 83rd Congress. See I.R.C. §§ 7851 and 7852, which expressly repealed the 1939 Code.

Code remained virtually unmodified until 1969, when it was amended by the 1969 Tax Reform Act.[7] It seemed, at the time, that major revisions in tax law would take place approximately every fifteen years, which was not overly burdensome on tax practitioners, tax students, or tax professors.

Unfortunately, that pattern would not last. The next significant revision was the Tax Reform Act of 1976.[8] Then things really started to happen. Another massive reform took place in 1981, with the Economic Recovery Tax Act (ERTA) of 1981.[9] Then came the Tax Equity and Fiscal Responsibility Act (TEFRA) of 1982,[10] and the Deficit Reduction Act (DEFRA) of 1984.[11] Congress seemed destined to drive tax students over the edge with acronyms, if not with constant changes in the tax law.

Due to public outcry over the complexity of the federal income tax, Congress promised to bring simplicity and fairness to tax legislation. Instead, it enacted the Tax Reform Act of 1986, which, among other things, created the Internal Revenue Code of 1986.[12] This was supposed to be the Tax Reform Act to end all tax reform. Yet Congress has continued to amend the Code on a regular basis since 1986, including some fairly major changes in recent years.

Accordingly, there is very little that can be gained from memorizing the current state of the tax laws, which will probably change before you graduate, and will certainly change several times while you are in practice. Furthermore, there is even less to be gained by reading hornbooks which tell you what the law was when those hornbooks were written. Instead, you must learn how to read the Internal Revenue Code to be able to determine the current state of the tax law at any time.

Fortunately, while the substantive tax laws constantly change, the language used to express those laws through the Internal Revenue Code has remained the same. Thus, if you learn the language of the Code, you will always be able to apply the tax laws, no matter how much they may change in the future.

That is why the primary purpose of this *Student's Guide* is to help you to learn how to read and employ the provisions of the Code for yourself. After all, it is much better for you to be able to understand the law itself than for you to read what someone else thinks the law says.

In addition to those sections that teach you how to comprehend the Code, Chapter 6 of the *Student's Guide* will introduce you to some of the principles of federal taxation that never change. Chapters 7 and 8 discuss the important judicial and administrative declarations (most notably tax cases, regulations and Revenue Rulings), which interpret the provisions of the Code, and the final chapters of this work are dedicated to application of the tax law through problems and examinations.

---

[7] P.L. 91-172.

[8] P.L. 94-455.

[9] P.L. 97-34.

[10] P.L. 97-248.

[11] P.L. 98-369.

[12] P.L. 99-514.

Chapter 2

ORGANIZATION OF THE CODE
(There Is a Method to This Madness)

§ 2.01 THE CODE MENU

If you have ever used a computer, you know that each program is capable of performing only those functions indicated by the program menu. However, even if you have not used a computer, you have probably ordered food from a restaurant menu. If you have used either type of menu, you have acquired the technical skills necessary for using the Internal Revenue Code. After all, the Code is arranged in a logical and orderly fashion, much like a computer program or a restaurant bill of fare. If you keep this simple concept in mind as you approach your study of tax, you will never seek a deduction provision from an inclusion section, just as you would never order dessert from the entrees.

This chapter discusses the internal organization of the Code, which is simply the Code's menu. It is important for you to be familiar with the manner in which the Code is arranged because the language of most Code sections assumes a working knowledge of the Code structure.

The final part of this chapter, "Anatomy of a Code Section," examines the operation of a single Code section. This section will demonstrate that each Code section has an internal organization of its own. If you understand the relationship between the various subsections and paragraphs of a particular section, you will be well on your way to using the Code in an efficient and logical manner.

§ 2.02 CHAPTERS, SUBCHAPTERS, PARTS AND SUBPARTS

[In reading the following sections, you should skim through the Code, examining the subdivisions it contains.]

The Code is arranged by classifications that range from the broad and general to the specific and narrow. The entire Code includes income taxes, social security, excise taxes, estate and gift taxes and tax procedure. However, we are primarily concerned with the study of income taxation, even though the language of the Code is basically the same for all of the types of taxation it controls. The income tax provisions fall under Subtitle A of the Code.

Subtitle A embraces a tremendous volume of tax law. To be specific, Subtitle A encompasses six chapters. Fortunately, we are concerned only with Chapter 1 of Subtitle A, which deals with normal taxes and surtaxes. You will notice that as we move from general to specific in the Code, we increase the number of applicable subdivisions. Therefore, you should not be surprised that Chapter 1 of Subtitle A has no fewer than twenty-two subchapters (Subchapters A–V). In turn, each of these subchapters is divided into parts, each of the parts is divided into subparts, and finally each of the subparts is divided into sections. These divisions are important because many Code sections limit their own applicability to a particular part, subpart, or chapter. Thus, you should always be aware of where you are in the Code. For example, § 61 can be found in Subtitle A, Chapter 1, Subchapter B (Computation of Taxable Income), Part I (Definition of Gross Income, Adjusted Gross Income, Taxable Income, etc.). Subchapter headings, like "Computation of Taxable Income," will be very helpful as you determine the function of a particular section. That is, you can see from the heading that § 61 must give some sort of definition related to income for purposes of computing the tax. In fact, § 61 defines gross income.

As an aid to your understanding of the importance of the various subchapters, parts, and subparts under the Income Tax Provisions (Subtitle A, Chapter 1), you should look through the Code and explore the different topics. The following paragraphs use some specific subchapters of Subtitle A, Chapter 1 as examples to help you in your initial exploration of the Code.

[1] Calculating the Tax

Subchapter A of Chapter 1 deals with the determination of tax liability. While the sections used to calculate a person's or a corporation's liability are the first to appear in the Code (§§ 1-59A), they are actually the last step in your journey. After all, you cannot compute a tax liability without first knowing what types of items are taxable or deductible. These questions of taxability and deductibility, among others, must be answered by other sections of the Code. If you try to discover a tax deduction in a subchapter dealing with calculating the tax, you are ordering from the wrong part of the menu! The following paragraphs discuss how to find the answers to specific questions in the Code.

[2] Definitions

One of the most important subchapters in the Code, and one that you will become intimately acquainted with in your tax course, is Subchapter B (Computation of Taxable Income). Notice that you cannot calculate the tax liability under Subchapter A until you determine how much taxable income a taxpayer has under Subchapter B. However, the process of discerning how much taxable income the taxpayer has is a rather complex one. To calculate taxable income we need to know how much total or gross income a person had. We must be sure to exclude from that person's income any non-taxable items, and we must deduct from income any expenses or losses allowed by the Code. Therefore, Subchapter B provides us with parts defining income and delineating the items we can exclude from income or should deduct from income.

Part I of Subchapter B provides us with definitions that are essential to the process of calculating taxable income. After all, you cannot possibly expect to calculate taxable income without first knowing what the Code means by the phrase "taxable income." The definition sections under Subchapter B, Part I are §§ 61-66. You should pay special attention to §§ 61-63, which are at the heart of every Federal Income Tax course. Notice how § 63 defines taxable income by reference to the taxpayer's gross income and deductions. Thus, the definition of taxable income is inexorably intertwined with the definition of gross income under § 61. You will not find these definitions anywhere else in the Code. The specific applications of these definition sections will be explained in Chapter 6 of this *Student Guide*, which deals with tax constants. For right now, it is sufficient that you know where to find these sections and know what purpose they serve in the overall scheme of the Code.

The paragraphs that follow focus on inclusions, exclusions and deductions, which can also be found in Subchapter B.

[3] Inclusions

While § 61 provides that gross income includes income from whatever source derived, there are certain items of income that Congress has decided to enumerate specifically as inclusions in gross income. Thus, Part II of Subchapter B sets forth those sections that are called inclusion provisions.

Any time you are referred to a Code section between § 71 and § 90 inclusive, you know that you are dealing with a provision requiring inclusion in gross income. Notice that each inclusion provision is characterized by the language "gross income shall include . . .".

[4] Exclusions

Just as Congress has determined that certain items should be specifically included in gross income, it has concluded that certain accessions to wealth should be specifically excluded from the gross income calculation. Once an item is excluded from gross income, it can never be subject to tax, since taxable income is defined by reference to gross income (§§ 61 and 63), and the tax liability is assessed upon taxable income (§ 1).

Thus, by providing exclusion provisions, Congress has made a policy decision that certain items should be beyond the rather extensive reach of the Internal Revenue Service. The exclusion provisions are found in Part III of Subchapter B. More specifically, they are created by §§ 101 to 139A, inclusive. Not surprisingly, all exclusion provisions are characterized by the language "gross income does not include . . .".

You can understand some of the policy reasons behind exclusions simply by looking at the section headings. For example, § 101 provides that death benefits, such as life insurance proceeds, are excluded from gross income. As you become increasingly familiar with the Code, you will notice that there are many special provisions relating to the receipt of property upon the death of another.[1] You might say that Congress had adopted the "suffered enough" principle for property acquired from a decedent. That is, while Congress could tax the receipt of such property, it has made a conscious decision that the death of a loved one is bad enough for a taxpayer to face, without adding the burden of the imposition of an income tax on the receipt of the loved one's property. Without specific exclusion provisions like § 101, items such as life insurance proceeds and death benefits would be includible accessions to wealth under § 61.

[5] Deductions

Deductions found in Subchapter B, Parts VI and VII constitute another vital category of Code sections. Only the Code sections in these two parts create tax deductions for an individual taxpayer.[2] More specifically, the Code sections that provide for deductions are §§ 161 and 211. Deductions are quite different from exclusions, and you must be careful not to confuse the two concepts. Exclusions are items of wealth that are not taxed. On the other hand, deductions are expenses or losses incurred by a taxpayer that can be used to reduce the ultimate amount of the taxpayer's taxable income.

In addition, you should notice that there are really two types of deductions. The first type involves the philosophy that a taxpayer should only be taxed on his or her net income. It is a generally accepted truth that in business a person must usually spend money to make money. For example, if you owned a business that produced horror movies (e.g., "The Attack of the Internal Revenue Monster"), you might earn $500 from the sale of my products. However, if you spend $200 on employee salaries and $100 on advertising to promote your films, you would really have a profit of only $200 ($500 earnings less $300 in expenses). Thus, you should only have to pay a tax on your $200 profit. Congress recognizes that situations such as your movie business require that you be allowed to subtract from your earnings the costs related to creating those earnings; that is why we have the deductions that relate to expenses incurred in the production of income.

---

[1] *See, e.g.,* §§ 102, 1014.

[2] Part VIII of Subchapter B contain provisions dealing with corporate tax deductions.

The second type of deductions are those which relate to individual expenditures. Such deductions encompass such items as the expenses for the medical care of the taxpayer (§ 213). These deductions are purely personal in nature. They arise solely as a result of Congressional largesse, and are subject to frequent modification and even repeal. For example, the provision under § 163 that allows for a deduction for interest paid on funds borrowed for consumer goods (*e.g.*, your personal car) was greatly modified by the Tax Reform Act of 1986. Since 1991 there has been no deduction allowed for most types of consumer interest.[3]

It should be noted that, in addition to the deduction provisions, Subchapter B contains sections that specifically *prevent* certain expenses and losses from being deductible. Part IX of Subchapter B (§§ 261 through 280H) contains the menu for disallowance provisions.

The language common to deduction provisions is "there shall be allowed as a deduction in computing taxable income . . .". Not surprisingly, the language common to disallowance provisions is "no deduction shall be allowed for . . .".

[6] Basis and Determination of Gain or Loss

If you buy property for $10 and sell it for $15, it is easy to see that you have an economic gain of $5. Your $5 gain will most likely be included as gross income, which will subject you to tax. This simple and common sense principle is the underlying theory behind Subchapter O (Gain or Loss on Disposition of Property). Subchapter O covers the full range of what can happen whenever a taxpayer purchases or disposes of property. Notice that a taxpayer can dispose of property by giving it away, exchanging it for other property, destroying it, or losing it; sales, therefore, are not the only type of transaction covered by the term "disposition."

Part I of Subchapter O, which includes only § 1001, tells you how to compute gain or loss. Fortunately, taxpayers are not taxed on the return of their investment in the property. A taxpayer's investment, referred to in the Code as "basis," is determined by Part II of Subchapter O (§§ 1011-1023). It is important to note that § 1001 does nothing more than determine the amount of a gain or a loss. Since it is not an inclusion provision, it cannot cause gain to be included in gross income. Likewise, since it is not a deduction provision, it cannot allow a deduction for any loss calculated under its direction. Deductions and inclusions are items found in other portions of the Code menu. (For a complete discussion of basis, realization of gain, and recognition of gain, see Chapter 6.)

[7] Credits

Within the confines of Part IV of Subchapter A are creatures known as "credits." Credits dwell in §§ 21 through 54, and come in all shapes and sizes. The most important aspect of a credit is how it is applied to reduce a taxpayer's tax liability. Unlike deductions, which reduce taxable income *before* the application of the tax rates, credits are applied directly against the tax owed by the taxpayer. Thus, a taxpayer owing $30 in tax but having a $25 tax credit will need to pay only $5 to the government; $1 of credit is truly $1 of tax savings.

On the other hand, deductions save a taxpayer only an amount equal to the deduction multiplied by the taxpayer's top tax bracket. That is, $1 of gross income taxed at a rate of 28% would create a tax liability of 28 cents. If a taxpayer had a $1 deduction in addition to his income, he would have no taxable income ($1 gross income less $1 deduction). But note that the taxpayer would have only paid 28 cents in tax without the deduction. Therefore,

---

[3] I.R.C. § 163(h).

the $1 deduction only saved the taxpayer 28 cents, while $1 in credit could offset equally $1 in tax owed.

[8]   Other Subchapters and Parts

As you advance in your study of the Code, you will have the opportunity to explore some very specialized subdivisions of the Code. We have, therefore, taken this opportunity to provide you with a brief "road map" of some of the subchapters and parts you are likely to encounter along the way.

[a]   Corporate Tax

The corporate tax provisions are primarily covered by Subchapter C, which contains §§ 301 through 385. Subchapter C provides for the tax treatment for every facet of a corporation's life from its formation to its liquidation.

[b]   Partnership Tax

The tax consequences to partners are extensively covered by Subchapter K. Interestingly enough, the partnership tax provisions are organized in much the same fashion as the corporate tax provisions. The partnership provisions are §§ 701 through 777.

[c]   Trusts and Estates

Trusts and estates are taxable entities, much like the corporations covered by Subchapter C. You can find the provisions relating to trusts and estates under Subchapter J (§§ 641-692).

[d]   S Corporations

Finally, some corporations qualify for special treatment under the Code. Such corporations are treated essentially as partnerships in that they are not subject to tax. Instead, their income is taxed directly to their shareholders. To achieve this special status, a corporation must meet the requirements set out in Subchapter S (hence the name "S" Corporation). Subchapter S encompasses §§ 1361 through 1379.

§ 2.03   ANATOMY OF A CODE SECTION

As we have seen from §§ 2.01 and 2.02 of this chapter, the Internal Revenue Code is divided into Subtitles, Chapters, Subchapters, Parts, Subparts, and Sections. In much the same way, the sections of the Code are broken into subsections, paragraphs, subparagraphs, sentences, and clauses. What follows is an illustration of the anatomy of a Code section. For this purpose, we have chosen to dissect § 71, because that section is a good example of a moderately complex provision. After you have studied this illustration, you should try to perform similar dissections on other Code provisions. Do not, however, try this out on your little brothers or sisters at home![4]

---

[4] Subsections are denoted by lowercase letters. (*e.g.*, (a) (b), (c)). Paragraphs are denoted by Arabic numbers (*e.g.*, (1), (2), (3)). Subparagraphs are indicated by uppercase letters (*e.g.*, (A), (B), (C)). Sentences are indicated by lowercase Roman numerals (*e.g.*, (i), (ii), (iii), (iv)). Clauses are denoted by large Roman numerals (*e.g.*, I, II, III). You can find examples of clauses in § 72 (*e.g.*, § 72(e)(5)(D)(ii)(I)). "Flush" language: sometimes there is no letter or number next to the language in the Code. Instead, this language is flush against the margin. Thus, we call such a provision the flush language.

SEC. 71. ALIMONY AND SEPARATE MAINTENANCE PAYMENTS.

[Sec. 71(a)]

[SUBSECTION]

(a) GENERAL RULE.—Gross income includes amounts received as alimony or separate maintenance payments.

[Sec. 71(b)]

(b) ALIMONY OR SEPARATE MAINTENANCE PAYMENTS DEFINED.—For purposes of this section—

[PARAGRAPH]

(1) IN GENERAL.—The term "alimony or separate maintenance payment" means any payment in cash if—

(A) such payment is received by (or on behalf of) a spouse under a divorce or separation instrument,

(B) the divorce or separation instrument does not designate such payment as a payment which is not includible in gross income under this section and not allowable as a deduction under section 215,

(C) in the case of an individual legally separated from his spouse under a decree of divorce of separate maintenance, the payee spouse and the payor spouse are not members of the same household at the time such payment is made, and

(D) there is no liability to make any such payment for any period after the death of the payee spouse and there is no liability to make any payment (in cash or property) as a substitute for such payments after the death of the payee spouse.

(2) DIVORCE OR SEPARATION INSTRUMENT.—The term "divorce or separation instrument" means—

(A) a decree of divorce or separate maintenance or a written instrument incident to such a decree,

(B) a written separation agreement, or

(C) a decree (not described in subparagraph (A)) requiring a spouse to make payments for the support or maintenance of the other spouse.

[Sec. 71(c)]

(c) PAYMENTS TO SUPPORT CHILDREN.—

(1) IN GENERAL.—Subsection (a) shall not apply to that part of any payment which the terms of the divorce or separation instrument fix (in terms of an amount of money or a part of the payment) as a sum which is payable for the support of children of the payor spouse.

(2) TREATMENT OF CERTAIN REDUCTIONS RELATED TO CONTINGENCIES INVOLVING CHILD.—For purposes of paragraph (1), if any amount specified in the instrument will be reduced—

[SUBPARAGRAPH]

(A) on the happening of a contingency specified in the instrument relating to a child (such as attaining a specified age, marrying, dying, leaving school, or a similar contingency), or

(B) at a time which can clearly be associated with a contingency of a kind specified in subparagraph (A).

[FLUSH LANGUAGE]

an amount equal to the amount of such reduction will be treated as an amount fixed as payable for the support of children of the payor spouse.

(3) SPECIAL RULE WHERE PAYMENT IS LESS THAN AMOUNT SPECIFIED IN INSTRUMENT.—For purposes of this subsection, if any payment is less than the amount specified in the instrument, then so much of such payment as does not exceed the sum payable for support shall be considered a payment for such support.

As seen in § 71(c), the flush language is separated from subparagraph (B) of paragraph (2) by a full line of space. Furthermore, while subparagraph (B) is indented, the flush language begins at the same margin as subsection (c). Thus, the flush language applies to the entire subsection (c), not just to subparagraph (B). It is important to notice the degree of indentation of the flush language, because the indentation indicates which portions of the section will be controlled by the flush language. Therefore, if the flush language in § 71 began at the same margin as paragraph (2), rather than the margin of subsection (c), it would only control paragraph (2) and any subparagraphs thereunder.

You should notice several things about the above illustration, or any Code section you study, for that matter. First, you can see that subsection (a) provides a general rule that will control the section. There will generally be a subsection or subsections, which define the terms involved in the application of the section. In the case of § 71, subsection (b) gives those definitions. You will notice that subsection (b) specifically limits its scope to defining alimony "for the purposes of this section." Thus, there could conceivably be a different definition of alimony somewhere else in the Code. If, on the other hand, a subsection says "for purposes of this subchapter," its scope is much broader, and will apply to all sections within the given subchapter.

Another thing you should notice is that § 71 makes reference to § 215. Whenever one Code section makes reference to another Code section in this way, it is a shorthand way of incorporating the language of that other section. Thus, for example, when § 71(b)(2)(C) says "a decree (not described in subparagraph (A))," it is actually saying "a decree (not a decree of divorce or separate maintenance or a written instrument incident to such a decree)."

Chapter 3
CODE MATHEMATICS

§ 3.01   CODE MATHEMATICS

Not surprisingly, much of the fear of the study of taxation stems from the realization that taxation inherently involves mathematics. But you might be surprised to learn that the math used in tax is actually quite simple, once you learn the language of the Code. For example, the calculations most often required by the Code are easy addition and subtraction. Even the most difficult calculations that you will have to make are really just simple ratios that can be derived by using common sense. The trick is really to learn how, and when, the Code tells you to add, subtract, multiply, and divide.

Therefore, this chapter is designed to help you overcome your fear of mathematics as applied to the laws of taxation by familiarizing you with the language used by the Code to designate math functions. You will find that there are certain terms and phrases in the Code that are really mathematical operands, just like the plus sign (+) or the minus sign (−).

§ 3.02   THE CODE MATHEMATICAL FUNCTIONS

The following sections deal with the math functions used consistently throughout the Code. Because Congress uses words to stand for math symbols when writing the Internal Revenue Code, you must reconvert those words to symbols, in order to make required calculations. Unlike the substantive law of tax, the language used to indicate Code math has not changed. Therefore, once you have mastered Code math, you have done so forever, no matter what legislative changes take place in the future.

[1]   Addition: "The Sum of . . . Plus"

The Code tells you to perform math functions in a very specific way. In the case of addition, anytime you see the words "the sum of . . . plus" you know that the Code is telling you to add. It is very important that you remember that only those exact words give rise to addition, because a common student error is to misinterpret the word "and" as a signal for addition. In fact, the word "and" operates to require that both parts of a specific test be met in order for a Code section to apply. (See the discussion on Conjunctive vs. Disjunctive in § 4.03.)

For an example of a section requiring Code addition, look at § 1001(b). Section 1001 deals with the determination of gains and losses from sales and other dispositions of property. (Notice that this section does not indicate whether gains should be included in gross income. That question is answered by other sections of the Code, as we discussed in Chapter Two. The sole purpose of § 1001 is computation of gain or loss.) Section 1001(b) tells you how to compute the amount realized from the sale or exchange of property: *the sum of* any money received *plus* the fair market value of the property (other than money) received.[1]

Now, let us use some numbers as illustrations. Say that you sold a used copy of the Uniform Commercial Code (which is not to be confused with "The Code," which is, of course,

---

[1] Emphasis supplied.

the Internal Revenue Code). What would be your amount realized if you sold your UCC for $1 in cash and a contracts outline worth $2? The Code dictates that your amount realized is equal to the sum of $1 (the cash that you received) plus $2 (the fair market value of the property, other than cash, that you received). Therefore, you realized $3.

Skeptics might argue that the numbers used in the above illustration were overly simplistic, but the important thing to remember is that, as long as you know the amount of cash and the value of the property you received, all you need to do is simple addition to determine the amount realized.

As you study the Code, you will notice that many of its sections require addition. For examples of such sections, you might wish to look at §§ 1(g)(1)(B) and 165(h)(2)(A).

[2]   Subtraction: "The Excess of . . . Over"

Like addition, there are many times when the Code requires you to perform subtraction. The words that alert you that it is time to pull out your calculator and press the minus sign are "the excess of . . . over." An example of Code subtraction can be found in § 1001(a), which provides that the gain realized from the sale or other disposition of property shall be *the excess of* the amount realized therefrom *over* the adjusted basis.[2] Therefore, § 1001 tells you that to compute the gain from a disposition of property, you must subtract the basis of the property from the amount realized. Even if you do not know what basis and amount realized are at this point in your study of taxation, you can understand how these two concepts (see Chapter Six) relate in the determination of gain.

At this point, you might wonder why the Code does not simply say to subtract adjusted basis from amount realized when you determine gain realized. The answer to that question is a very important one. The Code is only concerned with positive numbers. Thus, it requires you to compute the excess of amount realized over adjusted basis. The following illustration will help clarify the difference.

Let us return to the sale of your used UCC, which we used to illustrate Code addition. As you will recall, we determined that your amount realized from that sale was $3. Now let us assume that you had an adjusted basis of $5 in the UCC at the time of the sale. If § 1001(a) simply required you to subtract adjusted basis from amount realized, in order to determine gain, you would have a gain of negative $2 (derived when you subtract your $5 basis from your $3 amount realized).

Of course, it is not very logical that you would have a gain of a negative amount. That is why the Code defines gain as the excess of amount realized over adjusted basis. In our illustration, since $3 does not exceed $5, the excess of $3 over $5 is zero. Therefore, the gain realized from the sale of the UCC was zero, not negative $2. Thus, any time the Code subtraction yields a negative number, your answer will be zero, because there is no "excess of . . . over . . . ." In fact, you might find it helpful to modify the Code subtraction function so that it reads: the excess [IF ANY][3] of . . . over . . . .

Some other Code sections that require subtraction are: §§ 1(g)(3)(A), 163(d)(4)(A) and 1212(b)(1). You might wish to plug some numbers into these sections, just to see how the Code subtraction of taking only the excess of one tax component over another differs from pure subtraction. If you remember that your choices in Code subtraction are either a positive result or zero, you should have no problem in applying Code subtraction as you learn the substantive provisions.

---

[2] Emphasis supplied.

[3] In fact, Congress has supplied the phrase "if any" as a parenthetical in some Code sections. *See, e.g.*, § 71(f)(3), (4).

[3] Multiplication: "Multiplied By"

Perhaps the most obvious of the Code functions you will encounter is multiplication. This is because the Code, in a rare display of common English usage, straightforwardly says "multiplied by" whenever it requires multiplication. You might wish to look at §§ 25A(h)(1)(A) and 132(f)(6).

In addition to the "multiplied by" function, the Code sometimes requires you to take a percentage of something in order to apply a particular section. Section 170(b)(1)(B), for example, which deals with the charitable contributions deduction, requires such a computation. If you can work a calculator, you can perform the math necessary to make the computations involved in sections like § 170.

[4] The Code Ratio

Without question, the Code function that gives students the most trouble is something we affectionately call the "Code Ratio." Ironically, the Code Ratio is derived by translating common sense into the language of mathematics, and it is actually very easy to apply. Of course, in order to apply it, you must first recognize it.

Whenever you see the language "an amount which bears the same ratio to . . . as . . . bears to . . ." you will know that you are dealing with the infamous Code Ratio. The best way to examine the ratio is in the context of an actual Code provision. We have chosen § 72(b) for that purpose, because it deals with the exclusion ratio for annuities, which is generally the first Code ratio encountered by a tax student.

Section 72(b) provides "[g]ross income does not include that part of any *amount* received as an annuity, endowment, or life insurance contract *which bears the same ratio to* such amount *as* the investment in the contract bears to the expected return under the contract."[4]

While this provision might appear to be tremendously complex, it can easily be simplified in one of two ways.

The first way to simplify the Code Ratio is to understand in words what the Code is asking you to do with numbers. In the case of § 72, that requires some discussion of the taxation of annuities. Generally speaking, an annuity is a contract in which you pay some money now for the right to receive yearly payments in the future. For example, say you paid $1000 today for the right to receive $150 a year, for the rest of your life, with payments starting on your 65th birthday. Assume further that the average life expectancy is 75 years. Thus, when you purchased your contract, you probably expected to receive your annuity for 10 years. In purely financial terms, you paid $1000 today, hoping that you would receive $1500, or more, in the future, depending upon how long you actually lived. If you lived to 75, you would, therefore, expect a $500 profit on your investment.

The question is, how does the Code tax such a profit? After all, you should expect to get your $1000 investment back tax-free since the payment was made with post-tax dollars (see the discussion in Chapter 6). Since you will be receiving $150 per year, it will take you just a little under seven years to actually recoup your investment. On the other hand, the government will certainly want to tax you on your profit, and will want to do so as quickly as possible. In essence, you would like to wait until you have had all of your investment returns before you have to pay any tax, and the government would like to tax you on the profit first, while giving you your tax-free return of investment later. Interestingly enough, the Code requires a compromise between these two positions; it mandates that each payment be considered in part a return of investment, and in part a taxable accession to wealth, *i.e.*,

---

[4] Emphasis supplied.

taxable income. How much of an annuity payment should be treated as return of investment, and how much should be considered gross income, is really a matter of common sense. Since $1000 of the $1500 total you expect to receive is return of investment, ($1000/$1500) of each $150 payment should be return of investment, as well. Therefore ($1000/$1500), or (2/3), of each payment should be tax-free.

That is exactly what § 72(b) requires. It tells you to exclude from gross income the amount which bears the same ratio to the annuity payment you received as your investment bears to your total expected return. Using our example, the amount excluded from each annuity payment should bear the same ratio to the $150 annuity payment as your $1000 investment bears to your expected return of $1500. Expressed as a mathematical ratio, you would then have the following:

(Amount excluded/each payment) = (investment/total expected return)
or
(Amount excluded/$150) = ($1000/$1500)

All of which brings us to the second method of simplifying the Code Ratio. This method can be used even if you do not understand the underlying logic behind the ratio itself. In fact, all you need to be able to do to simplify the Code Ratio anytime it appears in the Code is to plug in the numbers. This is true because you will always know three of the four components involved in the application of a given ratio. For example, in the case of an annuity you will know what your investment is, what your expected return will be,[5] and the amount of each individual payment. The only unknown is the amount you can exclude from each payment. Returning to the numbers we used in our example, we can simplify the ratio as follows: First, we can multiply both sides of the equation by 150, which is the number being divided into the unknown.

150 × (amount excluded/150) = 150 × (1000/1500)

Next, we can simplify the equation, since 150 times the amount excluded divided by 150 must yield the amount excluded.

Amount excluded = 150 × (1000/1500)

Then, returning the ratio to words, you have an equation that will work anytime you wish to compute the exclusion ratio of § 72(b).

Amount excluded = (payment) × (investment/expected return)

Even if you are not comfortable with the algebra used to reach the above result, you can see that the result of that algebra is an equation that is very easy to apply. The same result can be obtained whenever you encounter the Code Ratio. Since the Code always expresses its ratio as "an amount which bears the same ratio to . . . as . . . ," you can express it as follows: the amount you are solving for (call it X) will bear the same ratio (fraction) to A as B (numerator) bears to C (denominator). Notice that all we have done is insert the letters A, B, and C where the blanks were before. You can then apply the ratio in its simplified form:

---

[5] Treas. Reg. § 1.72-5 defines expected return as the total annuity payments multiplied by the taxpayer's life expectancy as determined by reference to Treas. Reg. § 1.72-9, Table I. In essence, expected return is the amount the taxpayer would receive from the annuity if he survived for exactly the number of years specified in Table I.

X = (A)(B/C)
or, in words, X equals A times B divided by C

Remember, you will always know what A, B, and C will be. In § 72(b), A was the payment, B was the investment in the annuity, and C was the expected return.

> **PROBLEM 3:**[6] **Look at §§ 1011(b) and 1015(d)(6). How would you set up the ratios required by those sections? You do not need to know the meaning of the components of the ratios in order to set them up. However, when you learn the terminology used in these sections, you should think about the purpose of the ratio as applied to each section. Also, practice using some numbers in the ratios you have created. It really does not matter if the numbers you use are realistic, because numbers are simply placeholders. What is important is your ability to apply the Code language properly and consistently. For example, assume that you have met with Mr. Bill Able-hours, who is your firm's best client. He informs you that he received a gift of property worth $150,000 from his sister. He further instructs you that his sister had a basis of $100,000 in the property and that she paid $3,000 in gift taxes on the transfer. Can you tell Mr. Ablehours what his basis in the property will be under §§ 1015(a) and (d)(6)? [Hint: the total gift is $150,000. The net appreciation is $50,000 (the difference between the fair market value and the adjusted basis of the gift).]**

[5] "The Lesser (Greater) of"

The final mathematical function used by the Internal Revenue Code involves the use of a simple comparative. There are sections of the Code that require you to compare two or more numbers and to apply either the lesser (sometimes expressed as "the lower") or the greater of them. The Code uses the lesser/greater function as a limiting device. For example, look at § 1211(b). In general, that section allows taxpayers to take capital losses only to the extent of capital gains plus the lesser of $3000 or the excess of capital losses over capital gains. The effect of such a limitation is that a taxpayer will never be allowed to take more than $3000 in excess capital losses, because if the taxpayer's excess capital losses are greater than $3000, he will only be allowed $3000 (the lesser of the two). Thus, the comparative language "the lesser of" always establishes an absolute maximum amount.

On the other hand, as you might expect, whenever the Code uses the comparative language "the greater of" it always establishes an absolute minimum amount. For example, look at § 1(g)(1). It provides that a child will be taxed at her parents' rates on a portion of the child's unearned income. This, of course, assumes that the parent's tax bracket will be higher than the child's. There could, however, be cases in which the child's bracket is actually higher than the parent's. Thus, § 1(g)(1) provides that the tax imposed upon the child's unearned income will be "the greater of" the tax the child would have paid without the application of § 1(g), or the child's tax as recalculated, taking into account the application of § 1(g). By establishing an absolute minimum, which is the amount the child would have paid had there been no § 1(g) in the first place, the comparative function "the greater of" prevents taxpayers from using § 1(g) to lower the child's tax liability.

---

[6] The answers to problems presented at various points in this *Student's Guide* are provided in Appendix II.

Chapter 4
SOME IMPORTANT CODE VOCABULARY

§ 4.01 SOME EXPLANATORY REMARKS

The Internal Revenue Code is written in a language very similar to English. In fact, this similarity often gives tax students the greatest difficulty because each word used in the Code has its own precise meaning, even though that same word could have several meanings in English. Furthermore, there are many phrases used in the Code that require very specific interpretations. Thus, in order for you to use and understand the Internal Revenue Code, you must first learn some of its important vocabulary.

As you read this chapter, remember that every word and every phrase of the Code has a purpose. Congress does not use transitional phrases or flowery prose in writing the Code. Federal tax legislation is drafted for various reasons (*e.g.*, to raise revenue or promote social welfare);[1] it is not drafted for our reading pleasure. Of course, there are some hardened tax enthusiasts (generally referred to as "tax jocks" or "codeheads") who waterproof their Codes so that they can read them in the shower, but their numbers are (thankfully) few.

In any event, the next section of this chapter discusses how to resolve conflicts between Code sections which seem to require inconsistent results, while the remainder of the chapter introduces you to specific words and phrases you will need to know to speak the language of tax.

§ 4.02 GENERAL LANGUAGE VS. SPECIFIC LANGUAGE

Section 61 of the Code defines gross income as "income from whatever source derived." Many students have commented that defining gross income as income is like describing the flavor of vanilla as vanilla tasting. It is, therefore, helpful to know that, for tax purposes, income means any increase in or accession to wealth.[2]

On the other hand, § 102 states that gross income shall not include the value of property acquired by gift, even though a person who receives a gift has had a clear accession to wealth. Which section should you apply when one section seems to require inclusion[3] and another section seems to provide for exclusion? In applying the Code, the more specific provision will always override a more general provision. Thus, if you have a gift, § 102 allows you to exclude the value of the gift from gross income, even though you have enjoyed economic gain, because in § 102 Congress has shown specific intent to treat gifts differently than other sources of income.

Yet, there are certain types of gifts which receive even more specific treatment under the Code. The Supreme Court has held that, in order for a transfer of property to qualify as a gift for income tax purposes, it must arise from a "detached and disinterested generosity."[4]

---

[1] While there is little doubt that the income tax laws generate substantial revenue, they also serve to encourage taxpayers to engage in conduct which Congress considers to be helpful to society as a whole. For example, § 23 provides an inducement for taxpayers to adopt, § 170 provides an inducement for taxpayers to make contributions to charities, and §§ 219, 408, and 408A, which deal with Individual Retirement Accounts, provide an inducement for taxpayers to save money for their retirement. As the make-up of Congress changes, the social policies found in the Code usually change as well.

[2] C.I.R. v. Glenshaw Glass Co., 348 U.S. 426 (1955).

[3] Notice that § 61 alerts you to the fact that there are other provisions of the Code that will override its very broad statement of inclusion, when it says "except as otherwise provided in this subtitle." (*See* § 4.05.)

[4] C.I.R. v. Duberstein, 363 U.S. 278, 286 (1960).

For example, a birthday present to a child would certainly qualify as an excludable gift for income tax purposes. But consider an automobile prize given by a game show called "Spell Your Name!" Would you have gross income, or could you argue that the show had given you that car out of disinterested generosity? The answer to that question becomes quite clear if you look at § 74. Section 74 requires that prizes and awards be included in gross income. Thus, even if you could convince a court that the producers of "Spell Your Name!" gave you the car out of disinterested generosity, and it therefore should be excludable under § 102, § 74 would require inclusion of its value in gross income since it is a more specific provision.

The term "prizes" would also include scholarships, which are financial awards given by educational institutions. Should you have to include your scholarship to law school in gross income under § 74? Again, that question can be answered by reference to a statute which pertains directly to scholarships, § 117. Section 117 states that gross income does not include any amount received as a qualified scholarship (as defined by § 117(b)). Thus, even though § 74 requires inclusion of awards in gross income, § 117 carves out a specific exception for certain types of awards called "scholarships."

You should notice that scholarships are a type of prize, and that prizes are a type of gift. In fact, you could say that prizes are subsets of the larger set known as gifts, and that scholarships are a sub-subset of the prizes subset. Thinking in those terms can help you to discern which categories are more specific than others, which, in turn, can help you to decide which of several statutes should apply to your situation.

§ 4.03 CONJUNCTIVE VS. DISJUNCTIVE

In order to understand fully the importance of the difference between the conjunctive "and" and the disjunctive "or," you need only look to § 274(c)(2). In general, § 274(c) operates to limit otherwise allowable deductions for travel in foreign countries to the percentage of time the taxpayer actually spent on business. This rule is different from the rule for domestic travel, which allows taxpayers to deduct the full amount of their transportation expenses, as long as their travel is primarily business motivated.[5] Section 274(c)(2), however, provides that the limitation provisions of § 274(c)(1) shall not apply (and therefore, the general rules relating to domestic travel will apply to travel expenses outside the United States away from home) if—

> (A) such travel does not exceed one week,

> *or*

> (B) the portion of the time of travel outside the United States away from home which is not attributable to the pursuit of the taxpayer's trade or business . . . is less than 25 percent of the total time on such travel.

Whenever you have an exception to a Code provision that is stated in the disjunctive, as is § 274(c)(2), you only need to meet one of the requirements in order for the exception to apply. Consider the following hypotheticals:

QUESTION: Phil Tower travelled to France to engage in a business deal. All of the expenses of his travel would have been deductible under § 162 of the Code, had his trip been to Iowa, instead of France, but because his travel was outside of the United States, § 274(c) is called into play. Does § 274(c)(1) limit Phil's travel expense deduction, or will the exception of § 274(c)(2) prevail, if Phil spent four days in France? Seven days? Ten days?

---

[5] Treas. Reg. § 1.162-2(b)(1).

ANSWER: If Phil spent four days in France, the exception to section 274(c)(1), as enumerated in § 274(c)(2)(A) will apply. Foreign travel did not exceed one week, and all that is required for the exception to apply is that Phil meet one of the two tests. Likewise, the exception applies if Phil spent exactly one week in France, because he did not not exceed the one week requirement. In each of these cases, you did not even need to know how much of Phil's time was spent on pleasure, because, as long as his travel was one week or less, the exception would apply.

On the other hand, if Phil spent ten days in France, he failed the test of § 274(c)(2)(A), because his foreign travel exceeded one week. Yet, you cannot determine if the exception applies without first determining how much of Phil's time was actually spent on business. Since § 274(c)(2) is stated in the disjunctive, it will apply even if Phil's travel exceeded one week, as long as he spent less than 25% of his time on pursuits that were not related to his business, as required by § 274(c)(2)(B).

Conversely, since the limiting provisions of § 274(c)(1) can only apply if the exception under § 274(c)(2) does not apply, and since the exception will apply if EITHER Phil spends one week or less in France, OR he spends less than 25% of his time on pleasure, Phil must BOTH spend more than one week in France, AND he must spend 25% or more of his time on pleasure, in order for his deductions to be limited.

Now that you have seen how the disjunctive works as applied to section 274(c), we can formulate a rule that applies to any disjunctive in the Code. Whenever the Code gives you a test that may be satisfied by meeting one factor or another, then the only way you can fail that test is to fail both factors. You can express the above rule as a formula, as follows:

If A or B then C.

A and B are the parts of the test, and C is the result dictated by the Code when either part of the test is met. For example, in § 274(c)(2), A would correspond to the test requiring that the travel not exceed one week, while B would represent the requirement that the percentage of travel unrelated to a business be less than 25%. C would be the resulting exception to the general rule of § 274(c)(1).

Thus, if A then C, or if B then C.
Furthermore, if A, but not B then C, or
if not A, but B then C.

On the other hand, in order for C not to occur, you must have the opposite of A and B, which can be expressed as follows:

If not A and not B then not C.

The opposite of the disjunctive requires a conjunctive. Therefore, when the Code requires that you meet both prongs of a two part test in order to obtain a particular result, failure of either prong of the test will prevent that result. For example, look at § 132(b), which provides the definition of a no-additional-cost service. This definition is important, because no-additional-cost services are excluded from gross income by § 132(a).

Section 132(b) requires that for a fringe benefit to be a no-additional-cost service, it must be a service provided by an employer to an employee for use by such employee where:

(1) such service is offered for sale to customers in the ordinary course of the line of business of the employer in which the employee is performing services, *and*

(2) the employer incurs no substantial additional cost (including foregone revenue) in providing such service to the employee.

Thus, for a benefit to be considered excludable as a no-additional-cost service, it must meet both parts of § 132(b). Conversely, a benefit will not be a no-additional-cost service if the service EITHER: (A) is NOT offered for sale to customers in the ordinary course of the line of business of the employer in which the employee is performing services, OR (B) the employer incurs a substantial additional cost in providing such service to the employee. Again, you can establish an equation that will apply to any test in the Code requiring the conjunctive ("and").

If A and B then C.

Using § 132(b), A represents the requirement that the service be sold to customers in the ordinary course of the employer's business, B stands for the prong which mandates that the employer not incur a substantial additional cost, and C is the result that the fringe benefit will be considered a no-additional-cost service, if, and only if, both A and B occur.

Next, the converse of this equation can be stated in the following disjunctive:

If not A or not B then not C.
Therefore:
If A and not B, then not C.
If B and not A, then not C.

These equations, known by logicians as syllogisms, can be of tremendous help when you are trying to determine the applicability of a Code provision. You can use them any time the Code gives more than one test in a particular statute. As long as you understand the differences inherent in the Code's use of "and," and its use of "or," you will always understand which steps are required in order to analyze the issue at hand. These simple rules will apply, no matter what changes Congress might make in the Code.

§ 4.04 THE MAGIC PROVISION: "FOR PURPOSES OF . . . "

One of the major differences between Code language and English is that Congress has absolute power over Code language, but often has only a minimal command of the English language. The best evidence of this is that Congress can change the meaning of a word or phrase, or even the location of a country, through the provisions of the Internal Revenue Code. Such magic is performed by uttering the phrase "for purposes of . . . ," which has the effect of a Congressional "abracadabra."

If you look at § 274(h)(3), you will be able to see the mystical powers of the words "for the purposes of . . . " in action. In general, § 274(h) places restrictions on a taxpayer's ability to deduct the expenses of a convention held outside the North American area. Section 274(h)(3) says:

For purposes of this subsection[6]

(A) the term "North American area" means the United States, its possessions, and the Trust Territory of the Pacific Islands, and Canada and Mexico.

You are probably wondering what happened to Central America, Bermuda, The Bahamas, and Jamaica, all of which are considered part of North American by most experts on geography. Yet, in respect to the taxation of income, Congress has the ability to define a

---

[6] Emphasis supplied.

geographical region in any way it wishes. In fact, Congress could have included England in its definition of the North American area, if it so desired. The important thing to remember, is that whenever you see the phrase "for the purposes of," you know to expect a definition that will be unique and essential to your application of the statutory provision you are reading.

It is also important to note the limitations placed on special definitions given by the Code. Again using § 274(h)(3), you should notice that the definition of the North American area given in that paragraph applies only for the purposes of "this subsection" (subsection 274(h)). There could, therefore, be several different definitions of the North American area found at various locations in the Code, which are applicable only for the purposes of a particular section, subsection, or paragraph, as indicated in each definition. (See Chapter 2 for a discussion of the organization of Code sections.) Thus, the magic phrase "for the purposes of . . . " is always followed by words of limitation, which have the effect of restricting the applicability of the special definition to those parts of the Code indicated by the limiting phrase.

> **PROBLEM 4A: Study §§ 71(b) and 71(c) and answer the following questions:**
>
> **(1) Stu and Inci Pid were divorced on January 21, 2008, after three years of marital bliss (unfortunately, they were married for 24 years). The state court granting the divorce issued a written decree requiring Inci to pay Stu two bags of groceries each month as alimony. Will these payments be considered alimony under § 71(b)? Why, or why not? How does the phrase "for the purposes of . . ." affect your answer?**
>
> **(2) Assume the same facts as (1) above, except that instead of groceries, Inci was required to pay Stu $100 in cash each month? Is this alimony under § 71(b)?**
>
> **(3) Finally, assume that, in addition to the facts in (2) above, Stu and Inci had a child named Intre Pid, and that the $100 monthly payments to Stu would be reduced when Intre turned eighteen. How much of each payment will be defined as alimony? Would the fact that the state court defined the entire payment as alimony affect your answer in any way?**

§ 4.05 THE CODE RED FLAG: "EXCEPT AS PROVIDED"

When you are solving a problem in federal taxation, as in any area of the law, it is always important to make sure that the rule you are using applies to your particular circumstance. To that end, you must be certain that no other sections of the Code address your problem in a more specific manner (*see* § 4.02). Fortunately, the Internal Revenue Code often alerts you to the fact that there is another Code provision that might override the statutory language you are reading. This warning language is always expressed as "except as provided . . . ." Therefore, we call the phrase "except as provided" the Code "Red Flag."

To better understand how the Code Red Flag operates, look at § 61(a). As you probably know by now, § 61 defines the term "gross income" very broadly as "income from whatever source derived." Fortunately, § 61(a) immediately warns you that there will be exceptions to this general rule. Specifically, that section applies "*[e]xcept as otherwise provided*[7] in this subtitle." Notice that, like the "for the purposes of . . ." provision (discussed in § 4.04), the red flag language always establishes its own limitations. Thus, exceptions to inclusion of

---

[7] Emphasis supplied.

an item as gross income can occur througout subtitle A, which encompasses the entire body of income tax statutes. On the other hand, if you look at § 63(a), you will notice that the exceptions to the definition of "taxable income" are much more limited in scope, as that subsection states a definition that will apply, "except as provided in subsection (b)." In other words, the definition of taxable income given in § 63(a) will pertain to every taxpayer, unless that taxpayer falls under the ambit of § 63(b); you do not need to worry about any other exceptions.

> **PROBLEM 4B: Study §§ 101(a), 101(d), and 101(f). Make a statement that covers the tax consequences of every situation in which a taxpayer receives payments under a life insurance contract by reason of the death of the insured.**

§ 4.06 STRONG WORDS: "NOTWITHSTANDING ANY OTHER PROVISION"

Some Code sections stand alone. That is, Congress has decided that some areas of tax law are so important that the sections which govern those areas must have their own set of rules, which apply "notwithstanding any other provision." When you encounter these strong words, you know that Congress is telling you to ignore anything else you might have read in connection with the tax consequences of an item of income or deduction, because what you are about to read will apply despite anything else that may appear to be on point.

The classic example of a section which is self-governing is § 1245(a)(1). That section requires that gains from the sale of depreciable property be treated as ordinary income to the extent of the lower of the gain realized on the sale or the depreciation taken on the property. Further, the section states, except as provided in § 1245 itself, the gain treated as ordinary income "shall be recognized notwithstanding any other provision of this subtitle." Therefore, since the subtitle referred to is subtitle A, which addresses all statutes pertaining to income taxation, you must disregard any other statute which might allow, or even require nonrecognition in the case of dispositions of depreciable property, as only § 1245 is authorized to encompass such dispositions. For example, § 1031 provides that no gain will be recognized when a taxpayer exchanges property used in her trade or business for property of a like kind. Yet, § 1245(a) requires that gain from the disposition of certain depreciable property will be recognized "notwithstanding any other provision." I.R.C. § 1245(d). Therefore, § 1245(a) recognition overrides § 1031 nonrecognition. Fortunately, however, § 1245(b)(4) provides that gain will not be recognized when depreciable property is exchanged for other depreciable property of a like kind. Thus, exceptions to § 1245(a) must be found within § 1245 itself.

§ 4.07 SOME ADDITIONAL VOCABULARY

While §§ 4.02 through 4.06 of this chapter acquainted you with the most essential elements of Code vocabulary, the following paragraphs are designed to acquaint you with some of the other Code terms you are likely to encounter as you study federal taxation.

[1] Mandatory vs. Elective Language

While most of the provisions of the Code apply whether you want them to or not, there are some enactments which allow for elective tax treatment. Fortunately, it is very easy to distinguish mandatory declarations from elective ones, because of the Code language used to differentiate them. Mandatory provisions make use of the term "shall" to indicate that the taxpayer is required to do something. On the other hand, where tax treatment is optional, the Code will provide for a result "at the election of the taxpayer." To that end, examine §§ 1031(a), 1032, 1033(a)(1) and 1033(a)(2), and answer the following problem. (You need not know about nonrecognition provisions to answer the questions. However, you might find the discussion of nonrecognition in Chapter 6 to be helpful.)

> **PROBLEM 4C: Is § 1031(a) an elective provision; that is, can a taxpayer opt to recognize gain if she makes an exchange that is covered by § 1031(a)? How about § 1032? § 1033(a)(1)? 1033(a)(2)?**

[2] "Treated as" or "Considered"

Sometimes the Code requires you to pretend that a tax item is something other than what it really is. The best way to explain that rather cryptic statement is through a Code example. Section 1235 provides that a sale of all substantial rights to a patent "shall be *considered*[8] the sale or exchange of a capital asset held for more than one year." Thus, even if you held a patent for only two days, you would be treated as having held it for more than one year upon a sale of all of the substantial rights to that patent. Accordingly, even though you did not actually hold the asset for more than one year, you would be entitled to take advantage of the lower tax rates available for long-term capital gains (currently, the maximum rate for most long-term capital gains is 15%, while the maximum rate for ordinary and short-term gain income is 35%).[9] Other sections which use the term "treated as" or "considered" include §§ 64, 65, 1231, 1234, and 1239.

[3] "Including (But Not Limited To)"

The phrase "including (but not limited to)" always indicates that the items which follow are to be taken only as examples, not as an exclusive list. Thus, when § 61 states that gross income means income from whatever source derived, including (but not limited to) the fifteen items listed by that section, you know that items such as interest and rents are examples of gross income, but that there could be (and in fact there are) many other types of income which fall under the purview of gross income, even though they are not specifically listed.

[4] "But Does Not Include"

Section 1221 says "the term capital asset means property held by the taxpayer *but does not include*— . . . ."[10] The phrase "but does not include" serves as an indication that the list which follows will be exclusive. That is, only those types of property listed will be excepted from the general rule that capital assets are any property of the taxpayer. In other words, the whole world is a capital asset, except for those things listed as not being included as capital assets under § 1221(a)(1)-(8).

---

[8] Emphasis supplied.

[9] I.R.C. § 1. The Jobs and Growth Tax Relief Reconciliation Act of 2003 ("2003 JGTRRA") reduced the top tax rate bracket for ordinary income to 35% for 2003 and later years. Currently, the regular income tax rates are 10%, 15%, 25%, 28%, 33%, and 35%. Before 2003, the maximum rate at which most long term capital gains were taxed was 20%. The 2003 JGTRRA reduced the 20% long term capital gains rate to 15% (effective for sales after May 5, 2003). Even though the 2003 JGTRRA also reduced the top rate of tax on ordinary income to 35%, there is still a significant rate differential and premium placed on deriving capital gains rather than ordinary income.

[10] Emphasis supplied.

[5] "Allowed" vs. "Allowable"

When a taxpayer properly takes a deduction, we say that the taxpayer has been allowed that deduction. On the other hand, when a taxpayer does not take a deduction she could have properly taken, we say that the deduction was allowable. In the context of § 1016(a), you can see that a taxpayer's basis must be adjusted for the depreciation deductions allowable. This could mean that a taxpayer's basis is adjusted downward by a depreciation deduction she never actually used.

§ 4.08 A FINAL WORD

The words and phrases discussed in this chapter are some of the most important Code language you will encounter. As you might expect, the Code terminology discussed in this chapter is not exclusive. Therefore, you might find it helpful to make note of any new Code expression you might learn, because the language of the Code will remain consistent long after substantive provisions have been enacted, repealed, amended, modified, or simplified.

Chapter 5

USING A FLOW CHART TO FOLLOW COMPLEX SECTIONS

§ 5.01 VIEWING THE CODE AS A COMPUTER PROGRAM

When you insert a program disc into a computer, you give that computer the information necessary to perform any number of tasks related to the purpose of that program. Similarly, when you read the Internal Revenue Code, you give yourself the information necessary to answer questions related to federal taxation. Of course, unlike the computer, which is separate from its human user, you must serve as both hardware and user for the software known as the Internal Revenue Code.

One of the primary reasons for analogizing the Code to a computer program is that the Code, like computer software, is very meticulous. A program must dictate every step the computer takes; if any step is left out of the program, the computer will not complete the task. In much the same way, the Code controls every step you take in solving a tax problem. This is true even if steps which might seem obvious, or which you might perform in your head, without even a second thought. For example, when someone asks you to compute "2+2," you immediately think "4." Yet, the Code requires you to slow down your thinking process, in many cases, by forcing you to parse each problem into a particular series of steps. Congress, like the creator of computer software, assumes that unless the program is explicit, you will not be able to perform it. Therefore, some Code sections can become extremely detailed.

The fact that some Code sections are complex, however, should not frighten you, if you take a logical approach to applying those sections. After all, you can only perform one step of any section at a time, and you will find that no single step is really difficult. To that end, this chapter suggests a method for approaching some of the more complex provisions of the Code. The system proposed in this chapter closely resembles the device used for tracking complex computer programs, which is known as a "branch block."

In addition to explaining how the branch block method will help you to follow intricate Code sections, this chapter will also teach you how to diagram a complex section. Such a diagram, known in computer parlance as a flow chart, will be useful in helping you to get an overview of how the various steps of a section function together. To further aid in your understanding of flow charts, the final portion of this chapter contains a diagram of § 170, which is considered to be one of the more difficult statutes in the Code.

§ 5.02 THE BRANCH BLOCK

Simply stated, a branch block is a structure used in a computer program to tell the computer to perform either one block of statements or another. The choice of which block the computer performs will depend upon whether a given condition is true or false. In either case, once the particular block is performed, the computer will be told to go to the next series of tasks. The Internal Revenue Code, like a computer, employs the branch block in many of its more sophisticated sections.

You do not need to know anything about computers in order to understand the application of branch blocks. Before you look at how the branch block operates in connection with the Code, it might be helpful to think of how you use it in your every day life. For example, consider how a typical law student registers for classes. She might say "I'll take State Constitutional Law, if Professor Cooper is teaching it this semester. Otherwise, I'll take Domestic Relations." In branch block language, the student's statements could be expressed as: If Cooper is teaching State Constitutional Law, THEN I'll take it. If Cooper is not teaching State Constitutional Law, THEN I'll take Domestic Relations.

Notice the use of IF . . . THEN in the branch block. This tells you that you are testing a particular condition to see if it is true; if it is true, then a specified action will occur. If it is not true, then another action will take place. In either event, once the block is completed, you will go on to the next step, which would be, in the case of our law student, registering for the chosen class.

Now, let us see how sections of the Internal Revenue Code require us to use the branch block. Usually, the branch block is only a portion of a particular section. Sections like § 1011, however, are comprised entirely of branch blocks. You might find it helpful to think of such sections as "switchboards," since all they do is refer you to other sections of the Code. Section 1011(a), for example, is the switchboard for basis, because it tells you which sections or subsections to go to in order to determine basis. Expressed as an "if . . . then" statement, § 1011(a) would read:

> IF you want to determine basis for corporate distributions and adjustments, THEN go to Subchapter C.

> IF you want to determine basis relating to partners and partnerships, THEN go to Subchapter K.

> IF you want to determine adjusted basis, THEN go to § 1016.

> Otherwise, go to § 1012, or other applicable sections of this subchapter (subchapter O).

Therefore, the sole purpose of § 1011(a) is to direct you to some other part of the Code. But, if you examine subsection (b) of § 1011, you will have an opportunity to see an example of a branch block that operates exclusively within one Code section. In fact, § 1011(b) actually makes use of the "if . . . then" phraseology. As you can see, § 1011(b) states that IF you have a sale to a charity, which qualifies you for a deduction under § 170, THEN your basis shall be determined under § 1011(b).[1] Otherwise, you must refer to § 1011(a) in order to find out how to compute the basis, because § 1011(b) will apply only if you have a bargain sale to a charity. In either event, after you have completed the appropriate branch block, you will be able to proceed to the next step, which is the computation of basis under the provision indicated by the branch block.

If you can think of the steps involved in Code sections as simple branch block tests, you will be better able to approach difficult provisions. Unfortunately, you might find that some sections are so involved that even when you attack them one step at a time, you will have difficulty keeping track of all the steps they require. In those cases, you might find that making a diagram will help you; computer maniacs call such diagrams "flow charts." Therefore, the next few paragraphs of this chapter will explain how to approach and diagram Internal Revenue Code provisions.

---

[1] Section 1011(b) determines the basis that a taxpayer can use when she makes a bargain sale to charity. It is a good example of the Code Ratio, discussed in Chapter 3, in that a taxpayer's basis for determining gain from a bargain sale to charity shall be the amount which bears the same ratio to the total basis in the property as the amount realized from the sale bears to the fair market value of the property. Thus, if a taxpayer sold property with a basis of $20K and a fair market value of $100K, to a charity for $75K, the taxpayer would be allowed to use only a basis of $15K in computing her gain. The $15K is derived by the following equation: § 1011(b) basis = ($75K/$100K) x $20K. In essence, the government is saying that, since the taxpayer received cash equal to only ¾ of the value of her property, she should be able to use only ¾ of her basis in computing her gain. The reason that § 1011(b) applies only to bargain sales to charities is that charities are exempt from taxation. Therefore, any potential gain realized by the selling party which escapes taxation will never be taxed.

NOTE: There are certain sections which are called cross references. These cross references are very helpful, in that they alert you to other parts of the Code which might affect a given tax outcome. In essence, cross references are also examples of the branch block. A case in point is § 61(b), which alerts you to the fact that there are specific inclusions and exclusions which you must examine before you can determine whether an item of income is indeed gross income

§ 5.03 MAKING A FLOW CHART OF COMPLEX PROVISIONS

A flow chart is simply a diagram of the tests involved in a branch block. For example, consider the law student's dilemma discussed in the previous section of this chapter. In that case, the student would register for State Constitutional Law if Professor Cooper were teaching it that semester. Otherwise, the student would take Domestic Relations. A diagram of this very simple branch block would look like this:

Is Professor Cooper Teaching State Constitutional Law?

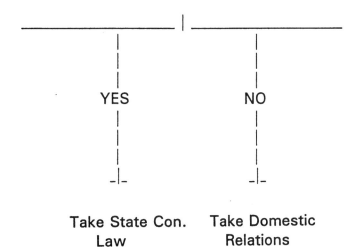

As you can see, this flow chart is extremely basic. Yet, if you heed the advice that you should only attempt to perform one step at a time, you will soon see that no single step of a flow chart will be any more complicated than the simple example above.

As you might expect, the complete flow charts you use in diagramming Code sections will generally be a bit more involved than the diagram of the student's dilemma. To that end, it will help you to develop a strategy as you approach complex statutes. Without such a plan of attack, you might discover that you will have no idea where to begin, because the starting points for some Code sections are not where you might expect them to be. The classic case in point is § 170, which is considered to be one of the most complex provisions in the entire Code.

Therefore, § 170 will be your guinea pig for the rest of this chapter. First, you will learn a logical approach to § 170; then you will see how that approach can be applied in a sample flow chart of that section.

§ 5.04 AN APPROACH TO A COMPLEX CODE SECTION: § 170

Section 170 controls the deduction for charitable contributions. Unfortunately, it is a very complex section, and you might find that it is quite difficult to apply if you simply read it straight through, without any attempt to organize it. On the other hand, if you approach § 170 in a rational manner, you will find that it is not impossible to understand.

One of the primary tools for approaching § 170, or any Code section for that matter, is good old common sense. Remember that the authors of the Code are not mystery writers; they want you to understand the tax laws as they apply to a given transaction. Thus, you should always think about how you would have dealt with the transaction at hand, before you even entered your first tax class. In the case of charitable deductions, you would have probably asked the following, common sense questions:

(1) Is my contribution to a qualified charitable organization?

(2) If so, how much of a contribution did I make?

(3) How much of my contribution is deductible?

(4) If part of my contribution cannot be deducted this year, will I be able to apply my excess contributions to another taxable year?

Those are the questions that are answered by § 170. Now, think about those questions a little bit more. Would it make any sense at all to determine the amount of your deduction before you determine the amount of your contribution? Of course not! After all, the amount of your deduction is completely dependent upon how much you gave to a particular charity. Thus, the order in which you tackle the problems presented by a charitable contribution must be dictated by common sense, as well. With these thoughts in mind, you can now turn to § 170.

Notice the subsection headings, because they will help you to determine which questions are being answered by the subsections they govern. Section 170(a) "Allowance of Deduction," for example, informs you that a deduction shall be allowed for charitable contributions as defined by subsection (c). Therefore, your starting point for the study of § 170 should be subsection (a), but then you must turn to subsection (c), not subsection (b), even though subsection (b) comes next in the Code. This is because § 170(b) provides for deduction "percentage limitations," which you know, from using common sense, cannot apply until after you determine whether your gift is to an appropriate charity, and if so, how much you gave to that charity. Notice that § 170(c) lists the types of organizations which are proper recipients of charitable gifts. If a gift is made to an organization which is not covered by § 170(c), then it is not a charitable contribution, and there will be no deduction allowed for it under § 170.

On the other hand, if a gift was made to a § 170(c) institution, then you must calculate the amount of the contribution. You have seen §§ 170(a), (b), and (c), none of which tells you anything about the amount of the contribution to be taken into account. Likewise, § 170(d) allows for a carryover in the event that there are "excess contributions," and you cannot possibly know if there are excess contributions until you know what your contributions are. Fortunately, § 170(e) tells you how to determine the amount of a contribution in the case of "certain . . . ordinary income and capital gain property." Therefore, after you have decided that the gift qualifies under § 170(c), you must go to § 170(e) to calculate the actual contribution.

[1] How Much Did I Contribute?

Section 170(e) is, in and of itself, a classic example of a complex branch block. It is a maze which must be run anytime contributions of property take place. The first question you need to answer when you confront § 170(e) is: was the contribution made in cash, or in appreciated property? If the contribution was purely cash, then the entire amount of the cash will be taken into account in calculating the contribution. This is because § 170(e) requires a reduction of the contribution amount only in the case of certain appreciated property. Thus, if the gift was $3000 in cash, the contribution would be $3000 for the purposes of § 170.

Conversely, if the contribution consisted of appreciated property, you would need to perform several tests under § 170(e). Common sense dictates that appreciated property be treated differently from cash. Although it makes sense that a taxpayer should have a potential deduction equal to the cash she gave to a charity, the government is not as anxious to allow the taxpayer a $3000 deduction when she contributed property worth $3000, for which she only paid $1. Thus, it should not surprise you that the amount of property taken into account for purposes of § 170 might be less than the fair market value of that property. Specifically, § 170(e)(1) dictates that the amount of any charitable contribution

> otherwise taken into account shall be reduced by the sum of:
>
> (A) the amount of gain which would not have been long-term capital gain . . . if the property contributed had been sold by the taxpayer at its fair market value (determined at the time of such contribution), and
>
> (B) in the case of a charitable contribution—
>
> (i) of tangible personal property . . . , if the use by the donee is unrelated to the purpose or function constituting the basis for its exemption . . . ,
>
> (ii) to or for the use of a private foundation (as defined in § 509(a)), other than a private foundation described in subsection (b)(1)(E)[F], [or]
>
> (iii) of any patent, copyright . . . , trademark, trade name, trade secret, know-how, software . . . , or similar property, or applications or registrations of such property, . . .
>
> the amount of gain which would have been long-term capital gain if the property contributed had been sold by the taxpayer at its fair market value (determined at the time of such contribution).

Therefore, when a gift of appreciated property is involved, you must ascertain whether that property would have generated ordinary gain, short-term capital gain, or long-term capital gain had the taxpayer sold it for its fair market value at the time of the contribution. If you determine that the property would have yielded ordinary or short-term capital gain, then the contribution must be reduced by the amount of such gain that would have resulted had the property in fact been sold (because § 170(e)(1)(A) applies). If you determine that the property would have yielded long-term capital gain, then the contribution may or may not be reduced by the amount of such gain that would have resulted had the property in fact been sold (depending on whether § 170(e)(1)(B) applies).

In essence, § 170(e)(1)(A) requires that no ordinary or short-term capital gains be taken into account in computing the contribution. In other words, if a taxpayer gave property for which she paid $1, and that property was ordinary or short-term capital gain property, then her contribution would only be $1, no matter what the fair market value of the property might be at the time of the contribution. For example, if the value of the property happened to be $3000 at the time of the contribution, then § 170(e)(1)(A) would require that the contribution be reduced by the amount that would have been ordinary or short-term gain, which would be $2999. Therefore, after you have determined that a contribution was made with appreciated property, instead of cash, your next step is to decide if, and to the extent that property is ordinary, or short-term gain property. If the property falls totally within the coverage of § 170(e)(1)(A), you will be finished with § 170(e) after you make the reductions required by that subparagraph.

If, however, the property contributed by a taxpayer would not totally give rise to ordinary or short-term capital gain, then you must go to § 170(e)(1)(B), to see if it might apply. Section 170(e)(1)(B) pertains whenever a taxpayer donates property which is long-term capital gain property, and which: (1) is tangible personal property unrelated to the charitable purpose of the organization; or (2) is given to a private foundation not described in § 170(b)(1)(E)[F]; or (3) is intangible intellectual property—which includes patents, certain copyrights, trademarks, trade names, trade secrets, know-how, and certain software.[2] (Do you see how the use of branch block diagrams might prove useful, here?) If § 170(e)(1)(B) operates, it causes the exact same result as § 170(e)(1)(A), which is a reduction in the contribution to the extent of the gain which would have arisen, if the property had been sold.

The purpose of § 170(e)(1)(B)(i) is to discourage taxpayers from giving personal property to charities, who have no use for such property, and will, in turn, sell that property for cash. Since charities are tax-exempt, they will not be taxed on the gain from such transactions. An illustration here would probably help you to understand the government's concern. Assume that Richie Nuvo, a famous art collector, donated his entire collection of wrestling posters to the Wrasslin' Hall of Fame, and that the transaction qualified as a charitable contribution under § 170(c). In this situation, the government will assume that (since the posters are related to the charitable purposes of the museum, which are to foster the historical and artistic preservation of wrestling artifacts) the museum will hold the posters for display to the public. Therefore, § 170(e)(1)(B)(i) will not operate to force a reduction in the amount of Richie's contribution (assuming that the Wrasslin' Hall of Fame is not a private foundation). On the other hand, if Prissy Propper donated her library, which contained selected works on manners and etiquette, to the Wrasslin' Hall of Fame, the government would be concerned that the curators of the Hall of Fame might sell the books, since they were unrelated to the purpose of the organization. Thus, Prissy's contribution would be reduced by subtracting the unrealized gain from its fair market value. Other examples of tangible personal property which are unrelated to the charitable function of an organization might include a baseball autographed by the 1999 Atlanta Braves given to a Catholic Church, or a pick-up truck given to the Museum of Science and Industry.[3]

The purpose of § 170(e)(1)(B)(iii) is to curb improper charitable tax deductions resulting from overvaluation of patents and other forms of intellectual property. Before enactment of § 170(e)(1)(B)(iii) in 2004, the amount of a charitable deduction in connection with the donation of many forms of intellectual property was equal to the fair market value of the intellectual property at the time of the contribution. The government, however, never fully articulated or formalized a standard or approach for determining the fair market value of donated intellectual property. As a consequence, valuation conflicts between donors and the government increasingly occurred as intellectual property grew in value and the practice of intellectual property donations also grew. In a major attack on intellectual property donations, Congress enacted § 170(e)(1)(B)(iii), which basically limits the amount of the charitable deduction to the taxpayer's basis in donated intellectual property. To encourage charitable giving of intellectual property, Congress deemed it appropriate to grant donors of intellectual property future charitable deductions based on the income received by the donee charity. This provision, § 170(m), allows the donor a deduction up to ten years for gifts of royalty producing intellectual property to public charities. The amount of the

---

[2] Private foundations not described in § 170(b)(1)(F) are usually referred to as non-operating private foundations.

[3] Of course, in the long run, whether a contribution is related to the exempt function of a charity is purely a question of fact. Regulation § 1.170A-4A(b)(2) requires the contributing taxpayer to show that "at the time of the contribution, [he] reasonably anticipated that the property would be used in a manner consistent with" the charity's exempt purpose.

charitable deduction is a percentage of the royalty income earned by the donee. The percentage declines over time. I.R.C. § 170(m)(1), (7).

In summation, when you approach § 170(e), you might find that using the following series of branch blocks will greatly simplify your task of calculating a contribution:

(1) Does the contribution consist of appreciated property? IF not, THEN go to (6). IF it does, THEN go to (2).

(2) Would the property have generated any ordinary income, or short-term capital gain, if it had been sold at the time of the contribution? IF not, THEN go to (3). IF it would have, THEN make the reduction in the contribution to the extent of that gain, under § 170(e)(1)(A), AND THEN go to (3).

(3) Would the property have generated any long-term capital gain, had it been sold at the time of the contribution? IF no, THEN go to (6). IF yes, THEN go to (4).

(4) Was the property contributed to a private foundation, other than a "good" private foundation?[4] IF not, THEN go to (5). IF it was, THEN reduce the contribution by the amount which would have been long-term capital gain, had the property been sold for its fair market value, at the time of the contribution, as required by § 170(e)(1)(B))(ii), and THEN go to (6).

(5) Was the property EITHER tangible personal property, unrelated to the purpose or function of the charity OR intellectual property (other than self-created copyrights or off-the-shelf software)? IF it was not, THEN go to (6). IF it was, THEN reduce the contribution by the amount of gain which would have been long-term capital gain, had the property been sold for its fair market value at the time of the contribution. THEN go to (6).

(6) Your contribution is the amount of cash given (if any) plus the value of the property reduced by steps (2), (4), and (5), to the extent those steps applied. Now, you are ready to go on to § 170(b), which defines the deduction limitations for charitable contributions. As you can see, § 170(e) is a branch block, in that no matter which of the reduction provisions of § 170(e) apply, if any, you will always end up at point (6), which takes you into the calculation of the actual charitable deduction.

[2] How Much of My Contribution Is Deductible?

Section 170(b) can be broken down into a series of fairly simple steps, much like § 170(e). In general, the legislature has determined that certain types of charitable contributions should be favored by the tax laws, while other contributions should be less favored, if not discouraged. Therefore, Congress has established four distinct deduction limitations in § 170(b). It will be your job to determine how these various limitations apply depending upon the type of property donated, and the type of charity to which it is given.

As you encounter § 170(b), you might find it helpful to divide charitable organizations into two categories: "good" charities, those listed under § 170(b)(1)(A), and "bad" charities, those listed under § 170(b)(1)(B). So called "good" charities include churches, universities, medical research facilities, private foundations described in § 170(b)(1)(F), and public institutions established for the general welfare of society as a whole. So called "bad" charities, on the other hand, include all qualified institutions which are not good charities. For the most part, the bad charities are private foundations not defined by § 170(b)(1)(F).

---

[4] That is, one not described in § 170(b)(1)(F).

Of course, Congress would not allow a deduction for a gift to a charity that was truly bad. In fact, the § 170(b)(1)(B) charities are actually favored by the tax laws, in comparison to most organizations. It is just in comparison with the most favored § 170(b)(1)(A) organizations that the bad charities seem to be disdained. That is because a taxpayer has a higher potential deduction for gifts to § 170(b)(1)(A) charities than he does for gifts to § 170(b)(1)(B) charities. Specifically, a taxpayers's maximum deduction for gifts to good charities is 50% of his contribution base,[5] while his maximum deduction for donations to bad charities is only the lesser of 30% of his contribution base, or 50% of his contribution base minus the deductions allowed under § 170(b)(1)(A). That is, the gifts to good charities must always be considered before the gifts to bad charities.

For example, if a taxpayer had a contribution base of $100,000, and she gave $5000 to the University of Alaska, a good charity, she could still give up to $30,000 to a bad charity. This is because $30,000 (30% of the taxpayer's contribution base) is less than $50,000 minus $5000 (50% of the contribution base minus the gifts to good charities). Conversely, if the taxpayer gave $40,000 to a good charity, she could only give $10,000 to a bad charity for the tax year in question, because $10,000 (50% of the contribution base minus gifts to good charities) is less than $30,000 (30% of the contribution base). Thus, in no event will a taxpayer's charitable deductions ever exceed 50% of her contribution base, because the gifts to good charities are always limited to 50% of the contribution base, and gifts to bad charities are limited to the lesser of 30% of the contribution base, or what is left of the 50% limitation, after taking into account the gifts to good charities.

Furthermore, § 170(b) differentiates between capital gain property and all other types of property when it defines the deduction limitations. As you may recall from the above discussion of § 170(e), contributions of long term capital gain property can be reduced, if they involve gifts of tangible personal property unrelated to the function of the charity, or if they consist of any capital gain property given to a "bad" private foundation, or if they involve gifts of intellectual property. A gift of land to a good charity, however, would not trigger reduction of the contribution amount, as land is not tangible personal property, nor is the contribution to a bad foundation, nor is the land intellectual property. In other words, a taxpayer giving capital real estate to a good charity could have a contribution equal to the fair market value of the property. For example, a taxpayer who paid $1 for a piece of land which appreciated in value to $500K, could have a contribution of $500K if he gave that land to a good charity. Thus, it would make sense that Congress might wish to limit the amount of the taxpayer's potential charitable deduction from the use of appreciated long-term capital gain property.

In fact, that is exactly what Congress has done in §§ 170(b)(1)(C) and (b)(1)(D). Section 170(b)(1)(C) limits the amount of the deduction generated by capital asset donations, not affected by § 170(e), to 30% of the taxpayer's contribution base. Section 170(b)(1)(C) requires you to take into account all contributions falling under sections 170(b)(1)(A) and (B), before you even consider a contribution under 170(b)(1)(C).

As if that was not enough to contemplate, § 170(b)(1)(C)(iii) gives taxpayers the option of having § 170(e)(1)(B) apply to reduce the amount of a contribution, even though § 170(e)(1)(B) would not otherwise have applied. If the taxpayer makes that election, then his contributions of capital gain property to good charities will be reduced by the long-term capital gain which would have been realized had the property been sold at the time of the contribution. The benefit of making the election is that the taxpayer will be able to take

---

[5] Section 170(b)(1)(G) defines contribution base as adjusted gross income, not taking into account any net operating loss deductions under § 172. In cases in which there is no net operating loss, therefore, contribution base is equal to adjusted gross income of the taxpayer. That is why you will often see the term "adjusted gross income" used in place of contribution base. Adjusted gross income is defined as gross income minus deductions listed in § 62(a). I.R.C. § 62.

advantage of the higher deduction limitations of § 170(b)(1)(A), instead of being constrained by the more restricted limitations under § 170(b)(1)(C).[6] The taxpayer should make the election provided by § 170(b)(1)(C)(iii) only if it will generate a higher current deduction. For example, assume that Genie Russ donated a long-term capital asset, land, to University of Florida, a § 170(b)(1)(A) good charity. Assume further that the land was worth $50,000, even though Genie only paid $1000 for it, and that Genie's contribution base was $100,000. While § 170(e) would not apply to reduce Genie's contribution, since she gave real property to a good charity (see the steps for § 170(e) in § 5.04[1]), under § 170(b)(1)(C) Genie's deduction would be limited to 30% of her contribution base, or $30,000, assuming that she made no other charitable transfers during the current year. Thus, of her $50,000 contribution, only $30,000 would be currently deductible.

Unfortunately, the election provided by § 170(b)(1)(C)(iii) would be of no help to Genie in this circumstance. If she made that election, she would be forced to reduce her contribution to $1000, because she would have had $49,000 of long-term gain had she sold the property at the time of the contribution. Therefore, she would not benefit form the increased deduction limit afforded to her by the election.

On the other hand, if Genie had paid $40,000 instead of only $1000 for the property, she would benefit by electing to have § 170(e)(1)(B) apply. This is true because, without the election, the most that Genie could deduct, according to § 170(b)(1)(C), would be $30,000 of her $50,000 contribution. If she made the election, however, she would be able to deduct $40,000 currently because the election would reduce her contribution to $40,000 ($50,000 − $10,000 that would have been long-term capital gain, had the property been sold), but would increase her deduction limit to $50,000 (50% of her contribution base).[7]

Finally, § 170(b)(1)(D) establishes a limitation on deductions arising from contributions of long-term capital gain property to bad charities. Deductions for such contributions are the most limited, as they can not exceed the lesser of 20% of the taxpayer's contribution base, or 30% of the taxpayer's contribution base minus the gifts covered by § 170(b)(1)(C).[8] This is true, notwithstanding the fact that § 170(e)(1)(B)(ii) requires a reduction in the amount of any contribution of capital gain property to a bad foundation. Furthermore, these types of generosity are accorded the lowest priority in the overall charitable deduction scheme, in that they are taken into the last of all current year contributions to be considered.

Now that you have studied the various rules governing the deductibility of charitable contributions under § 170(b), you can organize these rules into a branch block, just like the one used in discussing § 170(e). What follows is a suggested approach:

(1) IF the charitable contribution was made to a § 170(b)(1)(A) "good" charity, THEN, go to (2). IF it was not THEN go to (5).

(2) IF the contribution consisted of long-term capital gain property which was not affected by § 170(e)(1)(B), THEN go to (4). IF it did not, THEN go to (3).

---

[6] The disadvantage to the election is that it permanently reduces the potential deduction of the taxpayer. That is, a taxpayer who does not take the election might be entitled to a lower current deduction under the limitations of § 170(b)(1)(C), but he will be able to carry over his excess contributions for up to five years, meaning that they might be deductible at some time in the future. On the other hand, a taxpayer who elects to reduce his contribution might have a greater current deduction, but by reducing his contribution he reduces the amount of total possible (current plus carryovers) deductions he would have.

[7] As defined by § 170(b)(1)(G).

[8] Interestingly enough, a literal reading of § 170(b)(1)(D) would require a taxpayer to take into account even those capital gain contributions for which he made the election under § 170(b)(1)(C)(iii), when calculating his contributions of capital gain property. This is because the language of § 170(b)(1)(D)(i)(II) requires that all contributions to which § 170(b)(1)(C) applies be considered in setting the § 170(b)(1)(D) deduction limitations. Technically, property for which an election under § 170(b)(1)(C)(iii) is in effect is property to which § 170(b)(1)(C) applies, although this cannot be the intent of Congress, since the election causes capital gain property to be treated as contributions of non-capital gain property.

(3) Deduct the contribution to the extent that it does not exceed 50% of the taxpayer's contribution base, when it is added to all other, similar contributions (that is, those contributions of property to good charities, which either do not consist of long-term capital gain property, or consist of long-term capital gain property which is affected by § 170(e)(1)(B)). IF the aggregate contributions of such property exceed 50% of the taxpayer's contribution base, THEN go to (8).

(4) IF the taxpayer elected under § 170(b)(1)(C)(iii) to reduce the contribution as if § 170(e)(1)(B) had applied, THEN go to (3). IF he did not, THEN go to (6).

(5) IF the property was long-term capital gain property, THEN go to (7). IF it is not, THEN deduct the contribution to the extent that it, when added to all similar contributions (that is, contributions to bad charities not consisting of long-term capital gain property), does not exceed the lesser of:

(a) 30% of the taxpayer's contribution base, or

(b) 50% of the taxpayer's contribution base minus the deduction allowed under step (3), above (if any).

IF these contributions exceed the lesser of 30% of the taxpayer's contribution base, or 50% of the contribution base minus the deduction computed in (3), THEN go to (8).

(6) Deduct the contribution to the extent that it, when added to all similar deductions (that is, long-term capital gain contributions to good charities, not affected by § 170(e)(1)(B)), does not exceed the lesser of 30% of the taxpayer's contribution base. IF these contributions exceed the lesser of 30% of the taxpayer's contribution base, THEN go to (8).

(7) Deduct the contribution to the extent that it, when added to all similar contributions (that is, contributions of long-term capital gain property to bad charities), does not exceed the lesser of 20% of the taxpayer's contribution base, or 30% of the taxpayer's contribution base minus the deduction allowed by step (6).

(8) Contributions in excess of allowable limits may be carried over to another tax year, subject to carryover rules in § 170.

[3] Can I Carry Over My Excess Contributions?

In computer terminology, a program is often broken down into several smaller programs called "subroutines." So far, you have been introduced to two of the subroutines used by § 170. First, you used § 170(e) to calculate the amount of property contributed to a given charity. Then you discovered how to use § 170(b) in order to determine whether the amounts contributed were within the deduction limitations specified in that section. Neither of these subroutines make much sense in isolation, but as part of the overall determination of a taxpayer's charitable deduction for the taxable year, they are indispensable. Now it is time to turn your attention to the portions of § 170 which allow a taxpayer to carry over contributions which exceed the limits established by § 170(b). Fortunately, those provisions are the last of the subroutines found in § 170. Of course, you knew they had to be last, because common sense told you that you would need to calculate contributions before deductions, and deduction limitations before carryovers of excess contributions.

The statutes which govern carryovers of excess contributions are §§ 170(d)(1), 170(b)(1)(B) (flush language), 170(b)(1)(C)(ii), and 170(b)(1)(D)(ii). In fact, each type of contribution has its own carryover provision, even though § 170(d)(1) is the model for the other three. Section

170(d) works in conjunction with all cash and non-long-term capital gain contributions to good charities. This would include any capital gain contributions for which the election under § 170(b)(1)(C)(iii) was in effect.

Next comes § 170(b)(1)(B)(flush language), which relates to cash and non-long-term capital gain contributions to bad charities. Third in line is § 170(b)(1)(C)(ii), which controls carryovers of long-term capital gain property to good charities. Finally, there is § 170(b)(1)(D)(ii), which is the operative section whenever a taxpayer has made excess contributions of long-term capital gain property to bad foundations.

In effect, each of these carryover provisions allows a taxpayer to treat the excess contributions for the current tax year as a contribution of the same type of property to the same type of charity in a later year. There are, however, two slight catches. First, carryovers can be used only for the next five taxable years, and they must be used in order of time. That is, carryovers from 2008 would have to be used before carryovers from 2007, while those from 2007 must be used before those from 2006, and so on. Secondly, carryovers are taken into account after the current year's contributions to the same class of charity. This is important because the carryovers, when added to the current year's contributions, must not exceed the deduction limits set by the applicable portions of § 170(b).

For example, assume that X. Cessive had a § 170(d)(1) carryover of $30,000 because she gave excess cash and non-long-term capital gain contributions for 2006. Assume, further, that in 2007 she gave $45,000 to Alma Mater University, a § 170(b)(1)(A) good charity, when her contribution base was $100,000. Before she can use any of her carryover from 2006, X. Cessive must compare her current year's contribution of $45,000 to 50% of her contribution base, as mandated by § 170(b)(1)(A). This comparison will show that X. Cessive can deduct all $45,000 of her current contributions, because they do not exceed $50,000 (50% of her contribution base). On the other hand, X. will not be so lucky when it comes to deducting her carryover contribution, because she only has $5000 left of her deduction limit for the year ($50,000 total − $45,000 current contributions). Therefore, she will be able to deduct only $5000 of the excess contribution from 2006, with the remaining $25,000 being carried over as an excess to 2008. Since 2006 carryovers would have to be considered before 2005 carryovers, X. would not be able to use any of her 2005 carryovers this year (if she even has any), because she exceeded her deduction limit without exhausting her 2006 carryovers. Thus, if X. had any carryover contributions from 2002 she would lose them, since they expire after five years.

It is important to note that the carryover provisions, in conjunction with § 170(b), establish the following priorities for deducting charitable contributions:

(1) Current cash and non-long-term capital gain contributions to good charities.

(2) Carryovers of excess cash and non-long-term capital gain contributions to good charities, with a more recent year's carryovers having priority over an earlier year's carryovers, and with no carryover existing for more than five years.

(3) Current cash and non-long-term capital gain contributions to bad charities.

(4) Carryovers of excess cash and non-long-term capital gain contributions to bad charities, with a more recent year's carryovers having priority over an earlier year's carryovers, and with no carryover existing for more than five years.

(5) Current contributions of long-term capital gain property.

(6) Carryovers of excess contributions of long-term capital gain property, with a more recent year's carryovers having priority over an earlier year's carryovers, and with no carryover existing for more than five years.

(7) Current contributions of long-term capital gain property to bad charities.

(8) Carryovers of excess contributions of long-term capital gain property to bad charities, with a more recent year's carryovers having priority over an earlier year's carryovers, and with no carryover existing for more than five years. Notice that Congress had to establish the priority of carryovers from more recent years over those from earlier years in order to give the five year limitation period any meaning at all. Otherwise, taxpayers would opt to use their oldest carryovers first, so that they would not lose them.

You can use the above priority system whenever you determine a charitable deduction. In fact, this system will fit right into steps (1) through (8) of the branch block you used to calculate the deduction limitations (*see* § 5.04[2]). After all, the deduction limitations of § 170(b) apply to the aggregate amount of current and carryover contributions of specified types of property to specified classes of charities. The priority system just tells you which types of contributions are used up first, within each category of charitable contribution.

Now, we can take the steps we created in this section of Chapter 5, and diagram them. What follows is a flow chart of the complex computer program known as Code § 170.

See flow chart on following page.

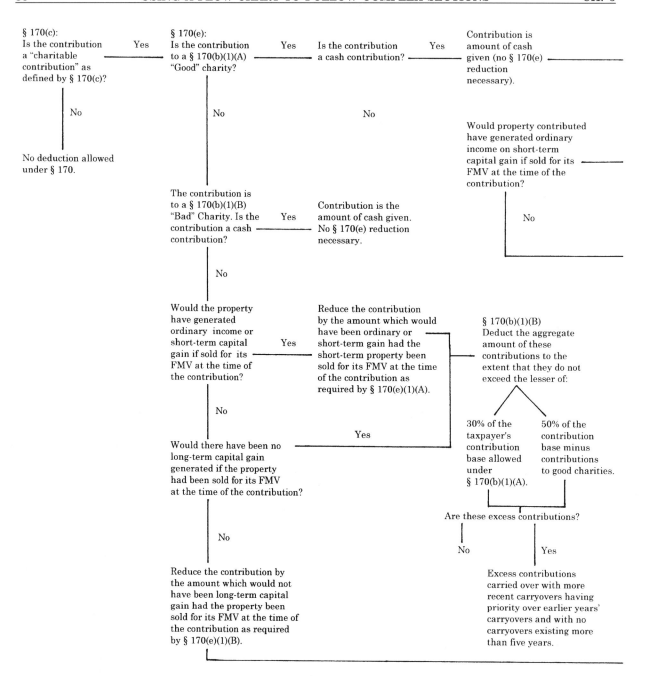

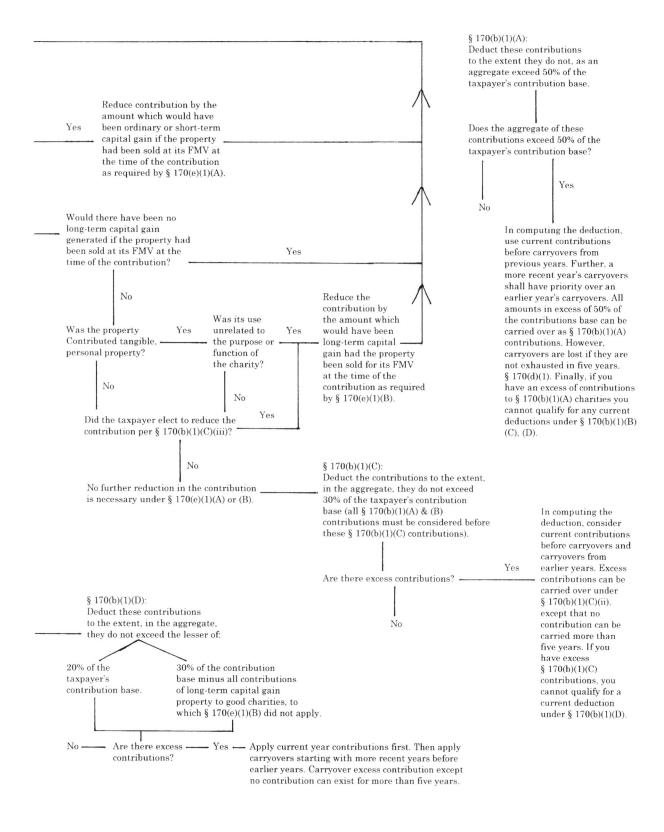

Chapter 6

THE TAX CONSTANTS
(Basic Concepts That Never Change)

§ 6.01 INTRODUCTION

In Chapters 2 through 5 you studied the mechanics and vocabulary of the language of federal income taxation, just as you might study any unfamiliar tongue. In this chapter, you will learn that there are some basic constants in taxation that will serve as practical reference points for applying the techniques you have mastered in the previous chapters. In effect, the previous chapters introduced you to what the Code is, and how it works, while this chapter will acquaint you with the basic economic motivations behind tax legislation. That is, this chapter deals with the "why's" behind Code language. To that end, you should notice that the vast majority of Code sections respond to problems raised by one or more of the tax constants.

§ 6.02 INCOME SHIFTING (OUR PROGRESSIVE RATE STRUCTURE)

Tax rates come and go. In the 1980's alone, the highest possible federal tax on a taxpayer's income dollar under § 1 of the Code decreased from 70 percent in 1981 to 33 percent in 1988. Furthermore, the number of marginal tax brackets decreased from thirteen in 1981 to two in 1988. Thus, the tax rates in the late 1980's were certainly less progressive than those of the early 1980's, because there were fewer intermediate steps between the highest and lowest brackets. In 1993, Congress changed the rates to create five brackets ranging from 15 percent to 39.6 percent. In 2001 and 2003, Congress once again changed the rates, reducing the top rate bracket for ordinary income to 35% for 2003 and later years.[1]

Even though Congress makes frequent changes in the actual tax rates, one basic principle does not change: as long as there are at least two tax brackets, taxpayers in higher brackets will be able to achieve tax savings if they can shift the incidence of taxation on their income to taxpayers in lower brackets. The greater the difference between the highest marginal tax bracket and the lowest marginal tax bracket in a given tax year, the greater the incentive will be to shift the incidence of taxation from one taxpayer to another.

The benefits of income shifting can be illustrated by a simple hypothetical. Assume that Ginger Vitas, a dentist, has earned enough income to place her in the highest possible tax bracket, which we will say is the 35% bracket for purposes of this example. This means that every dollar earned by Ginger for the remainder of the year will be split 65 cents for Ginger and 35 cents for the government in the form of taxes. However, any income earned by Ginger

---

[1] I.R.C. § 1. The Economic Growth and Tax Relief Reconciliation Act of 2001 ("2001 EGTRRA"), which became law in June 2001, reduced the top rate of tax on ordinary income from 39.6% to 35% over a six-year period. Under the 2001 EGTRRA, the highest marginal rate of tax on ordinary income for individuals was to be reduced as follows: For years 2001-2003, the top rate was to be reduced to 38.6%; for years 2004-2005, the top rate was to be reduced to 37.6%; and for 2006 and later, the top rate was to be reduced to 35%. In 2003, Congress passed significant tax cuts by accelerating the rate reductions in the regular income tax rates that were scheduled to be phased in under the 2001 EGTRRA. Specifically, the Jobs Growth Tax Relief Reconciliation Act of 2003 ("2003 JGTRRA") reduced the tax rate bracket for ordinary income to 35% for 2003 and later years. Now, the regular tax rates above 15% are 25%, 28%, 33%, and 35%. The maximum rate on gains from the sale or exchange of most capital assets held for more than one year is 15%. It is important to note, however, that tax rates projected for future years are always subject to change. Therefore, tax students and planners can never rely on tax rates for any future year.

before she reached the highest bracket was taxed at a lower marginal rate. In this case, Ginger has used her lower tax brackets to the full extent allowable, which makes her a share-cropper who must pay 35% of her earnings for the rest of the year to her landlord, the United States. Assume further that Ginger will be required to use some of her remaining 65% share to provide for her daughter, Dulce, an unemployed minor who is in the lowest possible bracket, which we will call the 15% bracket.

If Ginger earns a dollar, she will be left with 65 cents to provide for the care, feeding, and education of her daughter. On the other hand, if the daughter were taxed on the dollar earned by Ginger, there would be 85 cents left to provide for the daughter's support, after taxes. Thus, Ginger and Dulce would both benefit if they could establish a plan whereby dollars earned by Ginger are taxed to Dulce. The tax savings presented by this illustration are 20 cents, or 20% of each dollar earned by Ginger; she would be hard pressed to find an investment that would assure her that same 20% return! The reason for this result is really quite easy to explain; Ginger has fully utilized her lower tax brackets, while Dulce has not.

Another easy way to understand how income-splitting works is to take any amount of income and determine how much tax would be paid on that income by one taxpayer. Then, take the same amount of income and see what would happen if it were split by two taxpayers. You will notice that the two taxpayers pay less than one-half the taxes paid by the lone taxpayer, even though the total income earned is the same. You can try this test using the tax rates from any year. Even though the degree of benefit derived by income-shifting will vary depending upon the tax rates in effect during a given year, the fact that there will be a benefit from income-shifting will remain constant, as long as there are progressive tax rates, and as long as the income is shifted from a high bracket taxpayer to a low bracket taxpayer.

It is important to note that there is more than one way to shift income. While it is beneficial to shift the tax cost of income generation from a high bracket taxpayer to a low bracket taxpayer, it is equally beneficial to shift tax benefits from low brackets to high brackets. Tax benefits, which include such items as deductions, losses, and credits, reduce a taxpayer's ultimate tax liability. Deductions and losses reduce the amount of taxable income a taxpayer has. Since the tax rates are applied to taxable income under § 1 of the Code, each deduction from taxable income results in a reduction in tax owed equal to the deduction times the taxpayer's applicable tax rate. Or, in English, a taxpayer in the 35% bracket will save 35 cents for each dollar of deduction. On the other hand, a taxpayer in the 15% bracket will only save 15 cents for every dollar of deduction. Thus, a dollar of deduction is clearly worth more to the 35% bracket taxpayer in terms of tax savings. (For further discussion of deductions, see § 6.04.)

Fortunately, or unfortunately, depending upon your point of view, the government is very much aware of the potential for income-shifting that exists whenever progressive rates are involved. Thus, the Code has several sections which prevent tax avoidance through the vehicle of income-shifting. Some examples of such sections are §§ 1(g), 267, 704(e), and 7872.

PROBLEM 6A: How do the provisions listed above attempt to prevent the abuse of the progressive income tax rates? Can you find other sections which deal with the problem of income shifting? Now, look at § 102. Does the fact that gifts are not taxed as income give rise to possible income shifting through the use of gifts?

Income-shifting occurs most often between related taxpayers. After all, there are very few taxpayers who hate paying taxes so badly that they would be willing to shift some of their income to a non-relative, in order to receive tax benefits. In fact, it is never a good idea to avoid making more money, simply because you will have to pay taxes on that money. On the other hand, as in the hypothetical situation with Ginger and Dulce, above, there is usually an economic benefit other than the tax benefit involved in shifting income to a relative; the taxpayer would be paying for particular needs of that relative, irrespective of the tax consequences. Remember there are factors, other than the tax consequences, which must be considered in any transaction. You should never let the tax tail wag the dog!

It should also be noted that the term *relative* has a broader meaning in the realm of taxation than it does in the common usage of everyday life. In tax language, a shareholder can be related to a corporation, and a partner can be related to a partnership (*see, e.g.,* § 267(b)). The assignment of income to a relative is a matter of great concern to the courts, as well as the legislature. For example, the courts have held that a wage earner cannot avoid taxation on his salary simply by assigning the right to receive the salary to another taxpayer.[2] In addition, the owner of property cannot avoid the tax on the income generated by that piece of property unless he actually transfers the underlying interest that produces the income.[3]

§ 6.03   THE TIME VALUE OF MONEY (A QUESTION OF WHEN)

Which would you rather have, one dollar today, or one dollar next year? If you answered that you would take the dollar today, rather than waiting until next year to receive it, you are well on your way to understanding the concept of the time value of money.

In determining that you would rather receive the money today than next year you probably took into account factors such as interest and inflation. After all, you would certainly expect to receive some interest on your dollar if you invested it in the bank, so that even at a very modest rate, say 5%, your dollar would be worth $1.05 after one year. Furthermore, even if you decided to spend the dollar as soon as you received it, you could probably buy more goods or services for one dollar this year than you could next year, because of inflation. Inflation has become such a regular factor in the economy that you must consider it whenever you compare the present value of money to its value in the future. However, even in rare times of falling prices, a person can benefit from investing a dollar today, rather than waiting until next year to receive it.

Since taxation involves economic costs and benefits, it should not be surprising that the concept of the time value of money applies to tax legislation and planning. Thus, if you were asked whether you would rather receive a dollar from the government today, or next year, you should answer that you want your dollar today. However, there are quite a few taxpayers who rejoice when they receive a tax refund from the government each year. Whenever a taxpayer receives a refund from the government, he is merely receiving money that belonged to him anyway. After all, a refund occurs when a taxpayer overpays his tax. Thus, a taxpayer receiving a refund has allowed the government to use his money, interest-free, from the time of the overpayment until the time of the refund, which is the same as taking the dollar the next year, instead of today.

---

[2] Lucas v. Earl, 281 U.S. 111 (1930). In this case, a taxpayer had assigned half of his future income to his wife. The Supreme Court held that a taxpayer cannot shift the incidence of taxation on earned income, simply by assigning the rights to receive that income in the future to another taxpayer. That is, the taxpayer who earns the income is the taxpayer who will be taxed on that income. This case is especially interesting in that the taxpayer assigned his future wages to his wife prior to the adoption of the federal income tax in 1913. Thus, his motivation in making this assignment could not have involved tax avoidance. Furthermore, income shifting between spouses is really not a concern anymore because married couples must either file jointly, or as married filing separately. In either case, the amount of tax paid by the couple will be the same no matter which of the spouses actually earned the income.

[3] Helvering v. Horst, 311 U.S. 112 (1940).

Of course, there are some noneconomic reasons for overpaying taxes. For example, some taxpayers pay too much, simply because they do not want to take a chance on paying too little and incurring the wrath of the IRS. Other taxpayers argue that overpaying their taxes is a form of forced savings. In other words, they would have never saved the amount they overpaid to the government, so they see overpaying taxes as a way of hiding money from themselves. Yet taxpayers will always derive an economic benefit from paying the right amount of tax, instead of overpaying, because of the concept of the time value of money.

As you might expect, the time value of money is important in tax considerations other than whether a taxpayer should be happy about receiving a refund. In fact, it is a concept that has an impact upon every consideration by the taxpayer relating to the question of "when." That is, any taxpayer concerned about when to include an item of income, or when to take a deduction, should consider the effect of the changing value of money over time. The conventional wisdom in that regard leads to a basic tax planning maxim: accelerate deductions, defer income. You want to accelerate deductions, because deductions will reduce the amount of tax you owe in the current year, and will, therefore, increase the amount of dollars you will be able to use for investing or spending this year.

On the other hand, it is better if you can wait and pay a dollar of tax next year, instead of this year. That way, you, not the government, will have the use of the dollar for the current year. You can accomplish this task by waiting until next year to receive income, whenever possible. An easy example of income deferral is the Individual Retirement Arrangement (IRA), which allows a taxpayer to postpone paying the tax on income earned today until she retires. Another benefit of such an arrangement is that the interest generated by the account is accrued tax-deferred until the funds are withdrawn. Thus, by having an IRA, a taxpayer can use dollars that would have otherwise been given to the government in the form of taxes. (The provisions for IRA's are §§ 219 and 408.)

While tax deferral through the use of an IRA is clearly encouraged within the limits established by the Code, there are several provisions that prohibit either the acceleration of deductions, or the deferral of income. Even if Congress changes those provisions, or creates new ones governing timing, you should be able to see that the time value of money will always play an important role in matters of taxation. Some of the current provisions dealing with timing of income and deductions are §§ 83, 71(f), 72, 101(d), and 267(a)(2)(B).

PROBLEM 6B: How do the provisions listed above affect a taxpayer's ability to determine when income will be taxed, or deductions will be taken? Should you always follow the maxim which encourages deferring income and accelerating deductions?

Timing will always be an issue in federal income taxation. However, you should notice that other factors besides the time value of money will affect a taxpayer's decision, or the legislature's action, concerning when an item should be deducted or included. Specifically, you should consider the maximum tax bracket for a given year when you engage in tax planning. This is especially true if the taxpayer will be in a significantly higher tax bracket during the next year than he is for the current year. For example, a law student will probably be in a lower tax bracket as a struggling law clerk than she will be when she becomes a prosperous member of the Bar. Therefore, she might want to accelerate income so that it will be taxable while she is a clerk, and defer deductions so that they can be used against the higher bracket income she earns as a real lawyer. Thus, even though the time value of money is always an important consideration, it can be outweighed by one of the other tax constants, in this case the effect of the progressive tax rates. Notice that if the law student does choose to accelerate her income, she will, in essence, be splitting her income, not among different taxpayers, but among different tax years and tax rates.

§ 6.04 PRE-TAX VS. AFTER-TAX DOLLARS (THE BENEFITS OF DEDUCTIONS)

Anyone who has ever earned a paycheck realizes that there is a difference between what you make and what you keep. The primary cause for this disparity is the withholding of federal income taxes from an employee's paycheck. Thus, a taxpayer in the 35% bracket would need to earn $1.58 to take home $1, because of the federal income tax bite. In that instance, the dollar remaining for the use of the employee is called an after-tax dollar, because it is the amount the employee has left to spend free of the federal income tax. If the same employee earned exactly $1, he would only have 65 cents left to take home after the income tax had been withheld. Therefore, the dollar earned is called a pre-tax dollar, because the employee will actually have less than a dollar to spend on himself once the government takes its share of his earnings. As long as there is a tax on income, there will be a difference between the pre-tax value and after-tax value of earnings.

While the concept of pre-tax and after-tax dollars is most easily explained in a setting involving taxes withheld from employee salaries, it is a concept that is equally applicable in any situation involving taxable income. That is, anyone in the 35% tax bracket who earns $1.58 will owe the government 58 cents in taxes, even if the taxes are not withheld from the source of the income. Therefore, you might say that the only kind of dollars any taxpayer has to spend are after-tax dollars, because a portion of the pre-tax dollars actually belongs to the government *ab initio.* (We could not resist the temptation to use at least one Latin phrase somewhere in this book.)

However, there are times when taxpayers are allowed, and even encouraged, to use the government's share of their earnings to help pay for expenses. In fact, that is the basic premise behind the very familiar and popular tax item known as a deduction. Whenever the government classifies an expenditure as being deductible it is, in fact, helping to pay that expenditure. This amazing benefit results from the simple truth that $1.58 of income will be totally offset by $1.58 of deduction, leaving no tax liability on the part of the taxpayer. Therefore, if our taxpayer in the 35% bracket earns $1.58, and keeps it, or spends it in a way that is nondeductible, he will have to pay 58 cents in taxes, leaving him with a total benefit of $1. On the other hand, if he spends the money in a manner than gives rise to a deduction, he will owe no tax, and he will derive a benefit of $1.58.

For example, assume that the taxpayer needs to pay rent on his business office (see § 162), which costs him exactly $1.58 per month. (You can use any numbers in making this demonstration. I have used, rather redundantly, the ridiculous figure of $1.58 purely for simplicity.) The taxpayer will owe the $1.58 in rent, regardless of whether he earns any income this month, but assume that the taxpayer, indeed, earns $1.58. Notice that only $1 of the $1.58 belongs to the taxpayer. Yet if the taxpayer pays his rent from the $1.58 he earned, which is a deductible transaction, he will owe no taxes on his earnings, and his landlord will be fully paid. Thus, the taxpayer can use the government's share of his earnings to help pay his rent, and the government will let him get away with it!

The above, admittedly simplistic scenario, explains why taxpayers will always attempt to characterize payments as deductible, if possible. Congress might expand or limit the scope of deductible expenditures in the future, but as long as there are deductions, taxpayers will try to take advantage of them. One type of deduction that will probably remain a part of any future tax code, is the deduction for business expenses (§ 162). Business deductions represent an understanding on the part of the government that taxpayers have to spend money to make money. Therefore, a taxpayer's taxable business profit should be the result of a netting of business income with business expenses.

Of course, the government itself derives a benefit from many of the deductions it allows. For example, the deduction for charitable contributions (§ 170) encourages taxpayers to support charitable and educational institutions. The government would have to support such institutions to a much greater degree than it already does, if not for private contributions. Since the government would use tax dollars to support charities, it makes sense that taxpayers making contributions to charities would be entitled to a tax deduction. In effect, the charitable contributions deduction encourages taxpayers to do directly what the government would otherwise have to do indirectly.

> **PROBLEM 6C: The Manitoba Goon is a professional wrestler who has achieved the highest income tax bracket for the current tax year. Goon's daughter, Saskatoon, is in the lowest possible tax bracket. Given what you have learned about before-tax dollars, can you think of a way for Goon to shift income to Saskatoon using deductions? (*See* § 162(a)(1).)**

The tax benefit of using pre-tax dollars to pay for expenses is of major concern to the government. Therefore, many Code sections have evolved which prevent deductions for certain expenses. You should especially look at §§ 262 and 274, which disallow deductions for expenses which arise out of personal need or pleasure. For example, § 274(c) disallows the expenses related to the personal pleasure aspects of foreign travel. Further, that section places the burden of proving that a deduction should be allowed squarely upon the taxpayer.

Furthermore, the benefits of a deductible expense are worthwhile only when the expense itself is one the taxpayer ultimately needs or desires to make. For example, it never makes sense for a taxpayer to give money to charity, simply to obtain a tax benefit. After all, while it is true that a deduction allows the taxpayer to use the government's money to benefit the charity, most of the money given to the charity will be the taxpayer's. Remember, our $1.58 taxpayer could have paid his taxes and kept a dollar. If he gave the $1.58 to charity, he might avoid paying taxes, but he would lose the use of his dollar.

§ 6.05 BASIS

[1] The Nature of Basis

Many of the very basic principles of taxation are identical to the concepts you encounter every day in your non-tax life. That is, tax ideas are usually generated by common sense. For example, when you receive your salary, you are taxed on the income you have earned. However, when you deposit your after-tax paycheck in the bank, you are not taxed again every time you make a withdrawal from your account. You should expect to receive your money back tax-free, because you have already been taxed on the dollars in the bank. If you understand this simple transaction, you understand the purpose of the tax constant known as "basis."

As you have seen from § 6.04, the only type of dollars that a taxpayer has to spend are after-tax dollars. Therefore, when a taxpayer buys property, she does so with money that has already been subject to tax. This is true even if the government decides not to tax the dollars she uses, through the various exclusions found in the Code. After all, an exclusion simply means that the government has decided not to tax a particular type of income; the income itself was subject to the laws of taxation, although it was not ultimately taxed.

Thus, even if the taxpayer decides to buy stock, instead of depositing her money in the bank, she should be able to withdraw the money she has invested without incurring tax liability. Of course, when you think of property, such as stock, you do not generally think of withdrawing your investment. Instead, you most likely consider selling the stock. Yet, the tax effect is exactly the same; the taxpayer should be able to sell her shares of stock and receive her investment back tax-free. The amount she will be able to receive as a tax-free return of investment, or capital, is called her basis. Basis is another concept that will always be a part of the federal income tax system.

To illustrate the concept of basis, assume that Deja Vu, a famous dancer, decides to buy some stock in Two Left Feet, Inc. She uses the proceeds from her paycheck to buy 1000 shares of the stock at $1 per share. Therefore, her basis in the total shares of stock is $1000, while her basis in each share of stock is $1. If Deja sells all of her stock for $1000, she should owe no tax, because all that has happened is that she changed her form of after-tax dollars from cash, to stock, and back to cash again. Even if she sells all of the stock shares for $1500, she will still be able to receive her original $1000 investment, her basis, tax-free.

[2] Specific Basis Provisions

Now that you have an introduction to basis, it might be useful for you to study some of the Code sections that create, limit, or otherwise affect basis in property. Therefore, the following paragraphs are dedicated to a discussion of specific basis provisions: cost basis under § 1012, gift basis under § 1015, date of death basis under § 1014, and adjusted basis under § 1016. You should note that there is a common thread to all of these basis provisions: a taxpayer should be able to have her after-tax investment returned tax-free.

[a] Section 1012 Cost Basis

Section 1012 of the Internal Revenue Code states that the basis of property acquired by purchase or exchange shall be its cost. That section does not, however, give a definition of cost. Yet, if you remember the purpose behind having basis in property in the first place, which is to guarantee that a taxpayer will be able to recoup all of her after-tax dollars invested in the property, then you will have no problem understanding the definition of cost for tax purposes.

When you think in purely economic terms, you probably simply define cost as what you gave up in order to get something else. Thus, whether you paid $5000 in cash, or gave property with a value of $5000, you would say that your cost was $5000. Yet the tax definition of cost, which is the definition used by § 1012, does not rely upon the value of what you gave, but rather upon the amount of after-tax dollars you gave in order to receive property. Of course, this difference in the definition of cost will not have any impact upon a taxpayer using cash to buy property, since (one more time with feeling) the only kind of dollars a taxpayer has to spend are after-tax dollars. However, when a taxpayer uses her property to buy other property, there will be a major difference between the economic cost, and the tax cost in some circumstances.

To illustrate the difference between economic cost and tax cost, assume that April Fool, a famous rock star, has decided to exchange her electric drums for some glitter. Assume further that April paid $2000 for the drums, but, because of her tremendous fame, they are worth $5000. The glitter, on the other hand, is only worth $4500. What is the cost of the glitter to April? Your first inclination might be to say that since April gave up $5000 worth of drums, in order to receive $4500 worth of glitter, her cost is $5000; from a purely economic point of view, that would be correct. However, from a tax perspective April's cost must be determined by reference to the after-tax dollars she will have invested in the glitter. Clearly, her basis in the drums was $2000, because she paid cash for the drums. Therefore, April has at least $2000 after-tax invested in the glitter. But there is more; April does have economic gain, an accession to wealth, when she receives glitter worth more than what she paid for the drums, so it should not be surprising that she will be taxed on the difference between the basis of what she gave up, and the value of what she received (see § 1001 of the Code). In this case, April will be taxed on the difference between the basis of her drums ($2000) and the value of the glitter ($4500), which is $2500. Therefore, April's total tax cost when she purchases the glitter is $4500, which is derived from the amount she had invested in the drums, PLUS the amount of taxable gain generated by the receipt of the glitter. In other words, April's tax cost equals the value of the property she received, the glitter, NOT the value of the property she gave up. (For a complete discussion of the concept of gains derived from dealings in property, see § 6.06.)

Another example of tax cost occurs whenever an employee receives property in return for services. If April receives a $9000 sports car from her employer as compensation for her latest concert, she would indeed be taxed on the value of the car under §§ 61(a)(1) and 83. If she sells the car for $9000 in cash on the day she received it, she should not be forced to pay tax a second time on the $9000. Therefore, April's basis in the car must be $9000, which is the amount taxed when she received it; because she was taxed on the receipt of the $9000 automobile, she had $9000 in after-tax dollars invested in the car.

In any fully taxable transaction, the basis of property received is *always* the fair market value of that property immediately prior to the transaction.

[b] Section 1015 Gift Basis

Tax cost is the measuring of basis any time a taxpayer acquires property as compensation, or through purchase, or taxable exchange. But, what should be the taxpayer's basis in property acquired as a gift? After all, the donee of a gift does not, himself, have an after tax cost associated with the property he receives. On the other hand, the donor of a gift is not allowed a deduction for the gift, even though he has given up after-tax dollars in a transfer for which he received no economic consideration. Common sense would dictate, therefore, that the donee should be allowed to take the donor's basis in the property, because the donor has not been allowed to recoup the after-tax dollars he had invested. Section 1015, indeed, applies the aforementioned logical approach, in that it states that the donee's basis in a gift will be the same as the donor's basis immediately before the transfer.

[i] Split-Basis Under § 1015

Section 1015 does, however, contain some exceptions to the general rule that the donee takes the basis of the donor immediately prior to the transfer. First § 1015(a) provides that if the fair market value of the property is less than its adjusted basis immediately prior to the transfer, the basis for determining loss shall be the fair market value. This section, known as the "split-basis" provision, has the effect of preventing a taxpayer from transferring a potentially deductible loss to another taxpayer by gift. For example, if Woody had stock in the Dizzy Co. with an adjusted basis of $25 and a fair market value of $10, and he gave that stock to Buzz in a transaction qualifying as a gift under § 102, § 1015 would give Buzz a $25 basis for *most* purposes. Yet because Woody's basis was greater than the fair market value of the stock at the time of the gift, Buzz's basis for the purposes of determining loss would only be $10, which was the fair market value at the time of the gift. Accordingly, if Buzz later sold the stock for $8, he would only be able to take a $2 loss, which represents the economic decline in value of the property from the time Buzz received it. The $15 of loss inherent in the property at the time of the transfer is, therefore, not allowed as a deduction to Buzz since the loss occurred while the property was owned by Woody. Notice that if Buzz sold the property for $27, he would only have a $2 gain because the basis for determining gain would be $25. Oddly enough, if Buzz sold the stock for $13 (or for anything between $10 and $25, for that matter) he will neither have gain nor loss. His basis for determining loss would be $10, and his amount realized would be $13. Thus, he would realize no loss. On the other hand, his basis for determining gain would be $25, and his amount realized would be $13, so he would have no gain, either.

[ii] Part Sale/Part Gift

Another special rule relating to gift basis under § 1015 is the provision relating to transactions which are in part a sale and in part a gift. In other words, we need to know what basis a taxpayer has when she pays money or other consideration for property in a transaction which remains at least partly gratuitous. For example, assume that Bo Peep owned real estate knows as Baaacres, and that she had an adjusted basis in the property of $30K. Assume further that the property was worth $75K when Peep sold it to her brother, Bo Bridges, for $25K. Notice that even though Bridges paid money for the property, there was still an element of the transfer that was a gift. Specifically, Peep gave Bridges property worth $75K for a cost of $25K. Thus, there was a $50K gift in this transaction, even though it was also partly a sale. To determine the donee's basis on this transaction, we must look to the regulations under § 1.1015-4. That regulation tells us that when there is a part sale/part gift transaction, the donee's basis will be the greater of the donor's basis or the amount paid by the donee. Here, since Bridges only paid $25K and Peep's basis was $30K, Bridges will take a basis of $30K (the greater of the two). Had Bridges paid $50K for the property, on the other hand, his basis would have been $50K, since that was greater than Peep's basis of $30K. It is important to note that if Bridges paid $50K, Peep would have a gain of $20K under § 1001 of the Code and § 1.1001-1(e) of the regulations. Section 1.1001-1(e) of the regulations also provides that a donor will never have a loss on a part sale/part gift. This makes sense, because if the law allowed for a donor to take a loss on a part sale/part gift, donors would always sell the property for $1, rather than merely giving it away. In essence, therefore, the rules for part sale/part gift are the same rules for gifts, in general, provided that the donee does not pay more for the property than the donor's adjusted basis. If the donee does, in fact, pay more for the property than the donor's basis, the donor will have gain, and the donee will have a basis equal to his cost.

> **PROBLEM 6D: Sal Monella wants to give Swampacre to his daughter Ella. The property has a basis in Sal's hands of $7000, and it is worth $10,000. What is Ella's basis in the property if Sal gives it to her outright? What if Sal sold Ella the property for $50? For $7500?**

[iii] Section 1015(d)(6) Increase in Basis for Gift Tax Paid

One final special rule under § 1015 is that adjustment is made to the donee's basis for the gift tax paid by the donor. (We often have students who ask us whose basis is adjusted under § 1015 for gift taxes paid; who will have the property after the gift?) Section 1015(d)(6) states that the basis to the donee shall be increased to the extent that federal gift taxes were paid on the appreciated portion of the transfer. Thus, if Donald gave Minnie a gift of stock with a basis of $5K and a fair market value of $20K, and Donald was required to pay $4K in gift tax on the transfer, Minnie's basis would be the $5K basis Donald had plus ($15K/20K x $4K) (see a discussion of the Code ratio in § 3.02[4]). Thus, Minnie's basis would be $8K.

[c] Section 1014 Date of Death Basis

As you become more and more familiar with the provisions of the Code, you should be aware that certain relationships or situations tend to alter the general rules of taxation.

One situation that almost always involves special treatment is the death of a taxpayer. While there is no constitutional provision that requires the government to take it easy on taxpayers when they die, the income tax laws are generally more lenient for decedents and their beneficiaries than they are for other taxpayers. Such leniency might be due to the government's belief that the deceased taxpayer and his family have suffered enough, or it might be due to the fact that, as a planning matter, taxpayers can only make use of the special treatment for death once. Yet, in any event, the basis provisions clearly reflect the idea that death is a mitigating factor in taxation. Thus § 1014 provides that a person acquiring property from a decedent will take a basis equal to the fair market value of the property at the decedent's date of death.

In effect, the date of death basis can be of tremendous benefit to taxpayers, because the person acquiring property from a decedent can have a basis much greater than the after-tax dollars actually invested in the property. For example, if the decedent had a $40 basis in property worth $150, he would have a $110 gain if he sold the property. On the other hand, when the decedent dies leaving the property to his daughter, she will have a basis of $150 with no gain. Some other Code sections granting special tax treatment for situations involving death are § 101 (death payments), and § 102 (inheritance or bequest excluded from gross income).

[d] Section 1016 Adjusted Basis

Sections 1012, 1014 and 1015 indicate what a taxpayer's basis will be at the time he acquires property. However, as the taxpayer makes improvements on the property, or takes depreciation deductions connected with the property, he must increase or decrease his basis accordingly. Section 1016 dictates what adjustments must be made over the course of the taxpayer's ownership of property. Therefore, when the Code speaks of adjusted basis, it means the basis of the property when acquired as adjusted by § 1016.

Notice how § 1016 is consistent with the general concept of basis. When a taxpayer increases his after-tax investment by improving property, his basis will increase under § 1016(a)(1). Conversely, when the taxpayer removes some after-tax dollars from the property by taking a depreciation deduction related to the property his basis will decrease under § 1016(a)(2).

§ 6.06 REALIZATION AND RECOGNITION

Basis is an important tax principle, because it represents the amount of tax-free dollars a taxpayer can receive from the sale, exchange, or other disposition of property. By implication, therefore, any consideration the taxpayer receives in excess of her basis should be taxable as economic gain. This is indeed the result required by the Code under §§ 61(a)(3) and 1001.

Section 1001 defines gain realized to be the extent to which the amount realized by the taxpayer exceeds her adjusted basis. "Amount realized" is defined by § 1001(b) as the amount of cash plus the fair market value of property received by the taxpayer upon the disposition of her property. Section 1001(c) states that any gain *realized* by the taxpayer will be *recognized*, unless there is a provision in the Code to the contrary. Unfortunately, the Code does not define either realization or recognition, even though they are important constants in the scheme of taxation. The following paragraphs, therefore, are designed to acquaint you with the concepts of realization and recognition, which will always be members of the tax family.

[1] Realization

Section 61 requires a taxpayer to include all income, from whatever source derived, as part of his gross income. Case law[4] defines income as any accession to wealth. Therefore, any time a taxpayer's wealth is increased, he has income. When you consider how often property can appreciate in value, you can see how imposing a tax on every accession to wealth could be problematic.

For example, consider the poor soul who owns stock. Technically speaking, every time the value of his stock increases, he has an accession to wealth. Should the shareholder be taxed every time there is an up tick in the value of his stock? Should an owner of real estate be forced to revalue his property every year, or even every day, so that the government can tax him on any appreciation? Your answer to both these questions should be no. If the government taxed appreciation in the value of property as it occurred, there would be no need to calculate a taxpayer's basis, because the entire value of the taxpayer's holdings would consist of after-tax dollars. Instead, the government waits until the taxpayer disposes of the property in some way, before taxing any gain. Such a disposition is called a realization event.

Thus, when a taxpayer buys Z-Rocks Corp. stock for $1000 and it increases in value to $1200, there is no gain realized to the taxpayer. True, the taxpayer will probably say "I have $1200 worth of Z-Rocks," but the $200 difference between the stock's value, and the taxpayer's basis will simply be unrealized appreciation. This result makes sense when you consider the fact that the stock could very easily decrease in value the next day. In fact, the taxpayer risks fluctuations in the value of his stock, until he sells it, or exchanges it for other property. The sale or exchange which fixes the value of the stock to the selling shareholder gives rise to the realization of gain, or to the realization of loss if the taxpayer's adjusted basis is greater than the amount realized.

> **A NOTE ON VALUATION:** In your study of taxation, you will frequently encounter the phrase "fair market value." The fair market value is what a willing buyer would pay a willing seller, neither being under any compulsion to buy or sell. While the fair market value of some items, such as stock, can be easily obtained, there are many types of property that are not so easily or uniformly valued. For example, you might buy an automobile, loaded with all of the extras (engine, tires, etc.) for $9995. Your friend might pay $10,325 for the exact same automobile, with the exact same options. Which one of you paid market value? The answer is that you both did, as long as you both dealt at arms length with the dealer who sold you the car, and as long as you and your friend were not desperate buyers, and the dealer was not a desperate seller. Therefore, identical items can have different fair market values in our free market system.

Generally speaking, the government will presume that a transaction between taxpayers was for fair market value, as long as the transaction was at arms length, and that consideration paid by related parties is not fair market value. Related parties include corporations, partnerships, trusts and estates controlled by the taxpayer, as well as the taxpayer's family. (*See, e.g.,* I.R.C. §§ 267, 318.)

[2] Recognition

The mere fact that a gain or a loss has been realized does not mean that the taxpayer will necessarily have to report that gain as income under § 61 of the Code. However, when the taxpayer is required to report a realized gain as income, or is allowed to deduct a loss

---

[4] Commissioner v. Glenshaw Glass, 348 U.S. 426 (1955).

realized, he is said to have recognized a gain or loss. Thus a taxpayer can have a gain realized that is not recognized, but he cannot have a gain recognized unless he has a gain realized.

As you noticed before, § 1001(c) states that any gain realized will be recognized, that it will be taxed, unless there is a provision of the Code which states otherwise. Some Code sections which do not require recognition of a realized gain or loss (called, not surprisingly, nonrecognition provisions) are §§ 1031, 1032, 1033(a)(2)(A), and 1041.

You might be wondering why the Code gives special nonrecognition treatment for certain transactions. Nonrecognition treatment represents the government's position that there will be a more appropriate time to tax a particular gain. For example, if you owned a parking garage in Atlanta and exchanged it for a parking garage in New York, you would have a gain realized, as long as the fair market value of the New York garage exceeded the adjusted basis of the Atlanta garage. Yet you would not really liquidate your investment; you would simply change the location of that investment. A more appropriate time to tax you would be when you eventually sold your garage, or exchanged it for property that was totally different in nature.

You should notice that nonrecognition of a gain is different from exclusion of a gain. Nonrecognition merely defers the incidence of taxation to a later, more appropriate time, while exclusion is total forgiveness of gain. Thus it should not surprise you that the basis of property you receive in a nonrecognition transaction will generally be the same as the basis of the property you transfer. This makes sense, because the amount of after-tax dollars you will have invested in your new property will be exactly the same as the after-tax dollars invested in your old property, if you received the new property free of tax.

Therefore, using the adjusted basis of the Atlanta garage to illustrate, assume that the adjusted basis of the Atlanta garage was $70,000, and that the fair market value of the New York garage was $86,000. You would have a gain realized of $16,000 (amount realized minus adjusted basis). This gain would be recognized unless some provision of the Code called for nonrecognition. For the purposes of this example, you can assume that § 1031, a nonrecognition provision, applied to your garage exchange. Your basis in the New York garage will be $70,000, which is the same as the basis you had in your Atlanta property. If you then sold your New York garage for $86,000, you would have a gain realized and recognized of $16,000, which is equal to the gain that was deferred when you acquired the New York property.

Notice that when you sold your garage, you cashed out your investment. There can be no more appropriate time to tax you than when you totally liquidate an investment. If the government did not tax you on this sale, it would probably never be able to tax you; this is the government's last chance.

> **PROBLEM 6E: Cal Amity owned a dynamite factory that he used in his demolition business. The building had a basis of $400,000, and a fair market value of $1,000,000. Unfortunately, Cal decided to have a barbecue for his employees at his factory, which he hoped would be a real blowout; it was, and the factory was totally destroyed. What would be Cal's gain or loss realized, his gain or loss recognized, and his basis in his factory if:**
>
> **(1) the factory was uninsured?**
>
> **(2) the factory was insured for $750,000, and Cal used the insurance proceeds to take a long vacation?**
>
> **(3) the factory was insured for $1,000,000, and Cal reinvested the proceeds in a new factory building within two years of the explosion? (*See* § 1033.)**

§ 6.07   CASH EQUIVALENCE

By now, you have studied the concepts of basis, gain realized, and gain recognized. These constants would not be necessary if every transaction entered into by a taxpayer involved only cash. Of course, in the real world, taxpayers use various types of property, real and personal, tangible and intangible, in transacting their affairs. Thus basis, gain realized, and gain recognized are devices to insure that property transactions are treated identically to cash transactions.

For example, assume that Hal E. Tosis works at the Fresh Breath Clinic, which is owned by Pepper Mint. When Hal performs $500 worth of services for Pepper, she can pay him either in cash or in property. If Pepper pays Hal in cash, there is no question that Hal will have $500 worth of gross income under § 61(a)(1), and Pepper will have $500 less cash in her business. On the other hand, what will happen if, instead of cash, Pepper gives Hal machinery worth $500, but with a basis to Pepper of only $1? What will be the tax consequences to Pepper, and what will be Hal's basis in the machinery?

Pepper must realize and recognize a gain any time she uses appreciated property to pay a liability. If that were not the case, Pepper, and every taxpayer for that matter, would pay her debts with appreciated property. After all, Pepper only had $1 invested in the machinery. The rest of the value of the machinery is unrealized appreciation. Pepper should not be able to derive the same benefits by using appreciated property that she derives from using an equal value of cash. In fact, Pepper should be forced to realize and recognize a $499 gain when she uses the machinery to pay her obligation to Hal. Otherwise, Pepper would have a choice of using $500 or $1 to offset the same liability.

This result becomes obvious if you simply insert cash into the transaction. That is, assume that Pepper is not really transferring machinery to Hal, but that she is paying him $500 and Hal is returning the cash to Pepper in consideration for the property. In essence, that is exactly what is taking place for tax purposes. Clearly, if Pepper receives $500 in cash for her machinery, she would both realize and recognize a $499 gain. Furthermore, when Hal receives the $500 in cash, he will have $500 of gross income, and, in turn, when he transfers the cash for the machinery, he will have a $500 basis, because he will have $500 invested in the machinery after-tax.

You can simplify any transaction involving an exchange of property for services, or an exchange of property, by using the technique of inserting cash into the transaction. This makes sense, because property values are always expressed in terms of dollar equivalents. In essence, when you exchange property with another taxpayer in an arms length transaction, you are saying that the property you will receive is equal in dollar value to the property that you will transfer. Thus, it is not so strange to recharacterize your exchange as two simultaneous sales and purchases.

For the purpose of illustrating these simultaneous sales/purchases, assume that you want to trade your motor boat (adjusted basis $3000, fair market value $3500) for your neighbor's hot-tub (adjusted basis $1500, fair market value $3500). What you and your neighbor are actually saying is: "I will pay you $3500 for your property, and you pay me $3500 for my property." Thus, you will have a $500 gain realized and recognized on the sale of your boat, and you will have a $3500 basis in the hot-tub you purchased. Your neighbor will have a $2000 gain realized and recognized on the sale of his hot-tub, and he will have a $3500 basis in the boat he purchased. Of course, in reality, no cash changed hands. Yet, for tax purposes, it is much easier to understand the tax consequences of an exchange if you assume that each party paid the other an equal amount of cash for his property. After all, the Internal Revenue Code is, always has been, and always will be, based on the concept of cash equivalence where property is involved.

> **PROBLEM 6F: You have been appointed the executor of the estate of D. Cedent. Ms. Cedent's will requires that you pay $5000 to Benny Ficiary. However, when you are ready to make the required estate distributions, you notice that there is not enough cash in the estate to satisfy Benny's bequest. Therefore, you decide to give Benny stock with a fair market value of $5000, but an adjusted basis of only $1200. Will this distribution give rise to any gain to the estate? What will Benny's basis in the stock be? Can cash equivalence help you answer the above questions?**

§ 6.08   TAX ACCOUNTING

[1]   Introduction

The following paragraphs are intended as a very basic introduction to some of the accounting principles you will encounter in your study of federal income tax. No matter what headaches future tax legislation might cause, taxpayers will always have taxable years, and they will always have methods for reporting income known as accounting methods.

[2]   The Taxable Year

It is true that the types of taxable years allowed to a particular taxpayer can differ from tax reform to tax reform, but each taxpayer will, nonetheless, have a taxable year. Simply stated, a taxable year provides a frame of reference for determining a taxpayer's income, expenses and losses. Without a definite time period, it would be impossible for the government or the taxpayer to determine which losses should offset which income. Therefore, the government has decided that the most convenient time package for assessing the tax consequences of any given taxpayer is one year.

There are only two types of taxable years: the calendar year, and the fiscal year. The vast majority of individual taxpayers, S corporations, partnerships, and personal service corporations are required to use the calendar year as their taxable year. Calendar year taxpayers start with a clean slate each January 1, and close their books each December 31. Thus, as a general rule, only those items of income, deduction, loss, or credit actually occurring during the calendar year will affect the taxpayer's ultimate tax liability for that particular year.

The Code defines "fiscal year" to be any year other than a calendar year.[5] A taxpayer can adopt a fiscal year as his taxable year if his bookkeeping and accounting years naturally end on the last day of a month other than December. Generally speaking, a business's natural year ends with its heaviest income producing months.[6] Thus a citrus distributor which sells citrus from November to May each year, before closing down for the off-season, might consider having a year ending on May 31. Its new year would, therefore, begin on June 1 of each year. Since every taxpayer can only have one taxable year, it is important to note that a taxpayer with several businesses might be forced to choose a taxable year different from the natural tax years of any one, or all, of his businesses. The most likely candidates for fiscal years are large corporations.

---

[5] I.R.C. § 441(e).

[6] The taxpayer's natural year is subject to government approval. Likewise, once the taxpayer adopts a taxable year, he cannot change that year without prior approval of the Secretary of the Treasury. I.R.C. § 442.

[3] Accounting Methods

When you are an attorney and you perform services for your clients, should you be taxed on the income from your services as you earn it, or should you wait until you are actually paid before you are taxed? As long as the taxable year of performance and payment are the same, the method you use for reporting your income will not make a difference. That is, assume that you are a calendar year taxpayer, and that you perform $5000 worth of legal services for Dee Linquent on April 3, 2008, for which she pays you on December 3, 2008. You will report the $5000 as income on your 2008 tax return, irrespective of whether you are taxed when you earn income, or when you actually receive payment for the services you render. On the other hand, if Dee does not pay you until January 3, 2009, you can see that the year of inclusion will depend upon whether you report income as you earn it (2008) or as you actually receive it (2009). Based upon the concept of the time-value of money, discussed earlier in this chapter, it is clear that, given a choice, most taxpayers would want to wait to pay tax on their income until the last possible moment, which would be 2009 in the above hypothetical.

On the other hand, as a general rule, most taxpayers would prefer to take deductions as soon as possible. Therefore, if you incurred a deductible expense in 2008, but did not actually pay for that expense until 2009, you would probably want to take the deduction as soon as the liability arose, rather than waiting until you actually paid off the liability. It probably will not surprise you that the government does not allow taxpayers to choose the time of inclusion of every item of income or deduction. Instead, the government requires each taxpayer to choose the method of reporting income that most clearly reflects that taxpayer's income, deductions and loss as a whole. (*See* I.R.C. § 446.)

A taxpayer's choice of tax accounting methods is actually quite limited. In fact, you have already been introduced to the two available methods, although not by name. When a taxpayer includes income as he earns it, or takes deductions as the liability for those deductions is incurred, he is said to be an "accrual" method taxpayer. Conversely, when a taxpayer includes income only when he is paid,[7] or takes deductions only when he makes payment, he is said to be a "cash" method taxpayer. You can see that consistent methods of accounting must always be a part of income taxation.[8]

---

[7] There are instances when a cash method taxpayer will have to include income before he actually receives that income. Generally, those instances arise under the doctrine of constructive receipt, which is explained by Treas. Reg. § 1.451-2. Obvious examples of constructive receipt involve employees who ask to be paid after December 31 of a year, even though funds are available to pay them before that date (*e.g.*, Joseph Frank, 22 TC 945, *aff'd* without discussion on this point, 226 F.2d 600 (6th Cir. 1955)), or sellers of property who ask that their payments be postponed, in order to defer taxation (*e.g.*, Penn v. Glenn, 265 F.2d 911 (6th Cir. 1959)).

[8] The sections dealing with accounting method are I.R.C. §§ 451 and 461. As you might expect, there are some exceptions to the general rules of accounting, such as the doctrine of constructive receipt mentioned in note 7, *supra*. Some of the exceptions are statutory. For example, see § 691, which requires income not yet received by a cash-method decedent to be taxable to his heirs upon their receipt of the income. This rule prevents cash method taxpayers from having an advantage over accrual method taxpayers upon death. After all, an accrual method taxpayer who earns income and then dies will be taxed. Without § 691, a cash method taxpayer who did not receive what he earned would never be taxed, nor would his heirs under the § 102 exclusion for inherited sums.

Chapter 7

THE OTHER SOURCES OF THE TAX LAW

§ 7.01 INTRODUCTION

The purpose of this chapter is to acquaint you with the ways in which judicial and administrative bodies interpret the tax laws. In particular, this chapter discusses:

(1) the jurisdiction of courts to hear tax cases, and the weight of the authority which must be accorded to tax opinions issued by various courts.

(2) some of the important judicial doctrines which are not expressly dictated by the Code, but which complement the overall purpose of the legislation found in the Code.

(3) the purpose and authority of treasury regulations.

(4) the purpose and authority of rulings and advisories issued by the Internal Revenue Service.

While you will often find the proclamations of such bodies to be of great importance in your study of income taxation, you must remember that, ultimately, only Congress has the power to tax income.

§ 7.02 THE ROLE OF THE JUDICIARY IN TAX LAW

[1] Jurisdiction

While the primary focus of any study of federal income taxation must be the Internal Revenue Code, you cannot overlook the importance of tax cases. After all, these cases are judicial interpretations of the Internal Revenue Code. Generally speaking, by the time a law student enters her first class in Federal Income Taxation, she should be familiar with how to read and analyze cases. Yet, some of the courts empowered to render tax opinions will not be familiar to the beginning tax student. Therefore, it is important for a tax student (as opposed to a common, everyday law student) to learn which courts have jurisdiction over tax controversies.

[a] Trial Courts

Interestingly enough, there are three separate courts which have original trial level jurisdiction over tax matters. Those courts are the United States District Court,[1] the United States Claims Court,[2] and the United States Tax Court.[3] A taxpayer can choose which of these forums (or fora, for those of you who are Latin scholars) he wishes to enter, whenever there is a tax controversy which reaches the litigation stage. To a great extent, his choice will be dictated by whether he would rather pay a deficiency asserted by the Commissioner of Internal Revenue, and file for a refund, or simply contest the validity of the deficiency, without paying it unless he loses. The availability of a jury may also be of importance to an informed forum shopper.

---

[1] 28 U.S.C. § 1346(a)(1).

[2] 28 U.S.C. § 1346(a).

[3] I.R.C. § 7442.

Perhaps the most familiar of the tax trial courts is the Federal District Court. District courts derive their authority to hear tax cases from 28 U.S.C. § 1346(a)(1). In order for a taxpayer to gain access to the district courts, he must pay the deficiency asserted by the Commissioner and file for a refund. The requirement that the taxpayer pay before entering district court is known as the "full payment rule."[4] Unfortunately, the issue of whether the full payment rule requires the payment of penalties and interest, as well as the tax owed, has been unclear.[5]

You might wonder why a taxpayer would want to pay an amount that he contests in order to get into a district court. The answer is that a taxpayer can demand a jury trial in district court. As you can imagine, there are many cases when a taxpayer might feel that a jury will give him a more favorable verdict than will a judge. For example consider the case of Francine Schuster,[6] a Roman Catholic nun who provided nursing services in an area of the country in desperate need of such services. Sister Francine did not keep any of her earnings from her job as a nurse. Instead, she always transferred her wages directly to her religious order, pursuant to her vow of poverty. The Internal Revenue Service charged that Sister Francine should be required to pay tax on her wages, notwithstanding her vow of poverty. The Tax Court agreed. It seems reasonable to argue that a jury of ordinary taxpayers might have been more sympathetic to Sister Francine's arguments than a Tax Court judge.

The second type of trial court available to a taxpayer is the Claims Court. The Claims Court, which replaced the Court of Claims in 1982,[7] is similar to the federal district courts in that it derives its jurisdiction from 28 USC § 1346(a)(1). A taxpayer must tender full payment of an alleged deficiency in order to file for a refund in the Claims Court. Unlike the district courts, a taxpayer cannot demand a jury trial in the Claims Court. A taxpayer might choose the Claims Courts over the Tax Court because the Claims Court is reputed to be more likely to find in favor of taxpayers than is the Tax Court.

The final trial court available to a taxpayer is the United States Tax Court, which derives its jurisdiction from § 7442 of the Internal Revenue Code. The Tax Court, known as the Board of Tax Appeals until 1942, is required to have 19 judges.[8] These judges, who are appointed by the President, sit in various divisions, with only one regular Tax Court judge hearing any case. As you might expect, Tax Court judges are picked for their expertise in the field of taxation, which makes their opinions extremely valuable in shaping the laws of taxation. The chief judge prescribes the times and places of the sessions of the Tax Court with a view to securing a reasonable opportunity for taxpayers to appear before the Tax Court, with as little inconvenience and expense as possible.[9] Providing taxpayers with such a forum to litigate tax matters is the sole purpose for having the Tax Court. It is the only court of original tax jurisdiction which provides a taxpayer a forum in which to contest a deficiency asserted by the Commissioner without first having to pay that deficiency. Therefore, a taxpayer who does not have the necessary assets to pay the tax first, then file for a refund, will have access to a judicial hearing before his property can be attached by the government. Furthermore, there is a provision[10] for an expedited proceeding when the

---

[4] The "full payment rule" was first espoused in *Flora v. United States*, 362 U.S. 145 (1959).

[5] Compare, for example, *Kell-Strom Tool Co. v. U.S.*, 205 F. Supp. 190 (D. Ct. Conn. 1962), in which a taxpayer was allowed to bring a refund action without paying the accrued interest on the tax involved, with *Arnold v. U.S.*, AFTR 2d 82-6165 (N.D. Ohio 1982), in which a taxpayer was denied access to the district court because he had paid only the tax in dispute but not the interest.

[6] 84 T.C. 764 (1985).

[7] P.L. 97-164 (1982).

[8] I.R.C. § 7443(a).

[9] I.R.C. § 7446.

[10] I.R.C. § 7463.

amount of tax in dispute is $50,000 or less. Unfortunately, a taxpayer does have to give up something to enjoy the convenience of the Tax Court; he does not have the right to demand a jury trial.

When you read decisions of the Tax Court, you will notice that the opinions issued before 1977 list only the name of the taxpayer, even though the Commissioner of Internal Revenue is always the opposing party in Tax Court matters. You will also notice that some of the opinions are called Tax Court Memorandum decisions (or TCMs). These are decisions which the judges of the Tax Court have decided add nothing to the established body of the law. TCMs are not officially reported. On the other hand, Tax Court opinions which have been reviewed by the chief judge can be officially reported in the United States Tax Court Reporter. As you should expect, the officially reported Tax Court opinions carry greater precedential value than do TCMs.[11] In summation, only the district courts allow for a jury trial in tax controversies, and only the Tax Court allows for litigation without prior full payment. A maxim used by tax practitioners might help put all of this in perspective. If you have the facts on your side, go to district court. If you have the law on your side, go to Tax Court. If you have neither the facts nor the law, go to Claims Court.

[b] Appellate Courts

With the exception of Tax Court cases involving expedited procedures, in which judgments are final,[12] all tax cases can be appealed as a matter of right to the United States Circuit Courts of Appeals. District Court and Tax Court opinions are appealed to the Court of Appeals for the circuit in which the trial was heard. Thus if a taxpayer is heard by either the Tax Court sitting in Atlanta or the U.S. District Court for the Northern District of Georgia, his appeal will be heard by the Eleventh Circuit Court of Appeals. On the other hand, Claims Court decisions, which can be rendered in various parts of the country, are always appealed to the Court of Appeals for the Federal Circuit.

While it should not surprise you to learn that the Federal District Courts are bound to follow the opinions of the Courts of Appeals for the circuits in which they are located, you might be surprised to learn that the Tax Court has opted to be similarly bound.[13] That is, even though the Tax Court can rightly be viewed as one judicial body, the Tax Court has decided to follow the decisions of the Circuit Courts, even where the circuits conflict. Thus a taxpayer bringing an action in the Tax Court in Los Angeles, which is covered by the Ninth Federal Judicial Circuit, might face a different result than a taxpayer bringing a case with identical facts in the Tax Court in New York, which is in the Second Circuit.[14] This disparity has caused some writers to call for the creation of a Federal Tax Court of Appeals.[15]

In the event that a conflict in circuits does arise in a given tax controversy, the Supreme Court can grant a petition of certiorari to resolve the conflict. Although Supreme Court opinions are, of course, the highest possible judicial proclamations, they can always be overruled by an act of the legislature.[16] Therefore, whenever you read any case dealing with

---

[11] For a discussion on how to find the sources of authority discussed in this chapter, see Chapter 8: An Introduction to Tax Research.

[12] I.R.C. § 7463(b) provides that all decisions entered in cases involving the expedited procedures available for Tax Court disputes of $50,000 or less must be final.

[13] Jack E. Golsen, 54 T.C. 742 (1970), aff'd, 445 F.2d 985 (10th Cir. 1971).

[14] Two examples of cases reaching different decisions on the same issue are *Kenneth W. Doehring*, 33 TCM 1035 (1974), and *Paul E. Puckett*, 33 TCM 1038 (1974), which discussed the validity of subchapter S elections in identical circumstances, but with different results.

[15] *See, e.g.*, Sheppard, *Judge Tannenwald Calls for National Court of Tax Appeals*, 26 Tax Notes 117-118, Jan. 14, 1985.

[16] For example, I.R.C. § 1041, which was added to the Code in 1984 by P.L. 98-369, § 421(a), legislatively overruled *United States v. Davis*, 370 U.S. 65 (1962), *reh'g denied*, 371 U.S. 854 (1962). The *Davis* case held that a spouse transferring appreciated

tax law you must make sure that the Code has not changed with reference to any sections discussed by that case.

[2]   Important Judicial Doctrines

The various provisions of the Internal Revenue Code provide the framework for the tax laws. There are times, however, when the Code needs the help of the courts so that the legislative intent will be carried out. There are two important judicial doctrines that have, from time to time, been used to augment the Code.

[a]   Substance over Form

In its decision in *Knesch v. U.S.,*[17] the Supreme Court stated that questions of taxation must be determined by viewing what was actually done, rather than the declared purpose of the participants, and when applying the provisions of the Sixteenth Amendment and income laws enacted thereunder the courts must regard matters of substance and not mere form.

For example, the Code affords taxpayers ample opportunities for tax savings. A couple might derive tax benefits by divorcing and then remarrying. Yet if the sole purpose of the divorce were to reap a tax benefit, and the couple in fact remarried in a subsequent tax year, then a court can treat the couple as if they had never divorced in substance, even though the form of the divorce was proper.

The doctrine of substance over form is one of the judicial overlays that prevents taxpayers from using the Code language to establish tax benefits with transactions having no true substance. Therefore, you can expect to see it used most often in transactions where a taxpayer is dealing only with himself, or his family, since such transactions most readily lend themselves to creative structuring. Some examples of the doctrine as it has been applied, are *Miedanear v. C.I.R.,*[18] in which an author tried to shift income from his publications to a church he established, without actually giving up control over the royalties he purportedly transferred, and *Abbott v. Commissioner,*[19] in which a transfer of stock by a taxpayer to his corporation, which then sold the stock, was taxed as if the taxpayer sold the stock himself.

[b]   Step Transactions

The step transaction doctrine is a close relative to the doctrine of substance over form. In fact, the *Abbott* case, cited in the previous paragraph, represents both doctrines. The step transaction doctrine can be applied anytime a taxpayer tries to establish a desired tax benefit through the use of several steps which have no effect other than a tax savings. For example, § 267(a) prohibits a taxpayer from deducting losses incurred through sales or exchanges of property to related parties. A taxpayer might try to get around this prohibition by selling property at a loss to a third party, declaring the loss, and then repurchasing the property, so that he could sell it to a relative. A court might collapse this transaction as a sham by holding that the sale to the third party had no purpose other than to obtain the tax advantage, and that the transaction was actually only a sale by the taxpayer to his relative.

---

property in a divorce settlement would be forced to recognize gain, and that the spouse receiving the property would be entitled to a basis equal to the fair market value of the property transferred. Section 1041 provides that no gain shall be recognized to the transferring spouse, and the spouse receiving the property will take a basis equal to the basis in the hands of the transferring spouse.

[17] 364 U.S. 361 (1960).

[18] 81 T.C. 272 (1983).

[19] 342 F.2d 997 (5th Cir. 1965).

Therefore, in step transactions the court will often ignore those portions of a deal which serve no purpose other than to achieve the tax benefit. An example of the step transaction doctrine can be found in *Ellison v. C.I.R.,*[20] in which a limited partnership tried to avoid being taxed on the income it earned from an apartment building it owned by characterizing the income as part of the purchase price used to buy the property, and by transferring the income to the property's original owner. Notice how cases like *Ellison* can be used to espouse the doctrine of substance over form.

Without the step transaction doctrine and the doctrine of substance over form, taxpayers would be able to run rampant over the intent of Congress while staying within the literal language of the Code. These doctrines allow a court to ignore all or part of a taxpayer's actions, so that the intent of the tax laws can be preserved. Thus, the courts cannot write the tax laws, but they can have a tremendous impact on their implementation.

§ 7.03 TREASURY REGULATIONS

[1] What Are Regulations, and How Do I Use Them?

Students often refer to the treasury regulations as the "English translation of the Code." This is because the regulations, or regs, as hardened tax jocks call them, tend to be more detailed and illustrative than the statutes they compliment. Yet before the regulations can be of any help to you, you must know what they are, and how to use them.

[a] What Are Regulations?

Congress has granted general authority to the Treasury Department to promulgate regulations to interpret and give meaning to the Code. I.R.C. § 7805(a). Congress also has delegated specific rule-making authority to the Treasury Department in certain Code sections. *See, e.g.,* I.R.C. § 25A. As a result of the congressional grant of power, treasury regulations generally have the force and effect of law (as discussed further below).

Newly promulgated final regulations appear in the Internal Revenue Bulletin as Treasury Decisions (TDs). For example, Treasury Regulation § 1.61-1 was added by TD 6272, on November 25, 1957. This information always appears at the end of a regulation section. The date on which a regulation was issued can be especially helpful in that it will indicate whether the regulation reflects the latest changes in an amended Code section. If not, then the regulation will always be superseded by inconsistent language in a Code section. This is important because the Treasury often releases regulations several months, and even several years, after Congress enacts legislation.

Because of this delay, the Treasury will sometimes promulgate temporary and proposed regulations before it issues final ones. Temporary regulations are issued whenever the Treasury decides that there is a matter of importance which needs some form of regulation immediately. For example, when § 71, which deals with the taxation of payments for alimony and separate maintenance, was completely overhauled in 1984,[21] the Treasury decided that taxpayers might need immediate guidance on the new section. Therefore, regulation § 1.71-1T was released to fill the gap until the Treasury could study the provision more fully and issue final regulations. As of 2007, the Treasury Department has not issued final regulations to replace § 1.71-1T, so it is still a valid, albeit temporary, regulation.

In most respects, proposed regulations are similar to temporary regulations, in that they are designed to provide guidance to taxpayers until they are eventually adopted as final

---

[20] 80 T.C. 378 (1983).

[21] P.L. 98-369, § 422(a).

regulations. The only difference is that the Treasury fully intends for proposed regulations to become final regulations, either in their present state, or with minor modification, at some point in the future, while temporary regulations are only intended to be stopgaps. Thus, while both may be relied upon, long-range tax planning based on a temporary regulation may be eventually negated or modified by future Treasury pronouncements.

[b] How Do I Find the Regs?

Finding a particular regulation is actually quite easy, once you have the knack. All regulations have a prefix, followed by a period, followed by the Code section they regulate, finally followed by a dash and a series of numbers and letters. Take for example, § 1.61-1(a), which is pronounced "one point, sixty-one, dash, one a." The prefix for that reg section is "1." The prefix indicates the topic of the regulation. In this case, Chapter 1, which deals with income taxation, is the subject, while reg sections with the number 20 as a prefix are final estate tax regulations, and those with a 25 prefix are final gift tax regs. Some prefixes indicate regulations with very limited scope, such as regulations having the prefix 15a, which are always temporary regulations governing Code § 453, the Installment Sales Revision Act. As you might expect, you will usually be working with final regulations concerning income taxation, and thus will most often be using regs carrying the prefix 1.

The number following the prefix in a regulation section is the Code section being interpreted. Thus Reg. § 1.61-1(a) works in conjunction with Code § 61. You must use the Code section to find a regulation section, because reg. sections are arranged by the Code sections they compliment, not by their prefixes. Therefore, the regulations dealing with Code § 62 follow the regulations dealing with § 61, and so on.

Finally, the numbers following the dash indicate the internal organization of a regulation. That is, the drafters of the regulations use those to help you to differentiate and locate specific portions of a regulation. For example, while all of the regulations under § 61 deal with gross income, § 1.61-1(a) gives a general definition of the term gross income, while § 1.61-14 gives specific examples of miscellaneous types of income that should be included in calculating a taxpayer's gross income.

[2] Regulations as Authority

Most regulations are nothing more than the Treasury Department's opinion as to what the Internal Revenue Code says. After all, it is the Congress, not the Treasury, that is empowered to tax income from whatever source derived. However, no less of an authority than the Supreme Court has held that the regulations deserve to be given great weight, when they are not in direct contradiction to the Code.[22] Therefore, the regulations deserve your respect as long as you cannot show any direct conflict between them and the Code. Remember, the Code will always supersede the regulations. Of course, if the regulations err on the side of the taxpayer, he might wish to argue that the government should be bound by them, since taxpayers could be expected to rely on them.

There are, however, some regulations, called legislative regulations, which actually have the force of law. Legislative regulations arise any time Congress expressly delegates its legislative authority to the Secretary. For example, elections made under Code sections, such as the election allowed by § 1033(a)(2)(A), are to be "made at such time and in such manner as the Secretary may by regulation prescribe." By delegating its authority, Congress is basically saying, "we adopt the words of the Secretary as our own." Another example of a Code section which grants legislative authority to the Treasury is § 385(a), which states:

---

[22] Commissioner v. South Texas Lumber Co., 333 U.S. 496 (1948).

"The Secretary is authorized to prescribe such regulations as may be necessary or appropriate to determine whether an interest in a corporation is to be treated for purposes of this title as stock or indebtedness."

Regulations generally track the Code provisions they interpret, starting with a general rule, then moving into specific definitions and examples. See, for example, Reg. §§ 1.61-1 through 1.61-14. The examples and illustrations provided by the regs can be extremely helpful to you as you study the principles of taxation. For example, see Reg. § 1.162-5(b)(2)(iii) Example (1). That section provides several illustrations concerning the deductibility of educational expenses by an employee. You should notice that the examples given show you how the regulation section would apply to a specific set of facts.

In recent times, the Treasury has varied from its tried and true regulation formula, and has begun experimenting with regulations having a question and answer format. Such regs attempt to anticipate taxpayer questions concerning the legislation they interpret. Examples of the question and answer regulations are §§ 1.71-1T, and 1.1041-1T, which are temporary but still valid regulations issued in 1984.

§ 7.04 REVENUE RULINGS AND OTHER ADMINISTRATIVE PRONOUNCEMENTS

[1] Revenue Rulings

In addition to regulations, Code § 7805 empowers the Treasury Department to issue rules. This authority has been properly delegated to the Commissioner of the Internal Revenue, who issues various rulings and advisories designed to promote uniform application of the tax laws. While such pronouncements by the Internal Revenue Service can take many forms, the form most often encountered by tax students and practitioners is the Revenue Ruling (Rev. Rul.).

The Service issues Revenue Rulings in response to questions from taxpayers if those questions are determined to be of importance to taxpayers as a whole. There is no requirement that the government issue a ruling in response to a taxpayer's question, and, in fact, the Service refuses to issue rulings on some of the more controversial transactions.[23] Rulings are published weekly as part of the Internal Revenue Bulletin, and then become part of the Cumulative Bulletin (C.B.), a compilation of roughly six months worth of Internal Revenue Bulletins. Rulings always contain the last two digits of the year in which they were released and a number indicating the order in which they appeared in that year. They are cited by reference to the Cumulative Bulletin and page number in which they are contained. Thus Revenue Ruling 83-118 was the 118th ruling issued in 1983. It is found in 1983-2 C.B. at page 27, which means it was published in the second half of 1983 (those published in the first half would appear in 1983-1 C.B.). Fortunately, all you need to find any ruling is the ruling number itself, since the Cumulative Bulletins contain a numerical finding list, which indicates the page numbers where each ruling is located.

In terms of their legal authority, Revenue Rulings "do not have the force and effect of Treasury Department Regulations."[24] This is because they can be issued and withdrawn by the Service without formal approval by the Secretary of the Treasury. The greatest value of Revenue Rulings is that they let taxpayers know what position the Internal Revenue Service intends to take in a given fact situation. This can be of great use in tax planning.

---

[23] The reason for such reluctance is that controversial areas of tax often involve complex factual issues which do not lend themselves to resolution by a ruling. For example, the Service refuses to issues rulings on the question of whether an employee's compensation is reasonable under I.R.C. § 162.

[24] This statement appears in the beginning of the Cumulative Bulletins. *See, e.g.*, 1996-1 C.B. iii.

Courts do tend to give a great deal of consideration to Revenue Rulings because the Internal Revenue Service deals with the tax laws on a daily basis and is presumed to have a better knowledge of the Code than most taxpayers. A taxpayer should not, however, think that she is bound to accept a ruling as law, and, in fact, there are quite a few cases in which courts have held contrary to a position taken in a ruling.[25] Whenever you attempt to apply a ruling to a particular fact pattern you must always consider the effect of subsequent legislation, regulations, court decisions, and Revenue Procedures.[26] The Cumulative Bulletin has a list of current actions on previously published rulings, which lists the rulings that have been modified, amended, amplified, withdrawn, declared obsolete, distinguished or superseded.

[2] Acquiescence/Nonacquiescence

In addition to Revenue Rulings, the Internal Revenue Service lists its acquiescence, or nonacquiescence, to certain opinions of the Tax Court each week in the Internal Revenue Bulletin. An acquiescence will be issued only when the Service agrees to accept a holding by the Tax Court which was adverse to the government's position. As you might expect, a nonacquiescence will be issued when the Service refuses to abide by an adverse Tax Court determination. Neither acquiescence nor nonacquiescence in a Tax Court decision can have any effect on the taxpayer in that case. Rather, they serve to give other taxpayers, who might litigate similar facts in the Tax Court in the future, an indication of whether the government intends to pursue an issue that it lost.

You can usually find the list of acquiescences/nonacquiescences in the first few pages of each Cumulative Bulletin. Additionally, Tax Court opinions will have the symbol "(Acq)" included in the citation of opinions that enjoy acquiescence. Not surprisingly, opinions to which the government does not acquiesce will carry the symbol "(NA)".

A good example of a decision in which the Service issued a nonacquiescence is *Jenkins v. C.I.R.*, T.C. Memo 1983-667. In holding that country singer Conway Twitty could deduct as a business expense amounts he paid to Merle Haggard and other investors in his defunct fast food chain "Twitty Burgers," the Tax Court concluded with the following "Ode to Conway Twitty":

> Twitty Burgers went belly up
> But Conway remained true
> He repaid his investors, one and all
> It was the moral thing to do.
> His fans would not have liked it
> It could have hurt his fame
> Had any investors sued him
> Like Merle Haggard or Sonny James.
> When it was time to file taxes
> Conway thought what he would do
> Was deduct those payments as a business expense
> Under section one-sixty-two.
> In order to allow these deductions
> Goes the argument of the Commissioner

---

[25] Compare, for example, Rev. Rul. 81-69, 1981-1 C.B. 351, with *Cleveland Athletic Club, Inc. v. U.S.*, 770 F.2d 1160 (6th Cir. 1985). Revenue Ruling 81-69 required that a tax exempt social club have a profit motive before it would be entitled to offset unrelated business taxable income with losses from food sales to nonmembers. The Sixth Circuit in *Cleveland Athletic Club* refused to follow the ruling, holding that no such profit motive should be required.

[26] See § 7.04[4] for a discussion of Revenue Procedures.

The payments must be ordinary and necessary
To a business of the petitioner.
Had Conway not repaid the investors
His career would have been under cloud,
Under the unique facts of this case
Held: The deductions are allowed.

Showing that it had a sense of humor, the Service responded to the opinion with the following "Ode to Conway Twitty: A Reprise":

Harold Jenkins and Conway Twitty
They are both the same
But one was born
The other achieved fame.
The man is talented
And has many a friend
They opened a restaurant
His name he did lend.
They are two different things
Making burgers and song
The business went sour
It didn't take long.
He repaid his friends
Why did he act
Was it business or friendship
Which is fact?
Business the court held
It's deductible they feel
We disagree with the answer
But let's not appeal.
Recommendation: Nonacquiescence. [Action on Decision 1984-022]

[3] Private Letter Rulings

While the government can publish answers to taxpayer questions in the form of Revenue Rulings, it will most often answer such questions in a Private Letter Ruling (PLR) to the inquiring taxpayer. Even though such rulings cannot be relied upon by any taxpayer other than the taxpayer to whom they are issued (unlike Revenue Rulings),[27] § 6110 of the Code requires that they be available for public inspection. These Private Letter Rulings give a practitioner an idea of the government's thinking on a given subject.

[4] Other Administrative Pronouncements

In addition to Revenue Rulings, Acquiescences, and Private Letter Rulings, the Internal Revenue Service releases various determinations that are required to be available to the public under Code § 6110. The most important of these other types of pronouncements are Revenue Procedures (Rev. Proc.), which, among other things, provide taxpayers with the procedures for acquiring rulings or determination letters. Revenue Procedures appear in the part of the Cumulative Bulletin titled "Administrative, Procedural, and Miscellaneous."

---

[27] Rev. Proc. 2006-1, § 11.02, 2006-1 I.R.B. 48.

That portion of the Cumulative Bulletin also contains Delegation Orders, in which the Commissioner of Internal Revenue expressly delegates his authority to perform certain tasks to employees of the Internal Revenue Service, and Internal Revenue Notices, which provide guidance to taxpayers on such things as the inflation adjustment factor to be used for computing the windfall profit tax.

As if those were not enough, the first Revenue Procedure issued each year (*e.g.*, Rev. Proc. 2006-1)[28] discusses items called determination letters and information letters. Determination letters are generally used to rule on the qualifications of exempt organizations and employee benefit plans, while information letters contain only general information about a well-established interpretation of a principle of tax law, without applying it to specific facts. For example, in a December 4, 1975 information letter the Internal Revenue Service proclaimed that taxpayers could take medical expense deductions for the cost of resurfacing their houses in order to remove paint that had been shown to have levels of lead in sufficient quantities to cause a health hazard.

Finally, there are technical advice memoranda (TAM), which are discussed in the second Revenue Procedure issued each year (*e.g.*, Rev. Proc. 2006-2).[29] These memoranda are sent from the National Office of the Service to a district office when that district office seeks advice in considering a taxpayer's claim for a refund. While determination letters, information letters, and TAM's can be helpful in understanding the policies of the Service, they cannot be relied upon as precedent.

---

[28] 2006-1 I.R.B. 7-8.
[29] 2006-1 I.R.B. 89.

Chapter 8

AN INTRODUCTION TO TAX RESEARCH

§ 8.01 INTRODUCTION

We remember the first day we were called upon to do tax research in law school. We walked slowly and with great trepidation into that dreaded area of the library known as the "Tax and Labor Room." We had heard rumors that students entering that room would disappear, never to be heard from again. Fortunately, we survived our first encounter with the tax materials, and in the process, we discovered that tax law is generally easier to research than most other areas of the law. The purpose of this chapter is to acquaint you, in a very introductory way,[1] with tax research, so that you will be able to find the sources of the law discussed in Chapter 7. Of course, in the end, the only way to learn how to do tax research is to take that long and frightening walk into the tax area of your law library, and dig right in.

One assumption that we make in writing this chapter is that a student entering a course in federal income taxation already has some working knowledge of legal research. That is, we assume that tax students know how to use, and cite to, such materials as the United States Code, West's Regional and Federal Reporter system, and the Federal Register. If our assumption is correct, then, maybe without even knowing it, you already have the ability to find sections of the Internal Revenue Code, tax cases other than Tax Court opinions, and Treasury Regulations. After all, the Internal Revenue Code encompasses Title 26 of the United States Code. West's Reporter system, and the digests that service that system, cover all cases in the federal district courts (Federal Supplement), the U.S. Claims Court (Federal Supplement, Claims Court Reporter), the circuit courts of appeals (Federal Reporter), and the U.S. Supreme Court (Supreme Court Reporter). You can research an issue in federal tax in much the same way that you would research an issue in contracts, torts, evidence, civil procedure, or property. However, if you use general research materials when you research tax, you will probably find yourself inefficiently checking several resources in various parts of the library. Furthermore, there are some sources of tax law, most notably the Tax Court Reporters and the Cumulative Bulletins, which can only be found in the tax section of the library. By using materials designed specifically for tax research, you can save time and leg-work, since everything you need to use in researching a tax issue (statutes, regulations, rulings, cases, treatises, articles) will be in one area of your library.

Therefore, this chapter will focus only on the research materials peculiar to tax law.

§ 8.02 GETTING STARTED

[1] The Looseleaf Services

Tax students and practitioners have at their disposal regularly updated tax research services, which are generally referred to as the "looseleaf services." These services provide

---

[1] This chapter does not begin to cover all of the materials available for tax research, nor does it tell you how to use all of them. Instead, it is meant to help you know where to start the first few times you enter the tax library. You should be aware that all of the materials discussed in this chapter have their own instructions on how to use them. You should not hesitate to refer to those instructions.

For a complete guide to federal tax research, see Richmond, Federal Tax Research: Guide to Materials and Techniques (2007).

the user with full texts of the Code and regulations, legislative histories, case and ruling digests and citators, editorial explanations of the laws, pending legislation updates, and planning tips. The best known of these services are Standard Federal Tax Reporter, published by Commerce Clearing House (CCH), and Federal Tax Coordinator and Federal Tax Coordinator, 2nd, published by Thomson/Research Institute of America (RIA).

In most respects, the CCH and RIA services are identical. For example, they are both arranged by Code section. Therefore, if you know which Code provision controls the issue you are researching, you can go straight to the volume of Standard Federal Tax Reporter or Federal Tax Coordinator containing that provision. You can determine which volume you need by looking at the bindings, which indicate which sections are discussed in each volume. Once you have found the volume you need, you will notice that the publishers of each service have provided index tabs to aid you in locating the sections you want.

If, on the other hand, you do not know which Code section controls your topic, RIA and CCH provide two other methods for beginning your research. One of these methods allows you to look at the binding of each volume for general topic headings. For example, the binding of Volume 16 of RIA Federal Tax Coordinator indicates that particular volume covers the topics of business and investment expenses. As you might expect, you will gain access to very broad areas of the law using this approach to the looseleaf services, which is not a very efficient way to research a specific legal problem. The other and generally better method for getting into the looseleaf compilations is through the Topic Index Volume in RIA Federal Tax Coordinator and its Finding Tables in Volume 1. For CCH, it is simply called the Index Volume. Each index allows you to perform a search by subject, by case name, or by Internal Revenue proclamation (which would include Revenue Rulings, Revenue Procedures, and Treasury Decisions).

When you use the Index Volume of a tax service, you will be referred to a *paragraph* number. This is important, because the compilation volumes contain page numbers, as well as paragraph numbers, which may be a source of confusion to the novice. You can find the volume containing the appropriate paragraph or paragraphs by again looking to the outside binders.

No matter which of the three methods (Code section, general topics on the binding, or the index) you use, once you have gained access to your topic you will find a wealth of information at your fingertips. Included in the discussion of each section will be the regulations, the legislative history, editorial explanations, and a case and ruling digest arranged by issues. Of course, when you find the names of cases and the citations of rulings relevant to your subject you will want to read them, because you should never rely on a commercially prepared abstract.

[2] Computer-Assisted Research

One of the most important tools for researching the dynamic area of federal income taxation is the computer. The two widely recognized computer research programs which have federal tax data bases are LexisNexis and Westlaw. Each of these systems allows the user access to Code sections, legislative history, regulations, rulings and other Internal Revenue materials, and cases.

A person using LexisNexis or Westlaw to perform tax research must first gain access to the tax data base, because these systems contain databases on a multitude of subjects. Each system has instructions on how to reach the federal tax databases.

Once you are in the federal tax database, you will need to choose the file of documents you wish to search. For example, if you only want the computer to search cases, you must choose the "cases" file. Each of these systems allows you to restrict your search to certain dates, such as cases decided within the previous month or within the previous year, or ten years.

While LexisNexis and Westlaw online systems each cover the essential materials, such as the Code, regulations, cases, and administrative materials, the two systems offer access to other publications as well. Both offer treatises and excellent online classification systems of tax materials. The following is a very brief sampling of some of the additional publications available through each service:

LexisNexis

- NYU Institute on Federal Taxation (published by Matthew Bender now owned by LexisNexis), which encompasses the topic discussed at the yearly New York University Federal Tax Institute.

- Tax Analysts Publications.

- Law Journals, accounting journals and literature.

- Rabkin & Johnson Current Legal Forms with Tax Analysis.

- Shepard's Citations, which can be used to update your research and check for parallel citations.

- Tax Analysts Tax Notes Today and CCH Tax Day, which are tax newsletters.

Westlaw

- KeyCite Citations

- RIA Publications

- Warren Gorham Lamont Tax Journals

- Taxation Trial Pleadings, law reviews, journals and accounting literature

[3] Internet Sources

One of the most exciting advancements in tax research is the availability of tax information on the Internet. The following is a list of some of the websites giving access to a wealth of tax information, including IRS forms and publications:

- Basic Tools for Tax Professionals (from the Internal Revenue Service) (www.irs.gov/taxpros/article/0,,id = 118004,00.html)

- Federation of Tax Administrators (www.taxadmin.org/fta/link/Forms.html)

- The Official Government Site for downloadable and printable IRS Forms and Publications (www.irs.gov/formspubs/index.html?portlet = 3)

- Tax Analyst Online (www.tax.org/); interesting current news and tax information

- Cornell Law School LII Legal Information Institute (www.law.cornell.edu/search/index.html)

- Findlaw (www.findlaw.com/01topics/35tax/index.html); be sure to scroll to the end of the page for a searchable database of a variety of tax materials

- Georgetown Law Library Research Guides: Federal Tax Research (www.ll.georgetown.edu/lib/guides/federal_tax.html)

§ 8.03 FINDING TAX CASES

[1] Cases, Other Than Tax Court Cases

In the course of your research, you will often be referred to court decisions. While you are familiar with the West Reporter system, you will no doubt encounter case law compilations that work in conjunction with the looseleaf services. These collections are United States Tax Cases (USTC), published by Commerce Clearing House (CCH), and American Federal Tax Reports (AFTR and AFTR 2d Decisions Advance Sheets Volume), formerly published by Prentice-Hall and now published by Research Institute of America (RIA). USTC and AFTR volumes cover tax decisions from the United States Supreme Court, the U.S. Circuit Courts of Appeals, the Court of Claims, and the Federal District Courts. Should you need the official (West) citations for cases, AFTR and USTC conveniently provide them in the case headings.

Citations to AFTR and USTC are similar in form to citations to the West system. That is, the first number you see will be the volume number, followed by the reporter abbreviation. The next reference, however, is not to a page number, as it would be in a West reporter, but to a paragraph number, just like the paragraph references used in the looseleaf services. Therefore, the 1960 case of *Commissioner v. Duberstein* can be found at 363 U.S. 278, or at 80 S. Ct. 1190, or at 60-2 USTC 9515, or at 5 AFTR 2d 1626. Remember, you must look at *paragraph* number 9515 in volume 60-2 of USTC, or *paragraph* number 1626 in volume 5 of AFTR 2d to find the case, as these are *not* citations to *page* numbers.

Once you use the looseleaf service of a particular publisher, you will, for ease of use, be using that publisher's case compilation as well. It is important to note that some cases are reported in either USTC or AFTR, but not both. If you are sure that a case exists, but you cannot find it in one service, you will need to check for it in the other service.

[2] Tax Court Cases[2]

As was discussed in Chapter 7, Tax Court decisions can be divided into two categories: Published (or Regular) Opinions, and unpublished Memorandum Opinions. You can find the published opinions of the Tax Court in the official United States Tax Court Reports (TC) You can also find these Regular Tax Court decisions, in looseleaf form, in CCH Tax Court Reporter, or RIA Tax Court Reported and Memorandum Decisions. While Tax Court Memorandum (TCMs) opinions are not officially published, you can find them in several sources, most notably CCH Tax Court Reporter and RIA Tax Court Reported Memorandum Decisions.

§ 8.04 FINDING INTERNAL REVENUE PROCLAMATIONS

[1] Using the Cumulative Bulletin

The administrative proclamations most important to your research, which are Treasury Decisions, Revenue Rulings, and Revenue Procedures, will be published in the weekly Internal Revenue Bulletin. The Internal Revenue Bulletins are, in turn, republished as the hard-bound Cumulative Bulletin every six months. The Cumulative Bulletin contains a numerical findings list, which will give you the page number for a ruling when all you have

---

[2] Prior to 1942, the Tax Court was called the Board of Tax Appeals (B.T.A.). Therefore, you might find some early B.T.A. references. The official reporter for such cases was the B.T.A. Reports. Prentice Hall also published P-H B.T.A. Reports and P-H B.T.A. Memorandum Decisions.

is the ruling number. Additionally, the rulings in the Cumulative Bulletin are grouped by Code section. Thus, if you did not have a specific ruling in mind, but knew that you wanted some guidance on § 170, you could find all of the rulings dealing with that section in a given six month period. The Code references are given at the top of each page of the rulings portion of the Bulletin.

Revenue Procedures are found in the Administrative Materials in Part III of the Bulletin. Like the rulings, their page numbers within a Bulletin can be found through the numerical findings list.

[2]   Private Letter Rulings

Private Letter Rulings are the most important of the non-published government proclamations. You can find these through looseleaf services (CCH Private Letter Rulings, and RIA Private Letter Rulings), or you can gain access to them via one of the tax databases (LexisNexis and Westlaw).

§ 8.05   UPDATING YOUR RESEARCH

[1]   Citators

As you know from your first-year Legal Research course, you must always check the status of any cases that your research has found. The standard vehicle for this updating process is Shepard's Citations. If you are used to Shepard's, you will be happy to know that there is a Shepards designed solely for tax citations, which is called Shepard's Federal Tax Citator. Before you get too excited about the fact that you can rely upon an old friend for updating your research, you should learn to use the citators presented by CCH and RIA. The most extensive and complete citator for federal tax is the RIA Citator, which uses a method very similar to Shepard's, and even includes symbols like Shepard's. The CCH Citator is a bit easier to use than the RIA because it consists of only two volumes, rather than RIA's multiple volumes. On the other hand, CCH does not provide the same detailed coverage as the RIA version, because the editors of CCH do not give citations to all relevant cases, but rather choose only representative citations. Each of these citators gives citations to rulings, as well as cases.

Actually, you might find that the easiest way to check the continuing validity of the law you have found is to use one of the computer databases. LexisNexis and Westlaw are both capable of giving you the names of cases and cites of rulings which might affect your research.

[2]   Other Updating Materials

In addition to the Citators, the looseleaf services contain compilations of weekly updates and advance sheets to keep you current. You can update any material from CCH by referring to Volume 19, "New Matters." In that volume, you should check the paragraph numbers from Standard Federal Tax Reporter that were relevant to your research. If there have been any changes, you will be given a paragraph within Volume 19 that will supplement your search.

In much the same way, Volume 16 of RIA, which is the "Recent Developments" volume, allows you to check for changes in the paragraphs you have been using. If there are changes, Volume 16 will indicate a paragraph within Volume 16 which will explain current additions or deletions to the law.

§ 8.06 OTHER RESEARCH AIDS

What follows is basically a catalogue of some of the research tools available to tax students and practitioners. You should try to familiarize yourself with as many of these as possible while you are in law school so that you will know which, if any, of them you will want to use in practice.

[1] Other Looseleaf Services

In addition to the services provided by CCH and RIA there are two other widely used tax reporters. They are Rabkin & Johnson, Federal Income, Gift and Estate Taxation, published by Matthew Bender, now owned by LexisNexis, and Mertens, Law of Federal Income Taxation, published by The Thomson Corporation's brand, Callaghan & Co., the former publisher. Both of these services have separate Code, regulation, and treatise volumes, while Mertens also has a rulings volume.

Rabkin & Johnson is divided into Treatises, Code and Congressional Reports, and Regulations. A researcher can go directly to Code and Regulation sections covered in the Code and Regulation Volumes, or s/he can refer to the Index volumes in order to research a given subject or case. Mertens is divided into Treatise, Code, Regulations, and Rulings Volumes. The Treatise Volumes are similar to other legal encyclopedias, such as Corpus Juris Secundum.

Many researchers looking for Revenue Rulings prefer using Mertens to the Cumulative Bulletin, because Mertens publishes the rulings in their numerical order, while the Cumulative Bulletins publish rulings in the order of the Code sections they discuss. Therefore, Revenue Ruling 86-24 follows Revenue Ruling 86-23 in Mertens. In the Cumulative Bulletin Revenue Ruling 86-24 follows Revenue Ruling 86-80 (1986-1 C.B. 79-80).

[2] Tax Periodicals

You can most readily find tax articles through CCH Federal Tax Articles, or the Index to Federal Tax Articles (Warren, Gorham & Lamont which is now owned by The Thomson Corporation). These services list all articles related to tax, including those found in accounting and business related periodicals, as well as legal publications. Tax periodicals are also found online through LexisNexis, Westlaw, and Internet sources.

[3] Two Very Useful Tools

Last, but not least, two of the most useful services for tax planning are the Research Institute of America (RIA) Tax Action Coordinator, and the Bureau of National Affairs (BNA) Tax Management Portfolios. The Tax Action Coordinator provides useful information on the practical applications of tax law, as well as complete Code and regulation sections. It is arranged by subject, and can be accessed through an easy-to use index volume. The Tax Management Portfolios are spiral bound, in-depth discussions of very focused tax subjects. Each volume contains a discussion of the Code and regulations germane to the transactions being covered, as well as "working papers," which include sample forms and suggested checklists. You can reach the appropriate portfolio(s) through the Master Binder volume. Both of these services provide extensive case and ruling citations, while BNA also cites tax articles and books.

Chapter 9

FEDERAL INCOME TAX PROBLEMS

PROBLEM #1 GROSS INCOME

ASSIGNMENT:
Code: § 61
Regs.: §§ 1.61–1, –2, –3, –4, –5, –14

The Manitoba Goon is employed by the Universal Wrestling Association as a Professional Wrestler. Discuss the tax consequences to the Goon if the following happened in the current year:

1. He is paid a yearly salary of $150K.

2. He is given a $12K Christmas bonus for defeating Rusty Rhodes in a steel cage match with Texas Tornado rules.

3. He is paid a $40K bribe to throw his match against Bulk Brogan. Throwing a match is illegal. So are steroids!

4. He buys a Steinway Piano worth $1K and finds $700 in cash in the piano. (*See* C.I.R. v. Cesarini, 428 F.2d 812 (6th Cir. 1970).) What if he paid $1K for the piano, but it turns out to be worth $50K, because Elton John played it in a concert?

5. The Goon owns his own house. If he rented the house he would have to pay $900 per month in rent. Additionally, he grows tomatoes, which he eats himself. Those tomatoes would cost him $20 if he purchased them at a grocery store. Would your answer change if the Goon sold his tomatoes for a $5 profit, instead of eating them?

6. The Goon found a quarter in a Coke machine.

7. The Goon received $100 worth of medical care from Dr. M. Quackenbush in exchange for wrestling tickets worth $100. Will the Dr. have any income?

8. The Goon is given a parking space by his employer. The space would cost the Goon $600 per year, if he had to pay for it. (*See* § 132(f).)

9. The Goon is given a birthday cake by his fellow wrestlers. The cake cost $10. (*See* § 102(a).)

10. The Goon received $100K in punitive damages and $75K in compensatory damages from his mother in a defamation suit. She had defamed him by saying "he's such a nice boy." (*See* § 104(a)(2).) How would your answer be different, if instead he sued his mother for battery when she hit him over the head with a chair, and he received $75K as compensation for his injuries and $100K in punitive damages?

PROBLEM #2 EXCLUSIONS FOR GIFTS AND INHERITANCES

ASSIGNMENT:
Code: §§ 102; 132
Regs.: §§ 1.102–1(a), (b), (c), (f)(2); 1.132–1, –2, –3, –4
Case: C.I.R. v. Duberstein, 363 U.S. 278 (1960)

1. Transfers between family members are presumed to be gifts, while transfers between an employer and an employee are presumed to be compensation for services. Does this presumption make sense? For example, Father gives Daughter $5K in cash, while Employer gives Employee $5K in cash. How will these transactions be treated for tax purposes? What if Father had given Daughter the $5K in exchange for legal services she had performed for him? Do you see how transactions involving a transfer of the same amount of money or property will be treated differently for tax purposes depending upon the relationship of the parties involved?

2. Hirum owns the Mogen David Ham Company where he employs 100 workers. Which of the following transactions will qualify for the § 102(a) gift exclusion? The § 132 exclusion for fringe benefits? Any other exclusion provision?

   a. Hirum gives each of his employees a $5 ham for Christmas.

   b. Keepum, an employee, gives Hirum a $5 ham for Christmas.

   c. Hirum gives each of his employees a $100 clock-radio for Christmas.

   d. Hirum gives his son, who is also an employee of the company, a $100 clock-radio for the holidays.

   e. Hirum provides free coffee for his employees on a daily basis.

   f. Hirum provides doughnuts for his highly paid executives on National Doughnut Day.

   g. Hirum's highly paid executives are each given a posh office with a computer. They are also given memberships to the exclusive Trafe Country Club, even though no business is conducted there.

3. Beaver was in the business of selling real estate. Recently, Edward Haskell gave Beaver a tip that Gus, a fireman, wished to buy several acres of land. The tip turned out to be correct and Beaver made a huge profit on the deal. He wanted to show his gratitude to Haskell by giving him some land just west of St. Petersburg Beach, Florida. Although Haskell said such a gift was not necessary, Beaver insisted and recorded a deed in Haskell's name. Will the gift of land be excludable from gross income under § 102(a)?

4. For several years, Mary was an employee of the Glass Ceiling Corporation. When Mary died, the corporate board took note of her death and decided that, even though Mary was owed no salary by Glass Ceiling, she had been sadly under-compensated. The board elected to pay $15K to Mary's widower, Max.

   a. Will the payment to Max be an excludable gift?

   b. Why might the corporation (and Max) want to treat this as compensation rather than a gift? (See § 162 and the discussion of deductions in § 6.04.)

5. Which of the following will be excluded from gross income?

   a. A bequest of $20K to Daughter from Father's will.

    b.   Land received by an heir through intestate succession.

    c. $50K received by Niece in settlement of a contest she brought against the estate of Uncle. Niece claimed that she was left out of Uncle's will because of Nephew's fraud. (*See* Lyeth v. Hoey, 305 U.S. 188 (1938).)

    d.   A bequest of $2K to Attorney Shyster in lieu of payment for his services. (*See* Wolder v. C.I.R., 493 F.2d 608 (2d Cir. 1974).)

    e.   A bequest of $20K to Niece from Uncle's will. Niece is the personal representative of the will, which makes no mention of compensation for her services.

6.   Mr. Ed owned several office buildings. Upon his death, the rent from these buildings passed to Carol for her life, remainder to Wilbur and his heirs.

    a.   Will Carol have to include the rent in her gross income? Why or Why not?

    b.   Will Wilbur have to include the value of the remainder interest in his gross income?

PROBLEM #3 AWARDS AND SCHOLARSHIPS

ASSIGNMENT:
Code: §§ 74; 117

1. The American Medical Association gives a yearly award for the best article written by a physician concerning medical techniques. The award, $500, is paid at the end of a ceremony in which the winner is expected to make a brief presentation concerning her article. Should this year's winner include the $500 in her gross income? (*See* Rev. Rul. 58-89, 1958-1 C.B. 40. *But see* I.R.C. § 74(b).)

2. The citizens of Charleston, South Carolina are in the process of choosing their favorite sanitation engineer. The winner will receive a stipend of $100. Should the winner include the stipend in his gross income?

3. Are the value of the gold medals won at the Olympic games included in gross income? Why or why not?

4. Romeo won an all expenses paid vacation for two to Des Moines, Iowa on his favorite game show "Spell Your Name." The trip was valued at $500. Unfortunately, Romeo could not find anyone to take the trip with him, so he went alone. Should Romeo include the value of the trip in his gross income? If so, how much should he include?

5. Healthknit is a medical student at Scalpel U (an educational organization described in § 170(b)(1)(A)(ii)). Which of the following would qualify for the scholarship exclusion under § 117?

   a. Healthknit received $10K for use in paying his medical school tuition from a federal program which required him to work in Appalachia during his first five years after graduation. What if, instead, Healthknit received a full athletic scholarship?

   b. Healthknit received $5K from Scalpel U for his work as a lab assistant.

   c. Healthknit received a $5K scholarship from Scalpel U. The terms of the scholarship require him to spend 20 hours per week as a research assistant. Students at Scalpel U are generally required to spend only 10 hours per week as research assistants.

   d. Would your answer to (c) be different if Healthknit received a full academic scholarship paying for his tuition and books, and he decided to earn extra money as a research assistant? Be sure to address § 117(d) in answering this problem.

PROBLEM #4 GAINS DERIVED FROM DEALINGS IN PROPERTY

ASSIGNMENT:
 Code: §§ 61(a)(3); 1001(a); 1011; 1012; 1041
 Regs.: §§ 1.1001–1(a); 1.1011–1; 1.1012–1(a); 1.61–2(d)(2)(i); 1.1001–2
 Case: Crane v. C.I.R., 331 U.S. 1 (1947)

1. After suffering several financial set-backs, Mr. Bill decided that it was time for him to invest in real estate. His agent, Mr. Sluggo, arranged several deals for him. With respect to each deal below, determine: (1) whether Mr. Bill will realize any gain; and (2) what Mr. Bill's basis will be in the property acquired?

   a. Mr. Bill can pay $60K in cash for Bellyacre, which has a fair market value of $60K. Mr. Sluggo will keep $10K as his commission.

   b. Mr. Bill can buy Liabilityacre for $50K. He would pay $30K in cash plus assume an existing mortgage with remaining principal payments of $20K.

   c. Mr. Bill can buy Craneacre for $100K. He would pay no cash for the property, but would take the property subject to a mortgage of $100K. Mr. Bill *would not* personally be liable for the $100K mortgage.

   d. Mr. Bill can purchase Swampacre, which has a fair market value of $25K, by trading his 1959 classic Chevy worth $27K. Mr. Bill bought the Chevy in 1961 for $7K.

2. Fritz is an employee of Demo, Inc., a company engaged in the process of selling demonstrator automobiles. Normally, Fritz receives a salary of $7500 per month, but this month Demo, Inc.'s cash flow is a bit tight. Because of the liquidity problems, Fritz agrees to take a 1983 Honda Accord, valued at $10,000, in lieu of his salary. Unfortunately, Fritz soon finds out that his landlord will not take rides in Fritz's Honda in lieu of rent payments. Thus, Fritz sold the car for $8900.

   a. Did Fritz have any basis in the car? After all, Reg. § 1.1012-1(a) defines cost as the amount paid in cash or property, not services. (*See* Treas. Reg. § 1.61-2(d)(2)(i).)

   b. Will Fritz have any gain or loss on the sale of the car?

3. Mr. and Mrs. Right decided to get a divorce. As part of their divorce settlement, Mr. Right received 100 shares of United American Bank stock from Mrs. Right. The shares of stock have a fair market value (FMV) of $1000 each, but Mrs. Right paid only $100 per share when she bought the stock in 1970.

   Will either Mr. or Mrs. Right realize any gain on this transfer? What is Mr. Right's basis in the stock? (*See* § 1041.)

4. a. Thoughtful purchased an option to buy Wiseacre for $15K. If Thoughtful elects not to exercise the option but instead sells it to Mary for $20K what gain, if any, will he realize?

   b. What if Thoughtful exercised the option to buy Wiseacre, and he paid $100K for it in addition to what he paid for the option. What is Thoughtful's basis in Wiseacre?

5. The concept of basis has been likened to the idea of a bank account. Does this analogy make sense? If so, why?

PROBLEM #5 FUNDAMENTAL PRINCIPLES OF TIMING

ASSIGNMENT:
Code: § 83
Regs.: §§ 1.83–1, –2, –3, –4(b)

1. Sbgnv Sbgnvski is the famous soccer player-turned-field-goal-kicker for the Tampa Bay Boutonnieres professional football team. Even though Sbgnv (or "Sbg" as he is known to his teammates) is disappointed with the performance of the team, he is paid quite well for his efforts. In addition to his $1 million per game salary, he has received $10 million worth of stock in the team as bonus for his kicking proficiency. What will be the tax consequences (don't forget basis) to Sbg of the receipt of the stock if:

   a. His receipt of the shares was not subject to any restrictions or conditions.

   b. The shares were transferred to him subject to the condition that he would forfeit them if he did not stay with the team for at least five seasons, and this restriction was stamped on the face of the shares.

   c. The shares were stamped with the word "**NONTRANSFERABLE**".

   d. The same facts as (b) above, except that Sbg was killed by his own players in only his third season when he missed a field goal that would have given the team its first victory in seven years, and Sbg's son Szxyvd inherited Sbg's rights, if any, to the stock under state law.

   e. Two years later Sbg sold the shares he received in (b) for $11 million to a bona fide purchaser who was unaware of the restrictions on the stock. (*See* Treas. Reg. § 1.83-1(f) Ex. (2).)

2. Chancee was a real estate broker with Brooklyn Bridge Realty Company. Chancee's sales record was so good that her employer transferred to her a plot of land worth $200K in fee simple absolute subject to the condition that her sales would not fall below $1 million in the next two years. If her sales fell below $1 million in either of the next two years, the employer would take the property back. This condition was clearly evidenced on the face of the deed to Chancee. What are the tax consequences to Chancee if she exercised the election under § 83(b) and:

   a. The property had increased in value to $250K when the two years were completed and Chancee successfully met the requirements of her employer by selling at least $1 million of real estate in each of those years.

   b. Chancee failed to meet her employer's requirements in the second year, because she sold only $990K worth of real estate in that year, and, as a consequence, her employer repossessed the property.

   c. Chancee successfully met the requirements for ownership of the property by selling $1 million worth of property in the next two years, but the property declined in value and was only worth $175K when Chancee obtained unrestricted ownership of the property.

   Do these problems help you to understand why the election under § 83(b) is often called the gambler's choice?

PROBLEM #6 ANNUITIES AND LIFE INSURANCE PROCEEDS

ASSIGNMENT:
Code: §§ 72(a), (b), (c); 79; 101(a), (c), (d)
Regs.: §§ 1.72–4(A), –9 (Table V); 1.101–1(a)(1), (b)(1), –4(a)(1), (b)(1), (c)

1. The Lone Stranger died this year owning an insurance policy that would pay his designated beneficiary $250K but under which the beneficiary had several settlement options.

    a. What will the beneficiary have to include in gross income if he/she takes a lump-sum cash payment of the $250K?

    b. What if instead of taking a lump-sum the beneficiary merely leaves the money with the insurance company and they pay him $20K interest this year?

    c. What if Pronto is the beneficiary of the policy and he chooses to take $11K per year for life? Pronto has a life expectancy of 25 years.

    d. What if in (c) above the beneficiary had been the Lone Ranger's wife, Belle Starr, instead of Pronto? Starr also has a 25-year life expectancy. (*Compare* I.R.C. § 101(d), *with* Treas. Reg. § 1.101–4(a)(1)(ii). Which of these provisions should you follow? Why?)

2. Mr. Drysdale is employed by the First Bank of Beverly Hills. The bank makes a payment of $250 per employee each year to fund a group-term life insurance policy covering each employee. The face value of each policy under the plan is $50K. What does Mr. Drysdale have to include in gross income each year that the bank pays his group-term premium?

3. Timid Tom, a professional wrestler, is employed by the Florida Wrasslin' Corp. (FWC). FWC became fearful that Timid Tom might not survive his next match, a Texas Death match against Bullwhip Bison, so they acquired a $100K life insurance policy on Timid Tom's life. If Tom in fact dies during the match, what will FWC have to include in gross income if the policy named them as beneficiary, and:

    a. They actually purchased the policy on Tom's life (with Tom's consent)?

    b. They bought an existing policy from Tom for $50K, instead of taking out a new policy?

    c. What result in (b) above if Tom was a shareholder in FWC?

4. Oscar (who has a remaining life expectancy of 56 years) bought an annuity in 2007. Oscar paid $28K for the annuity which will pay him $1K per year for the rest of his life. There is no refund feature.

    a. How much of Oscar's $1K payment for this year will be included in gross income?

    b. If Oscar only lived two years after buying the annuity, would he be entitled to an income tax deduction for the loss he suffered on the annuity?

    c. If Oscar lived for 75 years, when would he have to stop excluding a portion of the annuity payments from gross income?

    d. Would your answer to these problems change if Oscar had been in extremely poor health at the time he purchased the annuity?

PROBLEM #7 GIFT BASIS (§ 1015)

ASSIGNMENT:
Code: §§ 1015; 1011(b)
Regs.: §§ 1.1015–4; 1.1001–1(e)

1. In 2007, as a token of his love and friendship, Kevin Arnold gave Winnie Cooper a diamond ring worth $20K. Kevin had received the ring from Becky Slater as a token of her love and friendship. Becky paid $16K for the ring when she bought it in 1996.

    a. What is Winnie's basis in the ring?

    b. What gain will Winnie have when she sells the ring for $22K in 2009?

    c. When gifts of property are involved, is § 102 really an exclusion provision? Explain.

2. Grandpa is interested in selling an antique that he received as a gift in 1925. Grandpa has no idea how much the donor of the gift paid for it. How will Grandpa's basis in the property be determined?

3. Sheriff Harry S. Truman gave F.B.I. agent Cooper a certificate that entitled him to free Dunkin Donuts for the rest of his life. The certificate cost Sheriff Truman $30K. Unfortunately, at the time of the gift the value of the donuts was only $24K.

    a. What will be Cooper's basis in the Donut certificate?

    b. What will be the tax consequences to Cooper if he sells the certificate to Audrey for:

        i. $36K?

        ii. $22K?

        iii. $27K?

4. Al E. Gator gave his good friend Georgia Bulldog a van so that she could drive to college football games on Saturdays. Al paid $15K for the van, which was worth $20K at the time of the gift. Al was required to pay $4K in gift tax on the transfer.

    a. What is Bulldog's basis in the van?

    b. How would your answer change if the van was only worth $10K at the time of the gift? Why?

5. Mary had a little land. Mary's basis in the land was $150K. Even though the land was worth $250K, Mary decided to sell it to Daughter at a reduced price.

    a. What are the tax consequences to Daughter and to Mary if Mary sold the land to Daughter for:

        i. $120K?

        ii. $160K?

        iii. $200K, and Mary paid $5K in gift tax on the transfer?

    b. How would your answer differ if instead of selling the land to her daughter, Mary sold it to a charity for $150K? (*See* § 1011(b).)

PROBLEM #8 DATE OF DEATH BASIS (§ 1014)

ASSIGNMENT:
Code: §§ 1014; 1001(e)
Regs.: §§ 1.1014–1, –3, –4, –5; 1.1001–1(f)

1. Ms. Stake died without a will. The only property she had, her classic Porsche 924 automobile, passed to her cousin Woody via intestate succession. (Ms. Stake hated Woody and would have certainly passed the property to "anyone else" had she known that Woody would get it.) Ms. Stake paid $10K for the car in 1975; the fair market value of the car upon her death was $32K. What is Woody's basis in the automobile?

2. Throckmorton (T) died on May 26, 2007, leaving Swampacre to Jeeves. T paid $15K for Swampacre in 1948, but the discovery of oil on the land increased its value to $2,000,000 by the time of T's death. Jeeves did not receive the property until June of 2008 because of state filing and probate proceedings. The value of the property when Jeeves actually received it was $2,500,000. What is Jeeves' basis in the property?

3. Jed Clampet bought Chez Marie, a fashionable boutique, for $1,000,000 in 1983. Shortly thereafter, Jed changed the boutique to a general store named Chez Granny. When Jed died in 2008, Chez Granny passed to Ellie May via intestate succession. The fair market value of the business was $250 at Jed's death. What is Ellie May's basis in the property?

4. Trusty (T) transferred the Sanford Arms Apartments into a trust. The trust provided that T would receive the income from the property for life, with the remainder passing to his heirs. The property was bought by T for $20K in 1942 but was worth $200K upon T's death.

   a. What basis will T's heirs have in the property if T reserved a right to revoke the trust at any time?

   b. What basis will the heirs have if the trust was irrevocable?

5. Planner possessed some highly appreciated real property. Planner, knowing about § 1014, decided to give the property to Ancient, who had one foot in the grave and the other on a banana peel. Ancient would then transfer the property back to Planner through his will. Will Planner's scheme work?

6. Hamlet died leaving Shakesacre to his son McBeth for life, with the remainder passing to his grandson Othello. The fair market value of the property was $100K upon Hamlet's death. How much gain will McBeth (25 years old) realize if he immediately sells his life interest for $92K?

PROBLEM #9 ASSIGNMENT OF INCOME

ASSIGNMENT:
Code: § 1. Skim §§ 269A; 671–678; 704(e)

1. What is the underlying purpose behind one taxpayer's attempt to assign income to another taxpayer?

2. Zaccaro was having an extremely good year in his real estate business. He had already earned $103K as of June 1, 2008, so he told his accountant to pay all of his future commissions to his wife Gerry, who had a yearly salary of only $35K. Who will be taxed on Zaccaro's future commissions? (*See* Lucas v. Earl, 281 U.S. 111 (1930).) Why is the Treasury concerned with assignments between spouses? (After all, most spouses file joint returns.)

3. Mr. Wrasslin' II wrote a book entitled *The Proper Application of the Sleeper Hold.* Who will be taxed on income generated:

    a. From the sales of the book if Mr. Wrasslin' II transferred all of the rights in the book to his son Mr. Wrasslin' II, Jr.?

    b. By the movie rights in the book if Mr. Wrasslin' II retained all rights in the book *except* for the movie rights, which he transferred to his daughter Maude Wrasslin'?

4. Mr. Estateplannin' II, a lawyer, drafted a will for Mr. Megabucks, a wealthy client. If Estateplannin' transferred all rights to income from his will drafting services to his daughter Suzy, who will be taxed on the income?

5. Ma and Pa Kettle own several acres of farm land in Orange County. At the present time, Ma and Pa receive $1,000 per month in rent for the property. Who will be taxed on the rental income in the following situations?

    a. Ma and Pa transfer only the right to receive the rental income to Jr.

    b. Ma and Pa transfer ½ of the property to Jr. in fee simple absolute.

    c. If in either (a) or (b) you determined that Ma and Pa would be taxed on the income, when will they be taxed?

    d. If in either (a) or (b) you determined that Jr. will be taxed on all or part of the income, will the fact that Jr. is 6 years old affect the tax consequences of the transaction? If so, how?

6. Leif was the income beneficiary of a trust which owned several apartment buildings. Leif was entitled to the use of the rental income from the property for life; the remainder belonged to Leif's sister Aftalief.

    a. Who will be taxed on the rental income if Leif assigns his entire life interest to his sister Afta?

    b. What if Leif assigned five years of his life interest?

7. Ari was a shipping executive with Tycoon, Inc. In 2007, Tycoon, Inc. decided to compensate Ari by paying him 5% of the profits of the corporation. By June 2008, Ari's share of the profits was $100K, and Ari informed the board of directors of Tycoon, Inc. that he would accept no future payments of compensation. Ari directed that the board "should do something worthwhile with the money." In accordance with Ari's wishes, the board of directors voted to give 5% of the profits from July–December of 2008 to the University of Saskatoon instead of to Ari. Will Ari have

to include the profits from July-December in his gross income? (*See* C.I.R. v. Giannini, 129 F.2d 638 (9th Cir. 1942).)

8. Dr. DeCay, a dentist, has sizeable income for the year. She wants to give money to her child Flossy (age 12), and she consulted you about the possibility of assigning her salary to Flossy. Can you recommend an alternative plan to the doctor which will satisfy her desire to give money to Flossy and have it be taxed at Flossy's presumably lower tax rates?

PROBLEM #10 DIVORCE AND SEPARATION

ASSIGNMENT:
Code: §§ 71; 215; 1041

1. Stu and Inci Pid have decided to break-up after one year of marital bliss (they have been married 22 years). Determine which of the following arrangements will be treated as alimony or separate maintenance payments (Assume that all divorce decrees or separation instruments begin in 2008.)

   a. Inci is to pay Stu $1K per year, in cash, pursuant to a written separation agreement. Stu will be living at his mother's house during the separation. The payments to Stu will cease upon his death. What if the payments were made in gold? Foreign currency?

   b. Pursuant to a decree of divorce, Inci is to pay Stu $12K per year in cash for five years. The payments will then be cut-back to $1K per year, until Stu's death. Stu will be living with his mother after the divorce.

   c. Pursuant to a divorce decree, Inci is to pay Stu $18K in cash in 2008. Inci will never have to pay Stu anything after she makes the $18K payment. He has gone home to mother.

   d. Inci and Stu devise a plan whereby they will get divorced, but remain living together. Inci will pay Stu $9K per year until Stu dies, thereby shifting income from Inci (a 35% bracket taxpayer) to Stu (a chronic 15% bracket taxpayer). Can a payment ever meet the requirements of § 71(b)(2)?

   e. Pursuant to a divorce decree, Inci will pay Stu (living with his mother) $9K per year until Stu dies. The decree specifically states that the payments will not be included in the income of the payee spouse.

   f. Pursuant to a divorce decree, Inci will pay Stu $5K per year for life and then $2K per year to a beneficiary designated by Stu to receive payments after his death.

   g. The divorce decree states that Stu will receive $300 per month from Inci until his death. However, the payments will be reduced to $100 per month when Stu's son, Q. Pid (who is living with Stu in Stu's mother's house), goes to college.

   h. What result in (g) above if Inci falls behind in her payments and can only pay $100 per month during 2010?

2. Mac MacDonald ("Big Mac") and Wendy Singlecheese ("Wendy") were married for seven years. On January 21, 2007, a final decree of divorce was entered in the Circuit Court of Pinellas County, Florida. The divorce decree specified that Big Mac was to make cash payments to Wendy, who had moved to Kentucky to live with Colonel Sanders, her uncle. The cash payments were to total $70K, but they were to cease upon Wendy's death. Wendy and Big Mac have no children.

   a. In 2007, Big Mac paid $25K to Wendy. In 2008, he paid $12K, and in 2009, he paid $1K. Will Big Mac be entitled to deduct any or all of these payments? What will be the consequences to Wendy?

   b. What will Big Mac be able to deduct if he has to make six equal payments of $11K each; the first payment will commence on the day after the divorce decree and the other payments will be made at 1-year intervals (i.e., the first payment is January 22, 2007; the second, January 22, 2008; etc.)?

c. What if in (a) above Big Mac had paid $1K in Years 1-7, $50K in Year 8, and $13K in Year 9; would he be able to deduct the payments?

d. What if in (a) above Big Mac had died in 2007 before he could pay more than $17K?

e. What if in (a) above Big Mac's payments were pursuant to a decree of support (sometimes called temporary alimony) rather than a decree of divorce or separate maintenance?

f. Big Mac, pursuant to a decree of divorce, was forced to pay Wendy (who was living away from Mac) 20% of his annual income in cash over the next 7 years. Big Mac's income in 2007 was $900K, in 2008 it was $100K, and in 2009 it was $150K. How much, if any, of the payments will Big Mac be able to deduct? Will there by any recapture?

g. What is the purpose of § 71(f)?

PROBLEM #11 DEDUCTIONS FOR LOSSES AND BUSINESS EXPENSES

ASSIGNMENT:
Code: §§ 62; 63(b),(c),(d),(e),(f),(g),(h); 162; 165(a),(c),(h); 274(a),(c),(h)
Regs.: §§ 1.62–1; 1.162–1, –2, –3, –4, –5, –6, –7, –8, –9, –15, –17(b);
1.165–1(a), –1(e), –7
Cases: Malat v. Riddle, 383 U.S. 569 (1966); Deputy v. duPont,
308 U.S. 488 (1940); Welch v. Helvering, 290 U.S. 111 (1933);
C.I.R. v. Groetzinger, 480 U.S. 23 (1987)

1. Attorney Foulup is a partner in the firm of Foulups, Bleeps and Blunders. The firm, primarily through Foulup's mismanagement, directed that the bonds of one of its most important clients be sold. Actually, the client did not want the bonds to be sold, and the sale resulted in a $25K loss for the client. If Foulups replaces the $25K, will he be entitled to a deduction? (*See* McDonald v. C.I.R., 592 F.2d 635 (2d Cir. 1978); Leon J. Greenspan, 29 TCM 1000). If you said that this is a deductible expense, will this be an "above-the-line" deduction or a "below-the-line" deduction?

2. Assume that Foulup (from problem 1) lives in a state that requires C.L.E. (continuing legal education) for its active bar members. Will Foulup be able to deduct his expenses for attending C.L.E. seminars? If yes, above or below the line?

3. What if Foulup, a litigation attorney, decided that he wanted to switch to the practice of taxation. Would his tuition expenses for attending an LL.M. program in taxation be deductible? What if, instead, Foulup went straight from law school into the LL.M. program?

4. a. Foulup went on a business trip to Des Moines. When he returned, the firm offered to reimburse him for his expenses. Foulup refused to accept the reimbursement, saying that he would simply deduct the expenses from his gross income. Can Foulup take such a deduction? Do you advise this course of action? (*See* Heidt v. C.I.R., 274 F.2d 25 (7th Cir. 1959).)

   b. Assuming that Foulup is reimbursed for his business trip expenses, what tax treatment will he have?

5. On Sunday, Foulup flew to Hawaii on business. After he finished conducting his business on Wednesday, he decided to spend Thursday and Friday just enjoying the beauty of the islands. He flew home on Saturday. What expenses of this trip, if any, will be deductible? Would your answer be different if Foulup's trip had been to the Bahamas, instead of Hawaii?

6. Business deductions are taken in computing adjusted gross income under § 62, while personal deductions are taken in computing taxable income under § 63. Which type of a deduction gets "better treatment" and why?

7. In 1985 Musky bought a Ford Lemon automobile for $5200. In 2008, Musky sold the car for $500. Will Musky be able to claim a loss deduction in 2008?

8. In 2008, Musky's home was robbed. The thieves took: jewelry with a fair market value of $25K and a basis of $10K; furniture valued at $800 and a $1000 basis; and paintings with a $3K fair market value and a $700 basis. Musky's adjusted gross income for the year was $110K. What deductible loss, if any, did Musky have from the theft of his property. (Assume that Musky was not insured.)

PROBLEM #12 CAPITAL GAINS AND LOSSES

ASSIGNMENT:
Code: §§ 1(h); 1211(b); 1212(b); 1221; 1222; 1223; 1231
Regs.: §§ 1.1221–1, 1.1223–1

1. Ms. Inglink owned a section of land known as Darwinacre, which she had inherited from her father. Since she wasn't in the business of dealing in property, Ms. Inglink decided to sell the property to Tarzan, who needed to use the land for his "Jungleland Amusement Park." Three years later, Tarzan sold the land to Cheetah, who was in the business of selling land to customers. What is the character of Darwinacre in the hands of each of these characters?

2. B. Fuddled sold her Confused.Com stock for $20K in the year 2007. What are the tax consequences of her sale if:

    a. She had purchased the stock for investment in 2005 for $14K, and she was in the 35% tax bracket?

    b. She had purchased the stock for investment in 2005 for $28K, and she had no other sales or exchanges for the year?

    c. She had purchased the stock for $11K earlier in 2007?

    d. She had purchased the stock in 2005 for $10K, held it for investment, and she was in the 15% tax bracket in 2007?

    e. How would your answers to the above questions change if the property sold in each case had been considered "section 1202 stock"?

3. Leo Lumberjack is in the business of delivering firewood to Maine residents. In the current year, Leo sold a parcel of land used in his business for $115K; he paid $100K for the land four years ago. Leo also sustained an uninsured loss as a result of the theft of his delivery truck that he used in his business for three years; at the time of theft, the truck had an adjusted basis of $10K and a value of $15K. What are the tax consequences on the land sale and truck loss?

PROBLEM #13 DEPRECIATION AND RECAPTURE

ASSIGNMENT:
   Code: §§ 167; 168; 179; 197; 1016; 1245; 1250
   Regs.: §§ 1.167(a)–1, –2, –3; 1.1245–1, –2, –3, –4, –5, –6

1. Jasper Whineberger is a business taxpayer. Jasper purchases a shredder to be used in the active conduct of his trade or business. The shredder is acquired and placed in service on January 15, 2008, at a cost of $10,000. Under the applicable Revenue Procedure, the shredder has a class life of 5 years. You may assume that the 40% rule of IRC § 168(d)(3)(A) is not applicable. Prepare a depreciation schedule for the shredder.

2. What if Jasper desires a different depreciation schedule than the one described in problem 1? What are his alternatives? Can he make an election under § 179?

3. Rush Limburger is a cash basis calendar year taxpayer. Rush owns a radio transmitter that he uses in his trade or business of promoting himself. The property is 5-year property and was purchased in 2008 for $100K. No § 179 election was made. What are the tax consequences to Rush if:

    a. He sells the transmitter for $25K in 2011, having taken a total of $80K in depreciation deductions?

    b. Same as (a) above except that Rush made the § 179 election?

    c. Same as (a) above but Rush sold the transmitter for $125K instead of $25K?

    d. Rush gave the transmitter to his daughter Sinead, and she sold it for $125K in 2011?

    e. Rush died, leaving the transmitter to Sinead, and she sold it for $125K, which was its fair market value at the time of Rush's death?

    f. Instead of selling the transmitter, Rush sold residential rental real estate with an adjusted basis of $50K for $600K. Rush has depreciated this property using the straight-line method of depreciation, and has properly claimed $15K of depreciation with respect to the property.

4. Best Cleaners, Inc. will purchase all the assets of an existing dry cleaning business from Comet Cleaners, Inc., including the following intangible assets: (1) a patent obtained by Comet on a dry cleaning chemical that does not dissolve buttons; (2) Comet's popular trademark "Buttons are our friend!"; (3) customer and supplier lists; (4) computer software; and (4) goodwill. The agreement between Best and Comet allocates the purchase price to the above items in the amount of their respective fair market values. Explain in general the tax consequences to Best Cleaners of the purchase of these assets.

PROBLEM #14 THE CHARITABLE DEDUCTION

ASSIGNMENT:
Code: § 170

Determine the (1) contribution, (2) deduction, and (3) carry-over for each of the following gifts:

1. a. Al Umni has adjusted gross income of $100K, and itemized deductions in excess of his appropriate zero bracket amount. Al was so excited this year when his college football team broke its 40-game losing streak by fighting to a 0-0 tie that he gave $55K in cash to the school (a § 170(b)(1)(A)(ii) charitable organization).

   b. What if in (a) above Al gave land which he had held for three months instead of cash? Assume the land had a basis of $50K and a fair market value of $100K.

   c. What if in (a) above Al had given the cash to the Sound Foundation (a § 170(b)(1)(B) organization)?

2. a. Martindale Hubble has adjusted gross income of $100K and has itemized deductions in excess of his zero bracket amount. Martindale donated $50K worth of Salvador Picasso paintings (some 50,000 paintings in all) to the Museum of Hotel Art (a § 170(b)(1)(A)(vii) charity). The paintings had a basis of $25K when Martindale purchased them in 1972.

   b. What if in (a) above Martindale had given the paintings to a church (a § 170(b)(1)(A)(iii) organization)?

3. a. Dweeb Einstein has adjusted gross income of $200K, and itemized deductions in excess of his appropriate zero bracket amount. Dweeb owns the patent on a pencil sharpening device that he invented, and has held the patent for more than one year. The patent has an adjusted basis of zero (because Dweeb immediately expensed his research and experimental costs under § 174(a)) and a fair market value of $100K. Dweeb gives the patent to a university (a § 170(b)(1)(A)(ii) charitable organization).

   b. What if in (a) above Dweeb bought the patent from an unrelated third party for $50K as an investment?

PROBLEM #15 NONRECOGNITION PROVISIONS

ASSIGNMENT:
Code: §§ 121; 1001(c); 1031; 1033; 1223; 1245(b)(4)
Regs.: §§ 1.1031(a)–1; 1.1031(b)–1; 1.1031(d)–2, Ex. 2

1. Paul Whitney owns an unencumbered sail boat with a fair market value of $15K and an adjusted basis of $8K. He exchanges the boat for real property owned by Terry Black which has a fair market value of $20K and is subject a mortgage in the amount of $5K. Terry has an adjusted basis in the property of $15K. The exchange *does not* qualify for any provision relating to non-recognition of gain under the Internal Revenue Code.

   a. In regards to Paul Whitney

      i. What is the amount realized?

      ii. What is the amount of gain or loss realized? Recognized?

      iii. What is Paul's adjusted basis in the acquired property? (*See* Philadelphia Park Amusement Co. v. United States, 126 F. Supp. 184 (Ct. Cl. 1954).)

   b. In regards to Terry Black

      i. What is the amount realized?

      ii. What is the amount of gain or loss realized? Recognized?

      iii. What is Terry's adjusted basis in the acquired property? (*See Philadelphia Park Amusement Co., supra.*)

2. Thomas Lott owns an apartment building which he holds for rental income purposes. Thomas had an adjusted basis in the building of $50K, and it has a fair market value of $100K. Tim Welch owns an apartment building for similar purposes. Tim has an adjusted basis in his apartment building of $110K. Tim's apartment complex has a fair market value of $100K. Larry and Tim exchange their apartment buildings in an exchange which qualifies for non-recognition of gain under I.R.C. § 1031.

   a. What are the income tax consequences to each party?

   b. Same as (a) above, except Tim Welch is a professional "dealer" in apartment buildings.

   c. Same as (a) above, except Thomas Lott sells his apartment building to Barry Burget and then uses the proceeds from the sale to purchase Tim Welch's apartment building.

3. Woody Shephard owns an apartment building with an adjusted basis of $50K and a fair market value of $70K which is subject to a mortgage of $40K. Ron Shotts owns a similar apartment building with an adjusted basis of $30K, a fair market value of $70K, and subject to a mortgage of $40K. Woody and Ron exchange their properties, each party taking subject to the mortgage in the acquired property.

   a. Does this qualify as an exchange under § 1031? If it does, what are tax consequences to Woody and Ron?

   b. Same as (a) above, except but Woody Shephard's building had a fair market value of $80K, and a mortgage on it of $50K. How does this change the result?

   c. Same as (a) above, except Woody Shephard's building has an adjusted basis of $50K, and a mortgage on it of $30K. In addition to exchanging property, Ron Shotts paid $10K in cash.

4. Elvis Peacock has a farm in Iowa which he wants to exchange for a farm owned by Steve Bryan in Checotah, Oklahoma. Steve Bryan wants to sell his property, but wants cash, not another farm. In the past, John Goodman had expressed an interest in purchasing Peacock's farm. Can you suggest a way to accommodate all parties?

5. Calendar-year taxpayer, Charles Follis, owned and leased an office and warehouse building with an adjusted basis of $120K. On January 13, 2008, the government condemned the building. On July 10, 2008, Charles received $180K in condemnation proceeds, and estimated that the entire $180K would be used to replace the original office and warehouse building with a new office and warehouse building.

   a. What is Charles' gain realized on the condemnation?

   b. What is the latest date Charles has to purchase qualified replacement property to not recognize the gain?

   c. Assuming Charles paid $200K for qualified replacement property within the prescribed time limit, what is Charles' basis in the new property?

6. On January 1, 2007, Leon Crosswhite, who is single and unemployed, purchased a principal residence in Charleston, South Carolina, for $200K. Determine the amount of gain, if any, that must be included in gross income in the following situations:

   a. Four years after the purchase, Leon sold the Charleston residence for $500K because he didn't like the sticky weather in Charleston.

   b. Twelve months after the purchase, Leon sold the Charleston residence for $500K because he obtained a job in Portland, Maine.

   c. Six months after the purchase, Leon married Leslie Visser who, at that time, moved into the Charleston residence. Title remained in Leon's name alone. Eighteen months after the marriage, Leon sold the Charleston residence for $500K, and filed a joint return with Leslie.

   d. Same as (c) above except that Leslie had been living in the Charleston residence since January 1, 2007.

PROBLEM #16 LIMITATIONS ON DEDUCTIONS: "AT RISK" AND "PASSIVE LOSS" RULES

ASSIGNMENT:
Code: §§ 465; 469
Regs.: § 1.469–5T

1. Risky Rick established a sole proprietorship, Krazy Kayakers, that manufactures and sells sea kayaks by the seashore. Risky contributed $50K and a piece of land worth $100K in which he had an adjusted basis of $25K. He also borrowed $300K on a non-recourse basis. In its first year of operation, Krazy Kayakers lost $125K. In its second year of operation, Krazy Kayakers had net earnings of $100K.

    a. What are the tax consequences to Risky under § 465?

    b. Same as (a) above, except the lender has recourse against Risky personally on the $300K debt.

2. Passive A. Gressive is a lawyer who earns $200K per year in his law practice. Passive also invests in a limited partnership, from which his share of net losses will be $55K in 2008. Assuming that Passive is at-risk to the extent of his share of the losses, to what extent will Passive be able to offset his earnings from his law practice with the losses from the limited partnership if:

    a. The limited partnership activities involve the production of motion pictures (like "Bambi Meets Godzilla")?

    b. The limited partnership losses arose from working interests in natural gas fields?

    c. Same as (b) above, but Passive is a general partner, rather than a limited partner?

3. Ma Kettle owns a grocery store in Portland, Maine. Ma's net income from her operation of the store is $75K per year, thanks in large part to her use of optical scanning equipment to checkout customers. Ma works at the store 40 hours per week. Ma also owns five apartments, which she rents to law students. In 2008, Ma's deductible expenses from the apartments will exceed her income from those apartments by $40K. To what extent will Ma be able to offset her grocery store income by the losses generated by the apartments if:

    a. Ma does not actively participate in the management of the apartments?

    b. Ma spends 10 hours per week managing the apartments?

    c. How would your answer to (b.) above, change if Ma's adjusted gross income for the year had been $150K? (Does § 62(a)(4) present any problems here?)

    d. What if Ma spends only 1 hour per week working at the grocery store? Does this give you any planning ideas?

    e. Generally speaking, what will happen if Ma has unused passive loss or credit carry-overs when she decides to dispose of the apartments in a fully taxable transaction?

Chapter 10

PRACTICE EXAMS

The best way to access your progress in any law school course is to take practice exams. You will find that forcing yourself to write out an exam answer within a specified time period will be an excellent way to diagnose your strengths and weaknesses in an area. The first part of this chapter contains an outline which offers one approach for studying for your tax exam.

The rest of this chapter contains five sample examinations. These practice examinations are designed to test your understanding of federal income taxation concepts and your ability to apply sections of the Internal Revenue Code. Approximate time allocations are given for each question. Answers to Practice Exams #1, #2, and #3 can be found in Appendix IV. We have not supplied answers to Practice Exams # 4 and #5, because you will best benefit from answering those on your own. We will be happy, however, to supply a model answer to Practice Exams #4 and #5, if you will mail or email us your answers.

Our addresses are:

Richard Gershon
Dean and Professor of Law
Charleston School of Law
P.O. Box 535
Charleston, SC 29402
rgershon@charlestonlaw.org

and

Jeffrey A. Maine
Associate Dean and Professor of Law
University of Maine School of Law
246 Deering Avenue
Portland, ME 04102
jmaine@usm.maine.edu

OUTLINE OF FEDERAL INCOME TAXATION

Topic	*Code Section*	*Regulation/Case*
Gross Income	61	1.61-1 through -6, -14 and *Glenshaw Glass, Cesarini, Old Colony Trust*
Exclusions for Gifts and Inheritances	102, 101(b)(1), 132	1.102-1(a), (b), (c); 1.132-1 through -4 and *Duberstein*
Awards and Scholarships	74, 117	
Gains Derived from Dealings in Property	61(a)(3), 1001(a), 1011, 1012, 1041	1.1001-1(a), 1.1011-1, 1.1012-1(a), 1.61-2(d)(2)(i), 1.1001-2 and *Philadelphia Park, Crane*
Fundamental Principals of Timing	83	1.83-1 through -3, 1.83-4(b)
Annuities and Life Insurance Proceeds	72(a), (b), (c); 79; 101(a), (c), (d)	1.72-4(a), -9 (Table 1); 1.101-1(a)(1), (b)(1), -4(a)(1), (b)(1), (c)
Gift Basis	1015, 1011(b)	1.1015-1; 1.1015-4; 1.1001-1(e)
Date of Death Basis	1014, 1001(e)	1.1014-1, -3, -4, -5; 1.1001-1(f)
Assignment of Income: Who	1; Skim 269A, 671-678, and 704(e)	*Lucas v. Earl, Giannini, Salvatore*
Divorce and Separation	71, 215 and 1041	
Deductions for Losses and Business Expenses	62; 63(b) - (h); 162; 165(a), (c), (h); 274(a), (c), (h)	1.62-1; 1.162-1 through -9, -15, -17(b); 1.165-1(a), (e), 1.165-7 and *Deputy v. duPont; Welch v. Helvering, Groetzinger*
Capital Gains and Losses	1(h), 1211(b), 1212(b), 1221, 1231, 1222, 1223	1.1221-1, 1.1223-1

Depreciation and Recapture	167, 168, 179, 197, 1016(a)(2), 1245, 1250	1.167(a)-1, -2, -3, 1.1245-1, -2, -3, -4, -5, -6
The Charitable Deduction	170	
Nonrecognition Provisions	121, 1001(c), 1031, 1033, 1223, 1245(b)(4)	1.1031(a)-1, 1.1031(b)-1, 1.1031(d)-2, Ex. 2
Limitations on Losses	465, 469	1.469-5T

CASE LAW

C.I.R. v. Glenshaw Glass Co., 348 U.S. 426 (1955): Income is defined as "undeniable accessions to wealth, clearly realized, and over which taxpayers have complete dominion." The source of receipts is irrelevant.

C.I.R. v. Cesarini, 428 F.2d 812 (6th Cir. 1970): Money found in piano was gross income in year reduced to undisputed possession under state law. Also in Reg. § 1.61-14.

Old Colony Trust Co. v. C.I.R., 279 U.S. 716 (1929): Although gross income, which includes both cash and non-cash benefits, is usually received directly by the taxpayer, gross income does not have to be received directly by the taxpayer. *Old Colony* involved the payment of employee's taxes by his employer.

C.I.R. v. Duberstein, 363 U.S. 278 (1960): Must have a detached and disinterested generosity in order to have gift exclusion. (Remember, in employer/employee relationship, presumption is no disinterested generosity.) Also in § 102(c).

Philadelphia Park Amusement Co. v. United States, 126 F. Supp. 184 (Ct. Cl. 1954): The taxpayer's basis in property received in a taxable exchange is equal to the fair market value of the property received. The concept of "tax cost basis" arises whenever property acquired other than by cash purchase is included in gross income (*e.g.*, treasure trove, prizes, property unlawfully received).

Crane v. C.I.R., 331 U.S. 1 (1947): All liabilities (recourse and non recourse) are part of amount realized when sold and amount paid when bought (pro taxpayer). Also in Reg. § 1.1001-2. The Anti-*Crane* provisions are in § 465 (where excess loss from a passive activity is limited to the amount at risk in that activity; nonrecourse liability is not generally considered an amount at-risk).

Lucas v. Earl, 281 U.S. 111 (1930): Cannot shift service income to family members. Service income must be taxed to person who earns the income (*i.e.*, cannot shift the incidents of taxation from service income.)

C.I.R. v. Giannini, 129 F.2d 638 (9th Cir. 1942): Where [right to] income is shifted by income earner timely giving up all control over where it goes (*i.e.*, I do not want it, and I do not care who you give it to) then the tax consequences are shifted. He did not control money that he told his company not to pay him. Giannini's company donated it to a university to establish an endowed chair in Giannini's name, but he did not exercise control over the income.

Suzy Salvatore v. C.I.R., T.C. Memo. 1970-30: Salvatore contracted to sell her gas station and transferred the rights to it to her children so they would pay the taxes in their bracket. Court said Salvatore had to pay the tax since she really did everything necessary to make the sale. In order to transfer the incidents of taxation by assignment of property interest, the assignment must occur before the taxable transaction.

Deputy v. DuPont, 308 U.S. 488 (1940): Whether an expense is ordinary or necessary is affected by time, place, circumstance and the nature of the expense. In this case, the Supreme Court denied a deduction to a taxpayer who paid a corporate debt for which he was not personally liable. The court reasoned that the expense arose out of the corporation's business, and not the taxpayer's.

Welch v. Helvering, 290 U.S. 111 (1933): "Ordinary" means customary/expected in business. "Necessary" means appropriate and helpful "Ordinary and necessary" does not necessarily mean habitual or regular. A one time expense can be ordinary. "Life in all its fullness must supply the answer to the riddle of what is ordinary and necessary." In other words, deductibility is a fact question to be determined by looking at all of the circumstances.

C.I.R. v. Groetzinger, 480 U.S. 23 (1987): To be engaged in a "trade or business" within the meaning of § 162, a taxpayer must be involved in the activity with continuity and regularity, and the taxpayer's primary purpose for engaging in the activity must be for income or profit. The Court held that an individual's gambling activities constituted a trade or business because they were pursued full time, in good faith, and with regularity, to the production of income for a livelihood. An activity will not qualify as a trade or business if it is a sporadic activity, a hobby, or an amusement diversion.

PRACTICE EXAM #1

PROBLEM I (90 minutes)

One of the worst things about being the fabulously successful tax attorney that you are (you were paid $400K in legal fees during 2007), is that all of your celebrity friends are in the habit of asking you for free tax advice. For example, during 2007 alone you estimate that you have given Zsa Zsa Zabor over $100K worth of free advice, and she hasn't even had the decency to say "Thank You, Dahlink." Accordingly, to deal with this problem, on December 14, 2007 you paid $10K to install the "Tax Hotline," a 1-900 number. Your friends can get tax advice from the hotline 24 hours a day, and they will pay $25 a minute (average call 5 minutes, under 18 ask your parents). You will be able to keep all of the money charged by the hotline, but you will have to pay the phone company a fee of $200 per year to keep the service operating.

At 9:00 a.m. on December 14, you received your first phone call. The caller was Woody Ellen who was seeking tax advice regarding his recent divorce from Mia Sparrow. Woody informed you that he will be required to pay Mia, pursuant to the divorce decree, $100K in 2007, $90K in 2008, $70K in 2009, and $20K in 2010. These payments, which will be in cash, will cease upon Mia's death or remarriage. Woody and Mia will be living "as far away from each other as possible." Woody will also be required to pay Mia $20K per year for child support, until all of her children, including Woody's girlfriend, reach the age of 25.

At 10:00 a.m. Major League Baseball (an old army buddy) called to inform you that she has been taking illegal kick-backs. This year alone she received $300K in exchange for her promise not to award a military contract to the St. Petersburg area. She gave the money to her son Minor, a 12 year old brat, who invested all of it in Blockbuster Video stock. Minor received $1400 in dividends from the stock in 2007. Also in 2007, Minor was given the rights to the rents from the Suncoastdome Apartments, which are owned in fee simple by his Auntie Trust. Minor received $4500 in rents during the year.

At 12:00 p.m. you got a call from Queenie Elizabeth, who owns a local restaurant called the "Windsor Palace Hot Dog Emporium." Queenie was upset because the restaurant burned down on December 13, 2007. The building had an adjusted basis of $50K and a fair market value of $200K, but she only received $120K from her insurance company. To make matters worse, that same night someone stole her family jewels. The jewels had an adjusted basis of $14K and a fair market value of $65K. Unfortunately, even though Queenie has an adjusted gross income of $130K, she decided not to waste her money buying insurance for the jewels.

At 2:30 p.m. Lizzie Borden called the Hotline. She told you that her parents had died in an unfortunate "ax"ident. Because of their death, she will receive $300K in life insurance proceeds from a policy she bought from her parents for $10K. The policy was worth $15K at the time Lizzie purchased it. Lizzie also received a payment of $11K from her mother's employer "40 Wax," a candle maker. The employer paid Lizzie the money in recognition of her mother's dedication to the company. Even though the company did not owe her anything, they wanted to help out the family following her death.

Finally, at 5:00 p.m. Ross Parrot called regarding some money he owes you for tax advice you had given him. To be precise, he owes you $75K. Ross, who is a little short of cash, told you that he would like to give you a building with a basis of $25K and a fair market value of $75K as payment for your services. Given the type of day that you have had, you decide to accept his offer.

What are the tax consequences of the above transactions? Please be sure to explain your answers.

PROBLEM II (45 minutes)

There are three parts to this problem; please be sure to answer all three.

A. Henry VIII and Ann Bowling, having been royal pains to each other for years, have decided to separate but remain married. According to their separation instrument, Henry will be required to sell Ann his royal bowling ball and give her his matching shoes. The ball has a basis of $500 and a fair market value of $300. The shoes have a basis of $50 and a fair market value of $60.

What will be the tax consequences to Henry and Ann, if Ann pays Henry $300 for the ball, and he gives her the shoes? What will be the tax consequences to Ann if she later sells the ball to King Burger for $300? Be sure to explain your answer.

B. Mr. Potato(e)head died owning land with a basis of $10K and a fair market value of $100K. According to Mr. Potato(e)head's will, the land was passed to his daughter Baked for life, remainder to his grandson Fried.

What are the tax consequences of the above transaction? What would be the tax consequences if Baked sold her life interest to Big Mac for $80K at a time when the life estate was worth 80% of the value of the property? Would your answer be different if Baked sold the life estate to Fried for $80K? Be sure to explain your answers.

C. Mat Robertson sold his collection of 2 Live Crew albums to his son Cliff for $25K, at a time when the albums had an adjusted basis of $2K and a fair market value of $50K. Because of the nature of this transaction, Pat was required to pay $4K in gift tax on this transaction.

What are the tax consequences of the above transaction? Be sure to explain your answer.

END OF EXAM

PRACTICE EXAM #2

PROBLEM 1 (45 minutes)

USelessAIR, the airline who's motto is "we go up almost as often as we come down" has contacted you to regarding the tax consequences of the following transactions which took place in 2007:

1. The airline sold 10 computers it had been using to book flights for its customers. They decided that booking customers was a mistake, because those customers actually expected to fly at the times printed on their tickets. The computers, which had an adjusted basis of $1100 each (reflecting the $400 USeless had taken in depreciation using the appropriate method), were sold for $1200 each.

2. The airline sold 1000 of the delicious meals normally served in flight to customers stuck on the ground in various airports around the country. The meals cost USeless a total of $500. They were sold for a total of $8000.

3. One airplane was totally wrecked when Rudolph the Red Nosed pilot forgot to take off the emergency brake while he was taxiing down the runway. Fortunately, there were no injuries. The airplane had an adjusted basis of $1 Million, reflecting the $9 Million of depreciation which USeless had taken using the appropriate depreciation method. USeless expects to receive a $4 Million payment from its insurer covering its loss. Of course, that check will be flown on a USeless Air flight, so it might take it a year to get to the company.

4. Finally, USeless had one of its office buildings condemned by the Federal government this year. The building was used by USeless as a training facility for its flight attendants until its condemnation. The government opted to keep only the building itself, allowing USeless to remove the whips, chains and leather goods so that they could be used at their other training facility on Devil's Island. The building, which was depreciated using the straight-line method of depreciation, had an adjusted basis of $100K. The government gave USeless $150K as compensation for the requisition.

> **What are the tax consequences of the above transactions? Be sure to explain your answers. Can USeless avoid gain recognition on any of the above transactions? If so, how?**

PROBLEM II (45 minutes)

Homer Simpson has had an interesting year, from a tax perspective. First, he sold 500 shares of Questionable, Inc. stock for $500 in March of 2007. Homer had purchased the stock for $10K in February of 2007. Homer also sold 10 shares of Prosperous, Inc. stock for $1K. Homer had paid $250 (total) for the shares in 1980.

More importantly, Homer has adjusted gross income of $100K for the 2007 tax year, and he would like to make some contributions to charity for the express purpose of minimizing his tax liability to the greatest extent possible. Homer has picked two possible charities to be the recipients of his bounty: Whatsamatta U., a § 170(b)(1)(A) educational organization, and the Save the Cockroach Foundation, a § 170(b)(1)(B) private foundation.

Homer has selected the following property as prospective gifts:

1. $50K in cash;

2. land held for investment, purchased by Homer in 1980 (Adjusted Basis of $10K, Fair Market Value of $40K);

3. stock purchased by Homer in 1950 (Adjusted Basis $45K, Fair Market Value $40K);

4. Inventory purchased in 1991 (Adjusted Basis $1K, Fair Market Value $6K);

5. Homer's personal furniture purchased in 1976 (Adjusted Basis $7K, Fair Market Value $32K).

Please inform Homer regarding the best plan for contributions for the year 2007. Explain your answer. Also, please advise Homer regarding the tax consequences of his stock sales for the year.

PROBLEM III (45 minutes)

M.T. Head, owner of a college bookstore, has been a client of yours for several years. Unfortunately, Mr. Head is one of those clients who acts first and then seeks your advice. For example, in 2007 and 2008, Head entered into the following transactions:

1. On April 1, 2007, Head purchased a 300 foot yacht worth 1.5 million dollars using $500K of cash and $1 million of nonrecourse debt. Head planned to rent the yacht to tourists on a daily or weekly basis. Unfortunately, there were few takers and Head's deductible expenditures exceeded his income from the yacht rentals by $520K. Head's only other sources of income are the $200K he netted from his lawn mower rental business and $100K from his business as a college bookstore owner. Head works 10 hours per week in his bookstore.

2. On April 7, 2008, Head traded his yacht (the Lead Balloon) for a yacht owned by R.U. Syrius (the Ugly Duckling). Head's basis in Lead Balloon immediately prior to the exchange was $1.5 Million, and its fair market value was $2 Million. The Ugly Duckling, which is also worth $2 Million, is subject to a $900K recourse debt.

What are the tax consequences of the above transactions? How would your answer to number 1 change if the liability was a recourse debt in 2007, which Head switched to nonrecourse debt in 2008?

END OF EXAM

PRACTICE EXAM #3

PROBLEM (120 minutes)

Taxpayer, who is single and has no dependents, has a calendar taxable year and reports on the cash receipts and disbursements method. In January 2008, Taxpayer embezzled $100,000 from his law firm and squandered the money on drugs. In February 2008, Taxpayer received an out-of-court settlement of $50,000 ($25,000 payment for pain and suffering and $25,000 payment for lost wages) resulting from a car accident in which a car driven by a drunk driver struck Taxpayer's car. Worried that he might have to pay tax on this money (embezzled funds and settlement), he generated cash from the following transactions.

On October 1, 2008, Taxpayer sold 100 shares of stock in X corporation to an unrelated third party for $15,000. He had purchased the stock as an investment on October 1, 2007 for $25,000. The stock paid no dividends. Taxpayer made a $1,000 interest payment this year on a loan through his brokerage house for the purchase of the X stock.

On October 10, 2008, Taxpayer sold 100 shares of stock in Y corporation to his sister for $10,000, its fair market value. Taxpayer acquired the stock as a gift from his father in 2006 when the stock was worth $15,000. Father paid $30,000 for the stock in 2002. The stock, which was owned free and clear, paid $500 in dividends in August 2008.

On October 15, 2008, Taxpayer sold his summer home located in Idaho (not his principal residence, but his only other residence) to his sister for $80,000, even though at the time of sale the summer home had a fair market value of $90,000. (Sister paid Taxpayer $50,000 cash and assumed a $30,000 mortgage on the property). Taxpayer's uncle, Don Corleone (who taught Taxpayer how to embezzle), devised Taxpayer the home in 2002. Uncle paid $25,000 for the home; at his date of death, the home had a fair market value of $45,000. Taxpayer did not work for his uncle. In 2007, Taxpayer borrowed $30,000 (home equity loan from The Money Store) and used all loan proceeds to make substantial improvements to the property. During 2008, Taxpayer paid $3,000 in interest on the mortgage which was secured by the summer home.

On October 30, 2008, Taxpayer sold to an unrelated third party for $20,000 the truck he used in his side trade or business of selling firewood to Maine residents (sole proprietorship). He acquired the truck on May 15, 2008 as a gift from his Cousin Leo. Cousin Leo purchased the truck for $15,000 on February 15, 2001 and used it solely in his trade or business at all times. In 2001, Cousin Leo did not utilize the section 179 deduction, but elected under IRC § 168(b)(5) to depreciate the truck under the straight line method. He did not purchase and place in service any other property during 2001. During 2008, Taxpayer sold 50 "cords" of wood for $5,000; he paid local farmers $2,500 for the cords.

Taxpayer had a long-term capital loss carry over from 2007 in the amount of $5,000, under IRC § 1212(b)(1)(B).

Analyze the tax consequences of all transactions. Also determine the amount and character of the carryover loss to 2009, if any.

END OF EXAM

PRACTICE EXAM #4

PROBLEM I (90 minutes)

As Fort Worth's most prominent tax attorney you have ridden the camel to success, as indicated by your $400K annual salary. In addition to this lucrative salary, you receive a membership to the Fort Worth Yacht Club worth $5K per year, and the firm pays for your parking each month. In fact, you are the only member of the firm to receive such benefits.

On May 7, 2007, as you were riding to your posh office at the beautiful Fort Worth Casino, you were kidnapped by aliens from the planet Codehead who took you into their spaceship. The aliens informed you that you had earned the reputation of being the greatest tax attorney in the Universe, and that they had travelled to Earth, at a cost of $4 million, in order to test your abilities. Should you pass this test, you will have riches and happiness beyond your wildest dreams, should you fail the Earth would be destroyed (and you would lose all of your billable hours for the month). The aliens tell you that the questions for the test will be taken from the sacred writings of the *National Enquirer,* which they discovered on their last trip to Earth.

First, the aliens tell you that Mortimer Snerd of Paris decided to divorce his wife Brunhilda when he found out that she was fooling around with Bigfoot. The divorce decree required Brunhilda to pay Mortimer in cash 15% of her profits as a banana importer. The decree further stated that payments would cease upon the death of Mortimer, and that Mortimer would be required to move out of the house, prior to receiving the first payment in 2007. The payments, based upon 15% of Brunhilda's profits would be: $150K in 2007, $45K in 2008, and $10K in 2009 (the aliens can see three years into the future). In 2007, Brunhilda also sold Mortimer some land in Texas. The land had a basis to Brunhilda of $50K, and it had a fair market value of $75K. Mortimer paid $60K for the land.

Next, the aliens told you the story of Clep Tomaniac, a man in Topeka, Kansas who stole $30K worth of equipment from his employer. Clep sold the stolen equipment to Donald Trump for $45K. Clep hid the $45K in a cookie jar, before he was arrested and given an all expenses paid trip to Sing-Sing prison. Famous Amos found the cookie jar, and was allowed under local law to keep the $45K contained therein.

The third part of the aliens' test deals with Donald Trump, who had $40K of long-term capital loss, $25K of short-term capital loss, $5K of long-term capital gain, and $27K of short-term capital gain in 2007. (You suggest that the aliens might wish to take Trump back to their planet with them when they leave.)

The fourth quiz deals with Joe, who owns an apartment that he holds for investment. The apartment has a basis of $45K and a fair market value of $125K. Joe loves Sally's office building and would like to acquire that building, for use in his manufacturing business. Sally has a basis of $118K in the building, which has a fair market value of $123K. Sally is willing to part with her building, but she would like to receive cash for it, and she has no desire to own Joe's apartment. Wanda loves Joe's apartment building, and she is willing to give Joe $125K in cash for it.

Finally, the aliens tell you that they would like to donate cash or property to a charity, but they do not even know where to begin.

Please help them. For the sake of the entire planet, please tell the aliens what the tax consequences of each of the above transactions will be. With respect to the fourth quiz, devise a plan whereby all of the parties will get the property of their dreams, while obtaining the best possible tax consequences. Be sure to explain your reasons for your plan.

[Note: The answer to this problem does not appear in Appendix IV of the *Student's Guide*. If you mail or email us your answer, we will be happy to "grade it," and supply you with a sample answer.]

PRACTICE EXAM #5

PROBLEM (90 minutes)

(a) Long Essay

Taxpayer, who is single and has no dependents, has a calendar taxable year and reports on the cash receipts and disbursements method. Until April 2008, Taxpayer, a retired professor, had a side trade or business. Taxpayer owned some raw, unimproved land (½ of an acre) in downtown Portland ("Cityland"). For a fee each day, he would allow people to park on Cityland. Because parking availability in downtown Portland is scarce, the business performed quite well, generating large profits the last three years.

On April 25, 2008, the government condemned Cityland, the real estate Taxpayer used in his trade or business. The government agreed to pay a condemnation award in the amount of $65,000, with $10,000 paid in May 2008 and $55,000 paid in December 2008. Taxpayer does not intend to use the $65,000 cash received to purchase any replacement property. Taxpayer acquired Cityland on January 5, 2005 from Mr. Smith (an unrelated third party) in an exchange for Taxpayer's five acres of swamp land located in Okeechobee, Florida ("Swampland"). Taxpayer had acquired Swampland in 2002 for $70,000 as an investment. Swampland had bad drainage and abutted a small highway. On January 5, 2005, the date of the exchange, Swampland was subject to a mortgage in the amount of $40,000, which Mr. Smith assumed. At the time of the exchange, Mr. Smith's Cityland was being held by Mr. Smith for investment purposes, had a fair market value of $100,000, and was not encumbered by a mortgage (*i.e.*, was held free and clear by Mr. Smith).

In addition to the above, Taxpayer (1) received $120,000 of parking fees during 2008, (2) paid $15,000 on an aggressive advertising campaign for new parking customers during 2008, and (3) had a long-term capital loss carry over from 2007 in the amount of $6,000, under IRC § 1212(b)(1)(B).

Assume Taxpayer had no other income, gain, loss, or deduction items during the relevant years.

> **Analyze fully the tax consequences to Taxpayer of all transactions, including the exchange of land that occurred in 2005. If you need to make assumptions, please state them. You DO NOT need to calculate Taxpayer's income tax liability under IRC § 1.**

(b) Short Essay

Eugene Amos was working as a cameraman at a 1997 professional basketball game when, in the course of the game, Dennis Rodman landed on several photographers, including Amos, and subsequently kicked him. Amos received medical treatment for injuries he claimed resulted from the incident and filed a police report. Amos and Rodman executed a settlement agreement and Rodman paid Amos $200,000. Amos excluded the payment from his gross income, but the IRS determined that the settlement amount was includable under § 61. The Tax Court recently determined that Amos was entitled to exclude $120,000 from gross income under § 104(a)(2). Relying primarily on the text of the settlement agreement, the Tax Court concluded that a portion of the settlement ($80,000) was paid in return for Amos' agreeing not to defame Rodman, publicize the incident, or assist in a criminal prosecution.

Do you agree with the Tax Court's decision? Explain.

[Note: The answer to these essays do not appear in Appendix IV of the *Student's Guide*. If you mail or email us your answers, we will be happy to "grade them," and supply you with sample answers.]

Appendix I

GLOSSARY OF TAX TERMINOLOGY

The following is a glossary of terms and phrases that you will encounter in your study of Federal Income Taxation. Citations following each definition are to sections of the Internal Revenue Code of 1986, as amended (§), sections of the Treasury Regulations (Reg. §), and chapters within this *Student's Guide* (Ch., §), where appropriate.

A

Accrual Method: A permissible method of tax accounting. An accrual method taxpayer includes income in the taxable year in which all events have occurred which fix that taxpayer's right to receive such income. By the same token, an accrual method taxpayer takes deductions in the taxable year in which all events establishing the liability, for which the deduction is claimed, have occurred. For example, an attorney using the accrual method of accounting would have income in the taxable year in which he completed work for a client, and determined his charges for that work, even though the client might not actually pay her bill until the following taxable year.

§ 446(c); Reg. § 1.446-1(c)(1)(ii); Ch. 6, § 6.08[3].

Adjusted Basis: The taxpayer's basis increased or decreased by expenditures, losses, depreciation, or improvements as required by § 1016 of the Code, and Reg. §§ 1.1016-2 through 1.1016-10. [*See* **Basis**.] Ch. 6, § 6.05.

Adjusted Gross Income: Gross income minus the deductions allowed under § 62. Generally speaking, the deductions listed in § 62 represent Congress' acknowledgement of the principle that taxpayers have to spend money in order to make money.

§ 62; Reg. § 1.62-1; Ch. 2, § 2.02[2], [5].

After-Tax Dollars: Dollars that have already been subject to tax. For example, an employee in the 28% tax bracket who earns $1 will only have $0.72 after taxes. Consequently, in order for the employee to have an after-tax dollar, he must actually earn more than $1. In essence, the only dollars that any of us can actually spend are after-tax dollars. It is important to note that amounts excluded from gross income have, in fact, been subject to tax, even though the government has chosen not to tax those items. Hence, a taxpayer who receives a gift of $1 will have $1 after-taxes, because gifts are excluded from gross income by § 102(a).

Ch. 6, § 6.04.

Amount Realized: The sum of the money received, plus the fair market value of property (other than money) received, plus the amount of liabilities received from the transferor in a sale, or other disposition of property. In other words, amount realized is the total amount of consideration received by a taxpayer in a sale or disposition of property.

§ 1001(b); Reg. §§ 1.1001-1(a) and 1.1001-2; Ch. 6, §§ 6.06, 6.07.

B

Basis: The total amount of a taxpayer's dollars which have already been subject to tax, invested in property. Because basis represents after-tax dollars invested in property, a taxpayer is entitled to have his basis returned to him tax-free when he sells or otherwise disposes of the property.

§§ 1011, 1012, 1014, 1015, 1016, 1041; Reg. §§ 1.61-2(d)(2)(ii), 1.1011-1, 1.1012-1, 1.1014-1 through 1.1014-8, 1.1015-1 through 1.1015-5, 1.1016-1 through 1.1016-5, 1.1041-1T; Ch. 6, § 6.05.

C

Cash Method: A permissible method of tax accounting, also known as the cash receipts and disbursements method. A cash method taxpayer includes income in the taxable year in which he actually or constructively receives payment. By the same token, a cash method taxpayer takes deductions in the taxable year in which payment of expenses is made. For example, an attorney using the cash method of accounting would not have income until his client actually paid his bill, even though the work for that client was completed in a prior taxable year.

§ 446(c); Reg. § 1.446-1(c)(1)(i); Ch. 6, § 6.08[3].

Cost Basis: The basis acquired by a taxpayer in a purchase or a taxable exchange. The taxpayer's cost is not computed in economic terms, but rather in terms of the amount of after-tax dollars the taxpayer has invested in property. Therefore, while cost basis is equal to the amount of cash paid plus liabilities acquired when a taxpayer purchases property, it is equal to the fair market value of property *received* in a taxable exchange.

§ 1012; Reg. § 1.1012-1; Ch. 6, § 6.05.

Credit: An amount which a taxpayer can apply directly against a tax liability. For example, if a taxpayer owes $10 of tax, but he has $3 of tax credits, she need only pay the government $7. A dollar of credit is more valuable than a dollar of deduction, because a dollar of deduction saves a taxpayer only the amount of tax he would have owed on a dollar of taxable income. For example, a taxpayer in the 28% bracket would owe $0.28 on a dollar of taxable income. Consequently, a dollar of deduction would save that taxpayer only $0.28.

§§ 21–54; Ch. 2, § 2.02[7].

Cumulative Bulletin (C.B.): A hard-bound compilation of the weekly Internal Revenue Bulletins. The Cumulative Bulletin is published every six months, and contains Revenue Rulings, Revenue Procedures, Treasury Decisions, and other administrative pronouncements.

Ch. 7, § 7.04, Ch. 8, § 8.04.

D

Deduction: An amount subtracted from gross income in computing taxable income. Some deductions, like the deduction for expenses incurred in a trade or business (§ 162), represent the government's acknowledgement that taxpayers should only be taxed on their net income from their business endeavors. Other deductions, like the deduction for charitable contributions (§ 170), reflect the government's desire to foster certain social policies.

§§ 161–249; Ch. 2, § 2.02[5]; Ch. 6, § 6.04.

E

Exclusion Provision: A Code section which provides that an increase in a taxpayer's wealth will not be included in his gross income. For example, when a taxpayer receives a gift of $50, there is no question that his wealth has been increased. Section 102, however, provides that gifts will not be included in gross income. Thus, § 102 is an exclusion provision.

§§ 101–140; Ch. 2, § 2.02[4].

F

Fair Market Value: The price at which property would change hands between a willing buyer and a willing seller, neither being under any compulsion to buy or sell and both having reasonable knowledge of relevant facts. Fair market is always a question of fact. Accordingly, if you buy a car from a dealer for $12,000, and your friend pays $11,500 for a car identical to yours from the same dealer, you have both paid fair market value, as long as you were both willing buyers, under no compulsion to buy, and you both had reasonable knowledge of the relevant facts.

Reg. § 1.170A-1(c); ch 6, § 6.06[1].

G

Gain: In tax terms, gain is the excess of a taxpayer's amount realized over his adjusted basis. Tax gain is different from pure economic gain. An example of the difference between tax gain and economic gain would arise when a taxpayer's factory, which had a basis of $50,000, and a fair market value of $75,000, was destroyed by a fire. If the taxpayer only had $60,000 worth of insurance, he would think that he had an economic loss of $15,000, the difference between his insurance coverage and the fair market value of his property. On the other hand, for tax purposes, the taxpayer would have a gain of $10,000, because his amount realized in the form of insurance proceeds exceeded his adjusted basis.

§ 1001(a); Reg. § 1.1001-1; Ch. 6, §§ 6.05–6.07.

Gross Income: All accessions to a taxpayer's wealth, occurring within a given taxable year, over which the taxpayer has dominion, and which are not excluded by some provision of the Internal Revenue Code. § 61; Reg. §§ 1.61-1 through 1.61-14; Ch. 2, § 2.02[3].

I

Inclusion Provision: A Code section requiring an accession to the taxpayer's wealth, from a specific source or activity, to be taken into consideration when calculating gross income.

§§ 71–90; Ch. 2, § 2.02[3].

Internal Revenue Code of 1986: A compilation of federal statutes relating to taxation, as amended to the present time. The Code, which is contained in Title 26 of the United States Code, is the primary source of the law of federal income taxation.

K

"Kiddie Tax:" Added to the Code in 1986, it taxes a child's unearned income at his parent's rates, if those rates are higher, and if the child is under eighteen. The purpose of the Kiddie Tax is to prevent parents from transferring money or property to their children merely to take advantage of the child's lower tax bracket.

§ 1(q); Ch. 6, § 6.02.

L

Loss: The excess of a taxpayer's adjusted basis over his amount realized. The tax concept of loss differs from the economic concept of loss. For example, Cal Amity owned an uninsured ship with an adjusted basis of $12,000, and a fair market value of $26,000. If Cal's navigational skills caused the ship to wreck, his tax loss would be $12,000 (the difference between his adjusted basis of $12,000 and his amount realized of zero), even though his economic loss would be $26,000, the value of the ship. It is important to note, however, that losses are only deductible if § 165, the "switchboard for losses," grants such a deduction.

§§ 165, 1001(a); Reg. §§ 1.165-1, 1001-1(a).

N

Nonrecognition: Section 1001(c) of the Code provides that all gains realized shall be recognized, unless some other section of the Code provides for nonrecognition. Nonrecognition provisions allow certain realized gains to escape taxation until a later, more appropriate time. For example, if an individual had a $58,000 basis in a rental building, and exchanged it for a similar rental building worth $67,000, he would have a gain realized of $9,000. This gain would be recognized, and therefore taxed, but for § 1031, which allows the deferral of gain recognized in like-kind exchanges. The basis of the new building would be $58,000, the same as the old building, and the gain would be recognized only when the new building is sold.

§§ 1031–1045; Ch. 6, § 6.06[2].

P

Private Letter Ruling: An Internal Revenue Service response to questions posed by a taxpayer. Private Letter Rulings are not precedent.

§§ 6110, 7805; Ch. 7, § 7.04[3].

Progressive Rate Structure: The element of the federal income tax which requires a taxpayer to pay taxes at rates corresponding to his relative taxable income. The basic premise behind progressive tax rates is that, as a taxpayer's income increases, so does his ability to pay taxes without facing starvation. Thus, a higher income person's top dollar should be taxed at a higher rate than a lower income person's top dollar.

§ 1; Ch. 6, § 6.02.

R

Realization: An event, such as the sale or exchange of property, which causes a taxpayer a tangible benefit or loss. For example, N. Vestor bought 25 shares of Major Motors stock for $4 per share. On Monday the shares were worth $20 per share, but Vestor decided not to sell them. Instead, he sold them on Tuesday, when they were only worth $6 per share. On Monday, Vestor had an unrealized gain of $16 per share, because he did not sell or exchange the shares, even though they increased in value. When Vestor sold the shares on Tuesday, however, he had a gain realized of $2 per share, because the sale fixed the amount of economic benefit Vestor would derive from the stock. § 1001(a); Reg. § 1.1001-1(a); Ch. 6, § 6.06[1].

Recognition: The inclusion of a realized gain in gross income, or, subject to § 165, the allowance of a realized loss as a deduction. [*See* **Nonrecognition**.]

§ 1001(c); Ch. 6, § 6.06[2].

Revenue Procedure (Rev. Proc.): An administrative proclamation, issued by the Internal Revenue Service, and published in the Internal Revenue Bulletin, which discusses tax procedures affecting the rights or duties of taxpayers.

§ 7.04[4].

Revenue Ruling (Rev. Rul.): A published, and therefore official, Internal Revenue Service response to a question raised by a taxpayer concerning the tax consequences of a specific transaction.

§ 7805; Reg. § 301.7805-1; Ch. 7, § 7.04[1].

T

Tax Bracket: The highest marginal rate of tax a person will pay on any dollar of income for a given year. For example, if the most tax a taxpayer must pay on any dollar of income is twenty-eight cents, he is said to be in the 28% tax bracket.

§ 1; Ch. 6, § 6.02.

Taxable Income: Gross income minus deductions and personal exemptions. The tax rates are applied to a taxpayer's taxable income.

§ 63; Ch. 2, § 2.02[2].

Tax Jock: A person who waterproofs his Internal Revenue Code, so that he can read it in the shower. Also known as a Codehead.

Taxable Year: The period during which a taxpayer calculates his federal income tax. For most taxpayers, the taxable year corresponds to the calendar year. Other taxpayers have fiscal years, which are usually twelve month periods ending on the last day of a month other than December.

§ 441; Reg. § 1.441-1 and 1.441-2; Ch. 6, § 6.08[2].

Treasury Decision (T.D.): An announcement, published in the Internal Revenue Bulletin, concerning the Treasury Department's decision to exercise its rulemaking authority under § 7805(a) of the Code. Treasury Regulations are initially issued as Treasury Decisions.

§ 7805(a); Ch. 7, § 7.03[1][a].

Treasury Regulations (Regs.): The Treasury Department's interpretations of the provisions of the Code. While the regulations are not law unless the Code gives them the force of law, they are given great weight as authority.

§ 7805(a); Ch. 7, § 7.03.

U

Unearned Income: Income from sources other than the taxpayer's own services or business endeavors. The primary examples of unearned income are interest and dividends.

§§ 1(q), 911(d)(2).

Appendix II

ANSWERS TO PROBLEMS CONTAINED IN THE TEXT

PROBLEM 3

Using the formula that X = [(A)(B/C)], the ratio required for § 1011(b) would be as follows:

"X" would stand for the portion of adjusted basis used for determining the gain from a bargain sale to charity.

"A" would stand for the adjusted basis of the property.

"B" would stand for the amount realized from the sale of the property.

"C" would stand for the fair market value of the property. Accordingly, the portion of the adjusted basis used for determining gain from a bargain sale to a charity equals [(the adjusted basis of the property) multiplied by (the amount realized from the sale divided by the fair market value of the property)].

An example using some numbers might prove useful. Say that the adjusted basis of the property was $15, and that you sold the property to charity for $30 (your amount realized), even though it had a fair market value of $45. Section 1011(b) tells you that the basis you could use for determining the gain from the sale of your property to charity would be ($15)($30/$45) = $10. In essence, that section is saying, "Since you sold the property for two-thirds (30/45 = 2/3) of its value, you should only be able to use two-thirds (10/15 = 2/3) of your basis for determining gain."

Now let us set up the ratio for § 1015(d)(6).

"X" would stand for the increase in basis due to gift tax paid.

"A" would stand for the amount of gift tax paid.

"B" would stand for the net appreciation in value of the gift.

"C" would stand for the amount of the gift.

Hence, the increase in the basis for gift tax paid equals [(the gift tax paid) multiplied by (the net appreciation in the value of the gift divided by the amount of the gift)].

Again, some numbers will be helpful. Assume that you received a Collector's Version of the Code from your Uncle Roscoe. Roscoe was forced to pay $2 in gift tax on the transfer, and the property, which he purchased for $10, was worth $20 at the time of the gift. That is, the gift had appreciated in value by $10 since the time Roscoe bought it. The basis you will take in the property will be increased under § 1015(d)(6) as follows:

Increase = [($2)(10/20)], or $1. In effect, § 1015(d)(6) says that you will get an increase in your basis to the extent of the gift tax paid on the appreciation in value of the property you received. Since $2 in gift tax was paid on the whole gift, and since the gift had appreciated in value by 10/20 (or 1/2), one-half of the tax paid (or $1) must have been paid on appreciation. Consequently, the increase in basis would be $1.

Under the facts of the problem, Mr. Ablehours would have a basis of $100K under § 1015(a). This basis would be increased by a portion of the gift tax paid under § 1015(d)(6) as follows: Increase = (net appreciation/total gift) × gift tax paid or ($50K/$150K) × $3K. [Net appreciaiton is $50K (FMV less AB) and the toal gift is $150K.] Accordingly, the increase in basis is $1K, so the donee's basis in the problem would be $101K.

PROBLEM 4A

(1) No, groceries cannot be alimony under § 71(b), as that section provides, "For the purposes of this section [t]he term 'alimony or separate maintenance payments' means any payment in cash." Therefore, no non-cash payment can qualify as alimony.

Notice that, even though the state court defined groceries to be alimony, they were not alimony for the purposes of § 71.

(2) The payments of $100 in cash per month would qualify as alimony only if

1. the divorce agreement did not designate that the payment would not be includible in gross income (§ 71(b)(1)(B)),

2. the couple was no longer living in the same household (§ 71(b)(1)(C)), and

3. there is no liability for Inci to pay anything after Stu's death (§ 71(b)(1)(D)).

All we know is that the payment was a cash payment, received by a spouse (§ 71(b)(1)(A)). Thus, all of the elements must be met in order for the payments to be alimony, for the purposes of § 71.

(3) Section 71(c) supplies the answer to this question. Section 71(c)(1) provides that no payment for the support of children of the payor spouse shall be considered to be alimony. Section 71(c)(2) provides that, for the purposes of paragraph (1), any amount which will be reduced upon the happening of a contingency relating to a child, shall be considered a payment for the support of a child of the payor spouse. Accordingly, the amount of the reductions in monthly payments to Stu that will take place when Intre reaches the age of eighteen shall be considered child support, not alimony. This would be true for the purposes of § 71, notwithstanding the state court's definition.

PROBLEM 4B

Because § 101(a) tells you that the only exceptions ("except as otherwise provided") to its general rule are to be found in §§ 101(a)(2), 101(d), and 101(f), you can make the following statement about any amounts received under life insurance contracts, if paid by reason of the death of the insured: All amounts received under a life insurance contract, and paid by reason of the death of the insured are excluded from gross income, unless:

1. The insurance contract was transferred to the payee for consideration, *and* (A) the basis of the contract in the hands of the transferee was not determined by reference to the basis of the contract in the hands of the transferror, *and* (B) the transfer was not to the insured, to a partner of the insured, to a partnership in which the insured was a partner, or to a corporation in which the insured is a shareholder or an officer.

2. The benefits are paid after the death of the insured, and are in an amount which is greater than the amount on the face of the policy.

3. The policy is a flexible premium policy issued prior to 1985, and the payments exceed the guideline premium limitations expressed in § 101(f)(2).

PROBLEM 4C

No, § 1031 is not an elective provision. Note that the language of § 1031 says no gain or loss "shall" be recognized when like-kind property is exchanged. Likewise, § 1032 is a mandatory provision as it requires that no gain or loss "shall" be recognized when a corporation transfers its stock in exchange for property or cash. Likewise, § 1033(a)(1) states that if a taxpayer's property is involuntarily converted to property similar or related in service or use, no gain or loss "shall" be recognized. Accordingly, if the state of South Carolina condemned your property, and replaced it with similar property, you would not be allowed to recognize a gain or loss. Section 1033(a)(2), on the other hand, is an elective provision. It gives the taxpayer the option of either recognizing gain or loss, or deferring gain or loss, when her property is involuntarily converted to cash. To elect nonrecognition here, the taxpayer must reinvest all the cash received through the involuntary conversion in similar property within two years of the involuntary conversion. (three years in the case of condemnations).

PROBLEM 6A

Section 1(g) prevents income-shifting by taxing the unearned income of a child under 18 at his parent's higher rate. Prior to the enactment of § 1(g), a parent could place money in a child's savings account, in order to take advantage of the child's lower tax bracket, and have the interest on the account taxed to the child. Section 1(g) greatly limits the utility of such a plan. Ironically, § 1(g) is broad enough to cover all unearned income of the child, not just the unearned income that resulted from a parental gift. Thus, a 13 year-old babysitter who places her earnings in a savings account might have to pay tax on her interest at her parent's rate. Fortunately, § 1(g)(4) ameliorates the over-inclusive nature of § 1(g), by providing an exemption for at least the first $1000 of the child's unearned income. (*See* §§ 1(g)(4)(A)(ii), 63(c)(5)(A).) Do you understand why I said that "at least" the first $1000 of unearned income would be excluded?)

Section 267 prevents family members, as defined by § 267(c)(4), or other related parties, as defined by § 267(b), from generating tax losses between themselves. For example, a father might sell land which has declined in value to his daughter, in order to create a tax loss, while keeping the property in the family. A deductible tax loss to a person in a high bracket can be as effective in saving taxes as an actual shift in income. Section 267 reflects the government's knowledge of that basic tax maxim.

Section 704(e) is a partnership tax provision, which is a codification of the assignment of income principles discussed in § 6.02. Section 704(e) limits income shifting in three ways:

(1) It prevents family members from shifting the income generated by their services to other family members in a partnership. Therefore, a doctor could not shift his service income to his minor children by making them partners in his medical practice.

(2) It prevents children from having an income share in the partnership greater than their relative contributions. That is, a child cannot be allocated 75% of the partnership income, when he contributed only 30% of the partnership property; he must, instead, be allocated only 30% of the income. This is necessary, because partnerships can, under state law, allocate their income any way they please. The Code, however, recognizes the potential for collusion in family business arrangements.

(3) It requires that the income of the partners must reflect reasonable compensation for services by any partner who gave a family member the property that family member contributed to the partnership. Thus, if Mother gave Son a building, which Son then contributed to a partnership, in which he and Mother were the only members, Mother's income must include reasonable compensation for services she renders to the partnership. This will prevent her from shifting income generated by her services to Son's lower tax bracket.

Section 7872 greatly reduced the effectiveness of one of the all-time favorite income-shifting devices, the interest-free-loan. Prior to Congress' adoption of § 7872, taxpayers could loan money to their children interest-free. Such an arrangement allowed a parent to shift the incidence of taxation without giving up control. That is, a parent who had money in a bank account earning interest might have been taxed on that interest at a rate of 50%. On the other hand, the parent could loan the money to a child, and have the child place the money in the same bank, while paying tax at a rate of only 14%. The benefit to the family was savings of 36 cents on every dollar of interest earned. In addition to the tax savings, the parent retained the legal right to demand repayment of the loan at any time, which gave him control without taxation!

Section 7872, however, requires that the parent be taxed as though he received a rate of interest determined by the Secretary of the Treasury, after having made a gift of that amount to the child. There are still some circumstances where interest-free loans will be nominally effective devices for tax savings, however, because of the exceptions provided in § 7872(c)(2). That section excludes *de minimis* loans (gift loans of $10,000 or less) from the imputed interest rules of § 7872. Of course, § 1(g) might restrict the utility of even *de minimis* interest-free loans. Do you see why that might be true?

Finally, while all of the sections discussed above limit the savings available to taxpayers through income-shifting, § 102 actually provides taxpayers with tax shifting opportunities. Section 102 allows taxpayers to receive gifts tax free. Consequently, a parent can give money to a child, the child can deposit the money in a savings account, and the interest earned on that money can be taxed at the child's rate, assuming that § 1(g) does not apply.

Furthermore, a parent could have property that he paid $2 for, but is now worth $15. If the parent sells the property, he will have a taxable gain of $13, which will be taxed at his rate. If, on the other hand, the parent gives the property to the child, and has the child sell it, the child will be taxed on the $13 of gain at the child's rate. Thus, gifts can be of great use in income-shifting, as long as the parent is willing to relinquish control over the property.

PROBLEM 6B

All of the listed sections affect the timing of inclusion in income or deductions from income. Section 83 requires an employee to include in his gross income property he received from his employer in the first year in which there is either no substantial risk of forfeiture, or the interest in the property is transferable by the employee. Section 83(b) gives the employee the option of electing to include the value of property that is subject to a substantial risk of forfeiture or is not transferable in an earlier year. An employee might make the § 83(b) election if he believed that the value of the property would increase significantly by the time that the property would have to be included under § 83(a).

Section 71(f) prevents a spouse from front-loading alimony payments to increase her deductions, while forcing lumping of income upon the spouse receiving the alimony. That section provides that if a paying spouse front-loads income, she will not be able to deduct a portion of her payment, even though the payment would qualify as income under § 71(b). By the same token, the recipient spouse would be required to include only that portion of the alimony payment that was not in excess of the limits established by § 71(f).

Section 72 governs the taxation of annuities. Generally speaking, an annuity is a contract in which the beneficiary pays a premium, or premiums, in order to receive a fixed yearly payment at a later date. For example, a taxpayer might pay an insurance company $10,000 in 2007 for the right to receive $1000 per year for the rest of his life, beginning in 2013. It is clear that, if the taxpayer lives to receive eleven payments, or more, he will have a gain, because he paid only $10,000 to begin with, and he will be receiving more than $10,000 in payments. But when should we tax that gain? The government would like to tax the gain as soon as possible, and the taxpayer would like to defer gain until as late as possible. Section 72 provides for a compromise, which treats each payment as partially taxable, and partially tax-free. For a discussion of § 72, see § 3.02[4].

Section 101(d) operates in much the same way as § 72. It applies whenever a taxpayer elects to receive life insurance benefits at a date later than the death of the insured. Section 101(d) provides that a portion of each payment from the insurance company must be included as income when it is received by the taxpayer, rather than allowing the taxpayer to defer taxable gain until she has recouped her entire investment. Finally, § 267(a)(2)(B) provides that the timing of income and deductions in transactions involving related taxpayers must match. For example, consider a taxpayer who is on the accrual method of accounting. That taxpayer would deduct expenses as soon as they arose, rather than waiting until they were actually paid. If the accrual method taxpayer borrowed money from a party who was on the cash receipts and disbursements method of accounting, deferral could take place, because the cash method lender would not have to include any interest payments in gross income until he had actually received them, while the accrual method borrower could deduct such interest payments when they became due. Thus, the borrower could deduct his December, 2007 interest payment for the year 2007, even though he did not pay it until January, 2008, while the lender would not have income, until he received the payment in January, 2008. If the borrower and lender had been related parties, however, § 267(a)(2)(B) would require the accrual method borrower to wait and take his deduction in the same year that the lender had income inclusion. Section 267(a)(2)(B) presumes that related parties will act in collusion to affect the timing of income and deductions.

Should you always follow the maxim which encourages deferring income and accelerating deductions? No. There are times when a taxpayer will wish to accelerate income and defer deductions. For example, assume that the maximum tax rate in 2007 was 35%, and that Congress decided to raise the maximum rate to 70% for 2008. High bracket taxpayers would clearly be better off by lumping as much income as they could into 2007's 35% rate, rather than deferring income until 2008, and facing 70% rates. By the same token, it would be wise for high bracket taxpayers to defer their deductions until 2008, when they will be worth savings of up to 70 cents per dollar, as opposed to only 35 cents per dollar. The moral is that you must look to the economics of each situation when you engage in tax planning, even though you will usually do well by deferring income, and accelerating deductions.

PROBLEM 6C

The Goon can save tax dollars, while providing for the support of his daughter, by paying her a reasonable salary for her services. That is, the Goon could hire Saskatoon to help him in his wrestling business. She could file, answer the phone, etc. Section 162(a)(1) would allow the Goon to deduct the payments to Saskatoon, as long as they were reasonable. Consequently, money earned by the Goon and paid to Saskatoon as salary would be taxed to Saskatoon only at her lower rates. For example, assume that the Goon paid Saskatoon $1000 in salary, and that the Goon was in the 35% tax bracket. Assume, further, that Saskatoon was in the 10% bracket. Saskatoon would only have to pay $100 in tax on her salary, leaving her a net income of $900. Had Goon kept the money himself, he would have had to pay $350 in tax, leaving a net of $650 to use for Saskatoon's support. (Note that § 1(g) does not apply to the earned income of a minor.)

PROBLEM 6D

Section 1015(a) provides that the basis of property received by gift shall be the basis of the property in the hands of the donor. Since Sal had a basis in Swampacre of $7000 at the time he gave his property to Ella, Ella will have a basis of $7000 as well.

But, what happens when Sal sells the property to Ella for $50? Any time a family member sells property to another family member for less than fair market value, the transaction is called a "part sale/part gift." Section 1.1015-4 of the Treasury Regulations provides that the basis of the transferee in a part sale/part gift shall be the greater of the basis of the property in the hands of the donor, or the amount paid by the donee. In this case, the basis of the property in the hands of the donor was $7000. The amount paid by the donee was $50. Thus, Ella's basis would be $7000 (the greater of the two).

Actually, you should be able to figure out the answer to this problem, without reference to the regulations, if you remember what basis is: basis represents the amount of after-tax dollars a person has invested in a piece of property. Thus, Sal had $7000 in after-tax dollars invested in the property when he transferred it to Ella. When Ella gave Sal $50 for the property, Sal took $50 out of the property tax-free, but Ella put $50 back into the property, leaving a total of $7000 after-tax invested in the property. Therefore, as long as Ella's payment to Sal is less than Sal's basis, the total after-tax dollars invested in the property, between the donor and the donee, will be the donor's basis. On the other hand, if Ella paid $7500 for the property, her basis would be $7500, because between Ella and Sal there would be $7500 invested in the property. That is also the result required by Reg. § 1.1015-4.

Notice that Sal would have received $7500 in return for property for which he paid $7000. This would cause Sal to have a gain realized of $500 on the transaction, because he received $500 more than he had invested in after-tax dollars.

PROBLEM 6E

(1) If Cal's factory were uninsured, he would have a loss realized of $400,000, notwithstanding the fact that the property was worth $1,000,000. Section 1001(a) states that the loss realized is the excess of adjusted basis over amount realized. Since Cal received no consideration in return for his factory, his amount realized, as defined by § 1001(b), would be zero. Thus, his loss realized would be $400,000 (adjusted basis) minus zero equals $400,000. Furthermore, § 1001(c) requires all losses realized to be recognized, unless otherwise provided in subtitle A of the Code. Since there are no exceptions to § 1001(c) in this instance, the loss will be recognized. The deductibility of a recognized loss is governed by § 165. Cal has no basis, because the factory is gone, and he has had his investment returned in the form of a tax loss (see § 165(c)(1)).

(2) If Cal had $750,000 of insurance, he would have a gain realized of $350,000 under § 1001(a), because his amount realized of $750,000 exceeded his adjusted basis of $400,000 by $350,000. This is true, even though economically it appears that Cal had a loss, since his factory was under-insured. The $350,000 gain realized should be recognized under § 1001(c), because there is nothing in the Code that allows for nonrecognition, when a taxpayer takes the proceeds of a disaster and goes on vacation. Gains from dealings in property are included in gross income because of § 61(a)(3). Moreover, Cal has no basis left, because he had $400,000 returned to him tax-free when he received his insurance proceeds.

(3) Finally, if Cal received $1,000,000 in insurance, but used it to rebuild the factory, he would have a $600,000 gain realized under § 1001(a). He would not, however, recognize a gain, because § 1033(a)(2) allows for nonrecognition of gain when a taxpayer uses the amount he received from insurance (not necessarily the actual dollars, just the amount) to buy property similar or related in service or use to the property destroyed. Section 1033(a)(2) is one of those "except as otherwise provided" sections referred to in § 1001(c).

The policy behind nonrecognition in cases like Cal's is that Cal is in about the same position he was in before the calamity at his factory, and there will be a more appropriate time to tax him later, for instance, when he sells the property. This same rationale governs the determination of Cal's basis in the new factory. Since Cal was able to avoid recognition of gain, it makes sense to say that he has not increased, nor for that matter decreased, his after-tax investment in the factory. Therefore, his basis in the new factory should be the same as his basis in the old factory. Not surprisingly, that is the result dictated by § 1033(b).

PROBLEM 6F

Any time a taxpayer uses appreciated property to discharge an obligation, he will have a gain realized. You can more easily understand that last statement if you substitute cash into a transaction in which a taxpayer uses appreciated property to pay a debt. Using the facts given in the problem, the estate owes Benny $5000. If the estate were to give Benny his $5000 in cash, and then sell him the stock for $5000, there would be no question that the estate would have a $3800 gain realized ($5000 amount realized minus $1200 adjusted basis) under § 1001(a). In essence, that is exactly what the estate is doing when it uses the stock to pay Benny his share of the estate.

If such transactions did not result in gain, taxpayers would always use appreciated property, instead of cash, to pay their debts. After all, the estate only had $1200 in after-tax dollars invested in the stock. If the stock could discharge Benny's bequest, without taxable gain to the estate, why would it ever want to pay $5000 totally in after-tax cash?

From Benny's perspective, he was entitled to receive $5000 tax-free (§ 102(a)). Had he received cash, he would have been able to use the cash to purchase property, which would have a $5000, § 1012 cost basis. The fact that he received stock, instead of cash, should not change that result; Benny's basis should be $5000, because the $5000 in property has been subject to tax by the estate. I.R.C. § 1014.

Now, let us change the facts a little bit. Instead of an estate and a beneficiary, assume that you were dealing with an employer and an employee. The employer did not have enough cash to pay his employee his $5000 salary, so he used stock with a basis of $1200 and a fair market value of $5000 to discharge his obligation. Like the estate, the employer would have a gain realized of $3800. Unlike the beneficiary, however, the employee would have income upon the receipt of the stock in exchange for his services (§ 61(a)(1)). Yet, the employee, like the beneficiary, would have a basis of $5000 in the stock, which can, again, be explained by inserting cash into the transaction.

If the employer had paid the employee $5000 in cash, and then sold the stock to the employee for the same $5000, you would have no problem understanding all facets of the transaction. That is, the employee would have $5000 in income, when he received the cash for his services (§ 61(a)(1)). In turn, the employer would have a gain realized of $3800 on the sale of the stock (§ 1001(a)). In addition, because the employee used dollars which have been subject to tax, under § 61(a)(1), to purchase the stock, he should have a § 1012 basis of $5000.

Consider what would happen if the employee did not take a $5000 basis in the stock. Section 61(a)(1) would still require inclusion of $5000 in income when he received the stock. Would § 61(a)(3) require another $5000 of gain to be included, if the employee sold his stock the next day for $5000? Of course not. The employee has already been taxed on the receipt of the $5000 in stock, and he should be able to sell it for $5000 without incurring any further gain. Thus, the receipt of property by an employee should be treated the same as the receipt of an amount of cash equal to the fair market value of the property received. (*See* Treas. Reg. § 1.61-2(d)(2)(i).)

Appendix III

ANSWERS TO CHAPTER 9 PROBLEMS

PROBLEM #1 GROSS INCOME

1. Under I.R.C. § 61(a)(1), the $150K salary is included in gross income. "Compensation for services" is the most common form of income.

2. Under I.R.C. § 61(a)(1), the $12K bonus is included in gross income as compensation for services. If in doubt, see Treas. Reg. § 1.61-2, which specifically lists bonuses as compensation income.

3. Income from illegal activity is taxable despite the recipient's legal obligation to make restitution. The Goon must include the $40K bribe in his gross income. *See James v. U.S.*; *see also* Treas. Reg. § 1.61-14 (stating illegal gains constitute gross income under § 61).

4. The Goon must include the $700 in gross income when the amount found is reduced to undisputed possession under applicable state law. *See C.I.R. v. Cesarini*; Treas. Reg. § 1.61-14. [Note: If he found a $700 watch inside the piano, he would include the value of the watch in gross income, and his basis in the watch would be its fair market value under "tax cost" basis notions. Treas. Reg. § 1.61-2(d)(2)(i)]. If instead, the piano simply turned out to be worth more than he expected, the Goon would not have income until he later sold it for a price (amount realized) greater than what he paid for it (adjusted basis). As a general rule, a taxpayer's bargain purchase does not generate income at the time of purchase; but may generate income when the property is sold. There is an exception when a bargain purchase occurs in an employment setting. For example, if the Goon paid $1K for the piano instead of its value of $50K because his employer owed him $49K in salary, then the bargain element (difference between fair market value and the amount paid) would be included in gross income. Treas. Reg. § 1.61-2(d)(2).

5. The Goon is deriving a benefit from his own property—that is, savings from not having to pay rent or buy tomatoes. This type of economic gain is called "imputed income" (the income attributed to the value of labor or property the taxpayer performs or produces for himself). A rigorous application of *Glenshaw Glass* would require that he include imputed income in gross income. Fortunately, the government has never sought to tax imputed income . . . for obvious reasons. It would be very difficult for the government to reach all imputed source income. Note that if the Goon does not eat the tomatoes himself, but sells the tomatoes for a profit, he would realize gross income. Likewise, if he exchanged his tomatoes for his neighbors cucumbers, he would also realize gross income.

6. Technically, under I.R.C. § 61(a), this is taxable as ordinary income because the quarter is an accession to wealth. *Glenshaw Glass*; Treas. Reg. § 1.61-14 (including treasure trove in gross income). Generally speaking, though, a quarter will not make any difference in the amount of tax owed. Have you ever reported a quarter you found in a Coke machine? We always take the position that we have lost at least as many quarters as we have found, so we are basically even. Not a very strong legal argument, we admit!

121

7. Because the Dr. rendered services and received tickets as compensation, he will have to recognize income to the extent of the fair market value of the tickets received (*See* I.R.C. § 61(a); Treas. Reg. § 1.61-2(d).) To determine if Goon has any gross income we would have to know what he paid for the tickets; if they were free then he has $100 gross income, but if he paid $100 for them there is no gross income for Goon. (See the discussion of basis in Problem 4 and § 6.05.) If you put cash into this transaction, it is much easier to understand. In essence what is really happening is that the Goon has received $100 worth of services from the Dr., and has paid the Dr. with a $100 bill; the Dr. has in turn, immediately given that same $100 bill back to the Goon, in exchange for the Goon's wrestling tickets. Of course, the parties did not actually pass the same bill back and forth, because they decided that the services and the tickets were the equivalent of $100 in cash.

8. Under I.R.C. § 61(a)(1), it appears as though the parking space is taxable because it is a "fringe benefit." However, I.R.C. § 132(a) excludes certain fringe benefits from income, including any "qualified transportation fringe." I.R.C. § 132(a)(5). Here, the parking space is a qualified transportation fringe as defined in § 132(f)(1)(C), (f)(5)(C). There is a limit; the maximum amount excludable from gross income shall not exceed $175 per month, adjusted for inflation. I.R.C. § 132(f)(2)(B), (f)(6). Since the parking space does not exceed the $175 per month limitation on qualified parking, the value of the parking space is not included in gross income. Goon clearly is better off economically, but Congress has elected not to tax this type of benefit.

9. Under I.R.C. § 102(a), gross income does not include the value of property acquired by gift, bequest, devise, or inheritance. Gifts clearly constitute an accession to wealth, but Congress has elected not to tax them. Otherwise, we would probably have to invite the IRS to our next birthday party!

10. Under I.R.C. § 104(a)(2), damages (other than punitive damages) on account of personal *physical* injury or sickness are excludible from gross income (§ 104(a)(2)). The $175K damages received on account of the defamation suit are not excludable. However, the $75K compensatory damages (and not the $100K punitive damages) received on account of the battery (a personal, physical injury) are excludable. Question: Why are compensatory damages ever income, when their sole purpose is to make the injured party whole? Is there really income if you are simply made whole?

PROBLEM #2 EXCLUSIONS FOR GIFTS AND INHERITANCES

1. If you consider that a family member will not seek a deduction for gifts given to family members, while an employer probably will seek a deduction for gifts given to employees, the distinction makes sense. First, if Father gives Daughter a gift of $5, it is non-taxable under I.R.C. § 102(a) because this section excludes from gross income the value of property acquired by gift, bequest, devise or inheritance. However, when an employer gives an employee a gift, it is taxable under I.R.C. § 102(c). Section 102(c) says that subsection (a) shall not exclude from gross income any amount transferred by or for an employer to or for the benefit of an employee. Section 102(c) appears to deny "gift" classification to all transfers by employers to employees. There are, however, limited exceptions to the § 102(c) inclusion rule. For example, Prop. Treas. Reg. § 1.102-1(f)(2) carves out an exception for extraordinary transfers to the natural objects of an employer's bounty if the transfer was attributable to the familial relationship of the parties. In addition, § 132(e) excludes certain *de minimis* fringes, and § 74(c) excludes certain employee achievement awards. Now, if Father gives Daughter money in exchange for legal services, it would be taxable to her under I.R.C. § 61(a) because it would not be a true gift since it would be in exchange for services. The motive of the donor determines whether the transaction results in a tax free gift to the donee. If the donor had mixed motives, the primary motive controls. In order to be excluded from gross income as a gift, the transfer must be made out of detached and disinterested generosity—that is, out of affection, respect, admiration, charity, etc.

2. a. Under § 102(c), the employees have gross income; however, it could be argued that the § 132(e) *de minimis* fringe benefit provision applies so that the hams are not taxable. [Note: It could also be argued that the hams are not taxable because they are "forced consumption," or because they are basically a no additional cost service, excludable from gross income under § 132(a)(1), (b).] It is likely Hirum will take a deduction for these business gifts (100 employees × $5 ham = $500). *See* I.R.C. §§ 162, 274(b).

   b. Under § 102(a), this is probably not taxable since it seems like a true gift (out of Keepum's detached and disinterested generosity). However, it could be argued that Keepum had an ulterior motive for giving his boss a gift.

   c. This is taxable under I.R.C. § 102(c). It is too valuable to be considered a *de minimis* fringe under § 132(e), unless the employer is huge and this is not a comparatively large expenditure (since to determine if something is de minimis one must look at the employer and employee and consider cost and frequency as factors). It could also be argued that this is an excludable working condition fringe benefit if it helps the employee at work (if it would have been deductible by the employee if the employee had paid for it herself). I.R.C. § 132(d).

   d. Under § 102(a), it would not be taxable if Hirum gave his son the radio for being his son, and his being employed is only incidental to the transfer. See Prop. Treas. Reg. § 1.102-1(f)(2), which deals with "familial" situations. (It must be proven that the gift/transfer is substantially related to the familial, rather than the employment relationship.) On the other hand, if Hirum gave his son the radio because he is an employee, and his being his son is the incidental occurrence, then it is gross income.

   e. Each cup of coffee is an accession to wealth. However, under § 132(e), the coffee qualifies as a *de minimis* fringe benefit, and so is excluded from gross income. *See* Treas. Reg. § 1.132-6(e)(1).

f. This is an excludable *de minimis* fringe benefit. *See* Treas. Reg. § 1.132-6(f). [Note: An employer is allowed to discriminate on *de minimis* fringe benefits and working condition fringe benefits (§ 132(j)(1)); *but not on* no additional cost items (§ 132(b)) or qualified employee discounts (§ 132(c)). *See* I.R.C. § 132(j)(1).]

g. To the extent the offices and computers are under control of Hirum most of the time, they are qualified working condition fringe benefits (as defined in § 132(d)) and are excludable from gross income under I.R.C. § 132(a)(3). An employer may discriminate with a working condition fringe benefit (I.R.C. § 132(j)(1)). The memberships in the private club are not excludable as *de minimis* fringes per Treas. Reg. § 1.132-6(e)(2), but you can argue that you utilize the membership to boost business and therefore it is at least partially a working condition fringe per Treas. Reg. § 1.132-5.

3. Probably no. The gift of land does not seem to proceed from Beaver's detached and disinterested generosity; this appears to be in a business context as in the *Duberstein* case. If Beaver deducts the cost of the land as a business expense, Haskell most likely has income.

4. a. This payment does not qualify as an excludable gift. I.R.C. § 102(c). Prior to 1996, an employee or employee's beneficiary could exclude up to $5K from gross income for a death benefit unrelated to insurance. This provision was repealed by the Small Business Job Protection Act of 1996.

b. The corporation can deduct reasonable compensation as an ordinary and necessary business expense under § 162(a)(1); however, the corporation cannot deduct a gift.

5. a. The 20K is excluded under § 102(a), because gross income does not include the value of property received by gift, bequest, devise, or inheritance. The phrase "bequest, devise, or inheritance" refers to money or property received under a will or under statutes of descent and distribution. Treas. Reg. § 1.102-1(a). Note that the decedent's donative intent is relevant. [Note: If gifts or inheritance produce income, such *income* shall not be excluded from gross income according to § 102(b).]

b. The value of the land received through intestate succession is excluded under § 102(a). As noted in the answer to (a) above, inheritance includes property received under intestacy statutes.

c. This is money that would have been left to her in the will except for the fraud, so it is still excludable under § 102(a).

d. The bequest is taxable to the attorney. Although the $2K is couched in terms of a bequest it is actually for services and therefore it is not excludable. I.R.C. § 102(c). It is disguised compensation.

e. There is a good argument that the $20K is excludable from Niece's gross income. I.R.C. § 102(a). However, the Service might make an argument that part of this should be taxable-to the extent of the amount to which Niece could have claimed for her services as personal representative, It would be nice to have more facts in determining Uncle's intent. For example, did Uncle bequeath money to his other nieces and nephews? If so, in what amounts?

6. a. The rent payments must be included in gross income because the gift is of income from property. § 102(b)(2).

b. No, the value of the remainder interest is not included in gross income. When Carol dies and he actually starts collecting rent from the property, then Wilbur will have to include the rent in gross income.

PROBLEM #3 AWARDS AND SCHOLARSHIPS

1. Yes, under § 74(a), the winner should include the $500 in gross income. Section 74(b) says gross income will not include amounts received as prizes or awards IF AND ONLY IF: (1) the recipient won without actively seeking the prize; (2) the recipient is not required to render substantial future services; and, (3) the award is transferred directly by the payor to a charitable organization. Therefore, this award would be excluded from gross income only if the physician had not entered the contest and if the money was transferred directly to charity.

2. Yes, the stipend is gross income, since under § 74(a) gross income includes amounts received as prizes or awards. This award is not excluded under § 74(b) because the requirements set forth above are not met. Nor is it excluded under § 74(c) (employee achievement award) because it is cash rather than tangible personal property. *See* I.R.C. §§ 74(c)(1), (c)(3), 274(j).

3. The value of the medals is taxable under § 74(a) since nothing in the Code excludes them from gross income. The Service has prosecutorial discretion, however, in whether to pursue the matter.

4. Romeo should include the portion of the trip that he utilizes. Since Romeo forfeited about half the value of the trip, he probably should not have to include that portion. Valuation is a factual question.

5. a. Healthknit should include the $10K in gross income because it represents payment for future services. *See* Treas. Reg. § 1.117-6(d)(5), Examples. If Healthknit receives a full athletic scholarship, this it is not really a payment for services, rather it is a qualified scholarship under § 117, so he would only have to include the amount received for room and board. I.R.C. § 117(c).

   b. This should be included in gross income under § 61 because the $5K is compensation for services regardless of the fact that Healthknit is a student.

   c. Assuming other students who are not scholarship recipients receive $2,500 for the required 10 hours per week, $2,500 of Healthknit's scholarship represents payments for services and must be included in Healthknit's gross income. If Healthknit establishes the remaining $2,500 is used for qualified tuition and related expenses, then $2,500 of the scholarship is excludable from Health-knit's gross income as a qualified scholarship. Treas Reg. § 1.117-6(d)(5), Ex. 5.

   d. Healthknit is employed as a research assistant and presumably receives a salary from Scalpel U. that represents reasonable compensation for the position of research assistant. In addition, Healthknit receives a qualified tuition reduction (as defined in § 117(d)). He includes his salary in income; the qualified tuition reduction does not represent payment for services and therefore is not includable in his gross income. Note that I.R.C. § 117(d)(5)[4] allows an exclusion for a tuition reduction for education at the graduate level. Without it, Healthknit would have income because § 117(d)(1) and (2) allows an exclusion for a tuition reduction for education "below the graduate level."

PROBLEM #4 GAINS DERIVED FROM DEALINGS IN PROPERTY

1. a. Mr. Bill will not realize any gain on the purchase of Bellyacre (which would happen, for example, if he exchanged appreciated property for Bellyacre). Mr. Bill's basis in Bellyacre will be what he paid, or $60K. I.R.C. § 1012 (defining basis as cost). The fact that Sluggo received a $10K commission from the seller is irrelevant and will not impact Mr. Bill's basis.

   b. Mr. Bill will not realize any gain, because this is a cash purchase. His § 1012 cost basis will be $50K-that is, the amount of cash paid ($30K) plus the amount of debt assumed ($20K). *Crane.*

   c. Mr. Bill will not realize any gain on this cash purchase. His basis will be $100K-the amount of debt incurred in the acquisition. The fact that the debt is nonrecourse is irrelevant, as debt incurred in acquiring property, whether recourse or nonrecourse, is included in basis. *Crane.*

   d. The exchange of the Chevy for Swampacre is a realization event ("sale or other disposition") within the meaning of § 1001. Mr. Bill's gain realized in the exchange is $18K-that is, $25K amount realized (fair market value of Swampacre received per § 1001(b)) minus $7K adjusted basis in the Chevy. Mr. Bill's basis in Swampacre will depend on whether the exchange is taxable or not. Under *Philiadelphia Park Amusement Co.* and tax cost basis notions, basis of property received in a taxable exchange will be the fair market value of the property received (and not the fair market value of the property given up). Here, Mr. Bill's gain realized is taxable because there is no applicable nonrecognition or exclusion provision in the Code. I.R.C. § 1001(c) (providing the general rule that all gains realized will be recognized unless otherwise provided in the Code); I.R.C. § 1031 (providing nonrecognition only for "like kind" exchanges). Accordingly, Mr. Bill's basis in Swampacre will be $25K, the fair market value of Swampacre at the time of exchange. A $25K basis in Swampacre makes since if we remember that Mr. Bill had a 7K basis in the Chevy, and then had gain of $18K.

2. Students usually suggest three possible answers:

   (1) His basis is $7500, and when he sells for $8900 he has a $1400 gain.

   (2) His basis is $10K, and when he sells for $8900, he has a $1100 loss (non-deductible in accordance with I.R.C. § 165).

   (3) Since he sold the car so soon and could only get $8900, that was the fair market value at time of receipt; as a result, his basis is $8900, and when he sells for $8900 he has no gain or loss.

   If services are paid for in property, the fair market value of the property taken in payment must be included in gross income as compensation. The Service would argue the fair market value at the time of receipt was $10K. Under tax cost basis notions, Fritz's basis in the car would be equal to the fair market value ($10K). When he sells the car for $8900, he would have a non-deductible loss (personal losses, other than personal casualty losses, are not deductible under § 165). *See* Treas. Reg. § 1.61-2(d)(2).

3. Mrs. Right is transferring appreciated property to satisfy an obligation. Although she may have gain realized, none of it will be recognized per § 1041(a) (providing no gain or loss shall be recognized on a transfer of property from an individual to a spouse or former spouse if the transfer is incident to divorce). Mr. Right is

receiving stock and it doesn't look like Mrs. Right is giving it out of detached and disinterested generosity—out of love, respect, admiration, etc., which is required under § 102. Section 1041(b)(1) provides, however, that the stock will be treated as acquired by gift. Hence, Mr. Right can exclude the value of the stock from his gross income under § 102. Under § 1041(b)(2), Mr. Right's basis will be the same as in the hands of Mrs. Right, or $10K.

4. a. An option is property. So, Thoughtful will have a gain realized of $5K—that is, $20K amount realized per § 1001(b) minus $15K adjusted basis in the option per §§ 1011, 1012.

    b. His basis will be the total of what he paid, or $115K ($15K for the option plus $100K for Wiseacre).

5. Money in a bank account represents dollars that have already been taxed. Therefore, if you put $10K of after-tax salary in a bank account, you can take it out without tax effects. Basis in property essentially ensures that the same dollars are not taxed more than once in the same taxpayer's hands. If you take after-tax salary proceeds of $10K and buy property and then you later sell the property for $10K, you have no taxable gain; you're just recovering tax free dollars that were already subject to tax.

PROBLEM #5 FUNDAMENTAL PRINCIPLES OF TIMING

1. a. Under I.R.C. § 83(a), he would include the entire amount of $10 million in gross income in the year he received the stock. Treas. Reg. § 1.83-1. His basis will be $10 million.

   b. Not included in gross income until the stock is substantially vested; but he must pay taxes on dividends as additional compensation. The gross income and basis will be the fair market value at time of the actual transfer in five years. Although Sbg could exercise his § 83(b) Gambler's Option, it would be quite risky. If this choice is made and the property is subsequently forfeited there is no deduction allowed; therefore the gambler's choice is good to use only if you are sure of getting the property and the property is definitely going up in value. The Tampa Bay Bouts also get a deduction when the stock vests. *See* Treas. Reg. § 1.83-1(f), Ex. 1. There is no gross income in the year of transfer.

   c. It has to be transferable in order to be considered owned. If nontransferable forever, then § 83(d) applies, and the government will find a value, usually fairly small, to tax Sbg on now. Of course he must include any dividends received in gross income.

   d. Here, Sbg dies while the stock is still substantially nonvested. Under Treas. Reg. § 1.83-1(d), any income realized on or after Sbg's death with respect to such stock (the dividends) is income to the son (the beneficiary). But wait . . . the stock is forfeited because the conditions were not met. So really nothing happens (but Sbg loses out (his life and his stock)). Sbg's right to the stock never vested, so his son has no rights.

   e. Sbg is the wrongdoer. He will have to pay tax on his gross income of the $11 million and he will have to give the $11 million to the corporation as well. [The bona fide purchaser is protected and will get to keep the shares.]

2. a. Chancee should include $200K in gross income when the employer transfers the plot of land to her. Note that she does not have to worry about the increased market value because the § 83(b) election is a "gambler's choice" election. She will not have to pay tax on the additional $50K until she sells the property and then it might be a capital gain. The Gamble Worked!

   b. She loses the Gambler's Choice Game! No deduction is allowed for the risk of forfeiture, so basically, she paid tax on $200K when she made the election. The flush language of § 83(b)(1)(B) says that if the election is made and the property is subsequently forfeited, NO DEDUCTION WILL BE ALLOWED IN RESPECT OF SUCH FORFEITURE.

   c. She paid too much tax too soon, but only to the extent of the tax on $25K. There is no longer a loss deduction allowance, so she will not be able to claim a loss until she sells the property, and that may be limited by other rules. This is not the worst case; (b) is worse because here she has $200K basis and if she sells it for $175K she can take a capital gains loss.

PROBLEM #6 ANNUITIES AND LIFE INSURANCE PROCEEDS

1. a. Nothing. Under I.R.C. § 101(a)(1), gross income does not include amounts received under a life insurance policy.

    b. Under § 101(c) he must pay tax on the money earned as interest. The $20K must be included in gross income, but the $250K is still excluded from gross income under § 101(a)(1).

    c. Pronto will receive a total of $275K and his basis is $250K. The excess, $25K of income, will be taxable as payments are received ($25K divided by 25 years equals $1K per year). Another way to figure it is as follows: Investment of $250K divided by the expected life of 25 years gives Pronto $10K a year that is excluded from gross income. So taxes must be paid on $1K per year.

    d. Belle Starr also needs to include $1K in income per year. Although Treas. Reg. § 1.101-4(a)(1)(ii) allows a $1K spousal deduction per year, it refers to a Code provision that has been repealed. Thus, the regulation is no longer applicable.

2. Nothing since the amount paid by the bank does not exceed the cost of $50K of insurance. *See* I.R.C. § 79(a)(1). An employee has to include in gross income only the amount paid on his behalf by his employer of an insurance policy that exceeds $50K.

3. a. Nothing, since § 101(a) excludes life insurance proceeds from gross income.

    b. Under § 101(a)(2), FWC can exclude $50K (their investment in the policy). "What they paid" can be excluded. This section discourages speculation on people's death to produce income.

    c. The payment is fully excluded under § 101(a)(2)(B). Even though FWC paid valuable consideration for the policy, it can exclude the entire amount of the insurance proceeds because Tom was a shareholder of FWC.

4. a. This problem requires us determine how much of each annuity payment should be treated as a return of investment, and how much should be considered gross income. Since $28K of the $56K total expected to be received is a return of investment, ($28K/$56K), or 50%, of each $1K payment should be a return of investment, excluded from gross income $500 excluded). $500K of each payment, then, should be included in gross income. I.R.C. § 72(b).

    b. Yes. He can take a deduction on his final return. Under § 72(b)(3), he can deduct the amount of the unrecovered investment. So, $28K less $1K equals $27K (only include the amount that is unrecovered).

    c. Oscar must stop excluding a portion of the payments after 56 years since, at that point, he has recouped all his $28K investment. Since he lived longer than his remaining life expectancy, he no longer gets this exclusion from gross income, and so must include $1K in gross income each year thereafter. *See* I.R.C. § 72(b)(2).

    d. No. The life expectancy table is not affected by poor health. But we would have advised him not to buy this investment.

PROBLEM #7 GIFT BASIS (§ 1015)

1. a. Under § 102 this is a true gift, given with detached and disinterested generosity. Winnie will have a gift basis in the property as set forth in § 1015(a), which says that the basis is the same as the donor's. Kevin's basis was $16K because he received a true gift under § 102 from Becky and took her basis of $16K under § 1015(a). Therefore, Winnie's basis will be $16K.

   b. Winnie's gain realized will be $6K-that is, $22K amount realized per § 1001(b) minus $16K adjusted basis per § 1015(a). I.R.C. § 1001(a).

   c. Yes. Gift recipients get to exclude the fair market value of the property received. No taxes are paid until the property is sold (or otherwise disposed of in a taxable transaction); at that point, taxes are only paid on gain realized and recognized (*i.e.*, the appreciation in value in the original donor's hands and the donee's hands). Notice the government has no problem shifting gain from the donor to the donee.

2. Under § 1015(a), when the donee is not sure of the donor's adjusted basis at the time of gift, the government will set basis at the property's fair market value at the time the gift was originally given (here 1925). This may be determined with the help of appraisers and old catalogues.

3. a. In the case of property acquired by gift, the donee's basis is generally the same basis the donor had in the property (so-called "transferred basis"). There is an important exception to the general transferred basis rule that potentially applies whenever the value of gifted property (at the time of gift) is less than the donor's basis. In such case, *for purposes of determining gain* by the donee on a later sale, the general rule still applies and the donee uses the donor's basis. However, *for purposes of determining loss* by the donee on a later sale, the exception applies. The donee's basis is not the donor's basis, but instead is the lower fair market value of the property. The effect of this exception is as follows: If a donee is gifted property that has declined in value in the donor's hands and the property continues to decline in value in the donee's hands, the donee's loss on a later sale of the property is limited to only the loss that accrued in the donee's hands. *See* I.R.C. § 1015 ("except" language). For gain determination, Cooper's basis is $30K; however, for loss determination, Cooper's basis is $24K. Note that this "split basis" rule creates an interesting situation if Cooper later sells the stock between $24K and $30K. There will be no gain or loss. *See* Treas. Reg. § 1.1015-1(a)(2).

   b. i. $6K gain realized ($36K amount realized -$30K adjusted basis for purposes of determining gain)

      ii. $2K loss realized ($24K adjusted basis for purposes of determining loss − $22K amount realized)

      iii. No gain or loss realized.

4. a. Bulldog can exclude the value of the van ($20K) from gross income under the § 102(a) gift exclusion due to disinterested generosity. Al cannot take any deduction for the gift. Al's basis was $15K under § 1012 because that's what he paid for the van. Bulldog's basis is determined under § 1015. Under § 1015(d)(6), Bulldog can increase his basis for gift tax Al paid. So, under § 1015, Bulldog takes Al's basis of $15K and increases it under § 1015(d)(6) as follows:

appreciation/fair market value of gift $\times$ gift tax paid

$5K/$20K $\times$ $4K = $1K

So Bulldog's basis is $15K plus $1K gift tax paid, or $16K.

b. Net appreciation is zero. So Bulldog will use split basis if she sells and would not increase basis by any amount. If you have a split basis, you will never increase basis for gift tax paid.

5. a. i. This is a part sale/part gift transaction. It appears that Mary realizes a $30K loss on the sale of the land to Daughter ($150K adjusted basis minus $120K amount realized). However, the regulations under § 1001 provide that no loss is allowed in a part sale/part gift transaction. Treas. Reg. § 1.1001-1(e). Daughter has a gift in the amount of $130K (the difference between what she paid and the fair market value) which is excluded from gross income under § 102. Daughter's basis is the greater of the amount she paid ($120K) or Mary's adjusted basis ($150K). So Daughter has a basis in the land of $150K. (§ 1.1015-4.)

ii. Mary realizes a gain of $10K under § 1001(a) ($160K amount realized minus $150K adjusted basis). [Note that Mary gets to recover 100% of her basis even though her amount realized is less than the land's fair market value. This would not be the case in a part sale/part gift to a charity.] Treas. Reg. § 1.1001-1(e). There is a gift to Daughter of $90K which is excluded under § 102. Daughter's basis is $160K (greater of Mary's adjusted basis or Daughter's amount paid). Treas. Reg. § 1.1015-4.

iii. This is a part sale/part gift with an increase in basis for gift tax paid. Mary realizes a gain of $50K ($200K amount realized minus $150K adjusted basis). Treas. Reg. § 1.1001-1(e). Mary makes a gift of $50K to Daughter, which is excluded from Daughter's gross income under § 102. Daughter's basis is $200K (greater of Mary's adjusted basis or Daughter's consideration) PLUS gift taxes paid by Mary with respect to the appreciation in the land. I.R.C. § 1015(d)(6); Treas. Reg. § 1.1015-4. The increase in gift taxes paid under § 1015(d)(6) is determined as follows:

[appreciation in value of land /(fair market value of land less consideration paid by Daughter)] x gift tax paid by Mary

[$100K/($250K − $200K)] $\times$ $5K

$100K/$50K $\times$ $5K = $10K

Only $5K of gift taxes were paid with respect to the transfer. Therefore, Daughter will get to increase basis by the entire $5K. In sum, Daughter's basis is $200K (greater of Mary's adjusted basis or Daughter's consideration paid), PLUS $5K gift tax paid (the entire amount), or $205K.

b. A bargain sale to charity works differently than a part sale/part gift to a family member. Section 1011(b) deals with bargain sales to charity.

First you need to apportion the basis between the amount sold and the amount given away:

amount realized/fair market value $\times$ adjusted basis = adjusted basis for determining gain

$150K/$250K $\times$ $150K

⅗ $\times$ $150K = $90K

So $90K is the adjusted basis utilized for purposes of determining Mary's gain. Mary will have a gain realized of $60K, that is:

$150K	amount realized minus
90K	apportioned adjusted basis
$ 60K	

This works as if she sold ⅗ of her property and donated ⅖ to charity; she only gets to use ⅗ of her basis, which comes to $90K.

PROBLEM #8 DATE OF DEATH BASIS (§ 1014)

1. Under § 1014(a)(1), Woody's basis will be the fair market value of the property at the date of Ms. Stake's death, that is $32K. Section 1014(a) says when one receives property from a decedent, the recipient's basis in the property is the fair market value of the property at time of death, provided that the recipient did not sell, exchange, or dispose of the property prior to death of decedent.

2. Jeeves' basis in the property, under § 1014(a)(1), is the fair market value of the property on the date of T's death, so it is $2 million.

3. Under § 1014(a)(1), Ellie May's basis in the property will be the fair market value at the date of Jed's death, or $250. This illustrates a "step down" in basis. It would have been best to have advised Jed to sell the business before his death and take the loss. Now, no one gets to realize the loss.

4. a. Under § 1014(b)(2), T's heir's basis will be date of death basis of $200K. The heirs had no rights until decedent died since the trust was revocable until his death; therefore the basis is $200K, the fair market value at the time of death.

    b. Because the transfer in trust was irrevocable, the beneficiaries will have the same basis as the donor under § 1015, in this case $20K. An irrevocable transfer is a completed gift at the time of the transfer rather than property acquired from a decedent, and thus the basis is determined under § 1015.

5. Maybe. Section 1014(e) could effectively serve to thwart this plan. If appreciated property is given back to the donor within one year of the donee's death, then the basis will be the adjusted basis of donor (and there will be no step up in basis to avoid the gain that is inherent in the property). Planner will be successful if Ancient lives for at least one year and one day and does decide to return the property to Planner through a will. Then, Planner would get the property back from Ancient with a basis equal to fair market value at Ancient's death. [Note that non-appreciated property does not get a step-up in basis. Section 1014(e) applies only to property that is appreciated at the time of the transaction.]

6. MacBeth will realize a $92K gain. His life interest is a "term interest in property." Under § 1001(e), MacBeth's basis for purposes of determining gain is $0.

PROBLEM #9 ASSIGNMENT OF INCOME: WHO

1. To shift the income into a lower tax bracket to take advantage of our progressive tax system.

2. Zaccaro cannot anticipatorily assign service income to his wife. Under *Lucas v. Earl*, the earner is responsible for the tax. Spouses are not really the problem in situations like this; it is the attempted assignment of income by parents to their children and grandchildren that concerns the government.

3. a. The son will have to pay tax because his father transferred all of his rights to the son, and therefore retained no rights.

   b. His daughter Maude will have to pay the taxes. Movie rights are property rights. Under § 1(g), Maude, if under age 18, will be taxed at the parents' rate on the royalty income (treated as unearned income).

4. Mr. E will be taxed because he did not transfer any property right to his daughter. Mr. E performed a service (will drafting). Income from services cannot be assigned.

5. a. Ma and Pa retain the underlying property interests so they are taxed on the property's rental income.

   b. Since Junior owns a ½ interest in the property, he is taxed on ½ of the income and Ma and Pa are taxed on the other ½.

   c. Ma and Pa are taxed when Jr. receives the rent.

   d. Under § 1(g), the "kiddie tax" applies because rental income is unearned income. Anything in excess of $1,000 will be taxed at his parents' highest marginal rate.

6. a. Afta. You do not always have to give away a fee simple absolute; you just have to give away all the rights you have.

   b. Leif. You do not always have to give away fee simple absolute, but you do have to give away all the rights you have.

7. No, as long as Ari had no control over who the recipient will be. *Giannini* tells us that a person can shift service income tax free provided he disclaims the income before earning it and does not control who gets it. Here, Ari disclaimed July-December income in June and he directed the money go to a worthwhile cause. He should not be taxed on the July-December income. [Note: What if Ari also served on the company's board of directors? Could it be argued that he indirectly controlled the recipient? What if Ari directed the board to give the income to one of five charities he listed, instead of directing the board to do something worthwhile with the money? Perhaps under these facts Ari would be taxed. As can be seen, the big issue is control.]

8. Dr. DeCay should hire Flossy, paying a reasonable salary to her. Dr. DeCay would be entitled to deduct the salary as an ordinary and necessary business expense (again, the salary must be reasonable). I.R.C. § 162(a)(1). Flossy would have earned income not subject to the kiddie tax.

PROBLEM #10 DIVORCE AND SEPARATION

1. a. Section 71(a) provides for the inclusion of alimony or separate maintenance in the gross income of the payee spouse or former spouse. Section 215(a) provides for a deduction from gross income for the payor spouse or former spouse. The payor's deduction is measured by reference to the payee's inclusion. I.R.C. § 215(b). Section 71(b) sets out specific criteria for a payment to constitute alimony for tax purposes. In this problem, the *cash* payment is alimony because it meets the requirements set out in § 71(b)(1):

   (1) the payment is received under a "divorce or separation instrument";

   (2) the agreement does not designate the payment as a *non*-alimony payment;

   (3) Stu and Inci are not members of the same household (an exception exists under § 71(b)(1)(C) if they are living together while under a temporary order for support); and

   (4) there is no liability to make further payments after the death of the payee spouse or substitute payments.

   Accordingly, Stu will have to include each payment (1K) in gross income, and Inci will deduct each payment.

   Payments in gold and foreign currency are not legal tender, and 71(b)(1) mentions only cash.

   b. This is alimony because it meets all the requirements set out in § 71(b)(1). Therefore, Stu, must include $12K in gross income during the first five years, then $1K a year for the remainder of his life, and Inci may deduct these amounts.

   c. This is alimony under § 71(b)(1); however, it is front-loading of alimony under § 71(f) and recapture applies. The first year excess is $3K because it is over $15K and Inci will be required to include it in gross income in the third post separation year; Stu will get a $3K deduction in the third post separation year.

   d. No, this is not alimony because one of the requirements of § 71(b)(1) is that the parties not live in the same household. The only time this requirement is waived is when the parties are living together under a temporary support order. *See* I.R.C. § 71(b)(1)(C), (b)(2).

   e. No, this is not alimony because it does not meet the test under § 71(b)(1)(B) since the parties stated that the payment is not includible as gross income. Since Stu won't include it in gross income, Inci cannot deduct the payment under § 215. This illustrates that whether a payment is considered taxable alimony to the recipient is to a significant degree a matter for negotiation between the parties. Within some limits, the parties can decide who gets taxed on the income. It's a bargaining chip.

   f. No, this is not alimony because it does not meet test under § 71(b)(1)(D) since Inci's liability to make payments does not cease after Stu's death. However, it could be argued that $3K/ year is alimony, and just the remaining $2K/ year (the amount of the substitute payments after death) is not alimony.

   g. Payments denominated as child support are not deductible by the payor and are not included in the gross income of the payee. I.R.C. § 71(c)(1). Here, nothing in the instrument designates part of the $300 payment as child support. Is any part of the payment disguised as child support? One hurdle to disguising child support as alimony are the rules of § 71(c) providing that payments which are reduced by the happening of contingencies related to the child are treated as child support. *See* Treas. Reg. § 1.71T(b) Q&A 17-18. Here, this is part alimony/part child support per § 71(c)(2)(A). The $200/month reduction in payment when child goes to college is treated as fixed for child support and, hence, is not considered alimony. Only $100/month is treated as alimony, and is included in the Stu's gross income and deducted by Inci.

h. Under § 71(c)(3), the payment is considered child support to the extent it does not exceed the normal child support payment.

2. a. This is alimony under § 71(b). However, because there is more than a $15K drop in payments between years, the government will view this as front-loading and attempt to recapture some of the tax deductions from Big Mac under § 71(f). Front-loading occurs when there are early large cash payments which dwindle in size over a short time-the first three years. The recapture occurs in the third year of post-separation payments, but it arises by reference to an analysis of first and second year post-separation payments. The recapture amount is the sum of the "excess alimony payments" from the first post-separation year and the second post-separation year. I.R.C. § 71(f)(2). The recapture computation is performed in reverse order, that is, we calculate the second post-separation year excess alimony payments and then the first year excess alimony payments. This is because one needs to know the second year recapture amount (called the second year "excess payments") to compute the first year recapture amount. Here are the steps:

(1) Find the second year excess payment, if any, per § 71(f)(4);

2nd yr E.P.	=	2nd yr pmts	–	(3rd yr pmts + $15K)
$0	=	12K	–	($1K + $15K)

(2) Find the first year excess payment per § 71(f)(3).

1st yr E.P.	=	1st yr pmts	–	[(2nd yr pmts – 2nd yr E.P. + 3rd yr pmts)/2 + $15K]
$3,500	=	$25K	–	[($12K – $0 + 1K)/2 + $15K]

(3) Add (1) and (2) per § 71(f)(2);

The total excess payments for Years 1 and 2 are $3,500 ($0 + $3,500)

(4) This amount is included in the payor's gross income for the third year of payments, as per § 71(f)(1)(A). Thus, Mac will have to report $3,500 of income in 2009 (while also deducting the 2009 payment of $1K).

(5) This amount is deducted by the payee in the third year, per § 71(f)(1)(B). Thus Wendy will deduction $3,500 (while also reporting the 2009 payment of $1K as income).

In sum: Mac will be able to deduct $25K in 2007, $12K in 2008, and $1K in 2009; however, in 2009, Mac must include $3500 in gross income. Wendy will have alimony income of $25K in 2007, $12K in 2008, and $1K in 2009; however, in 2009, Wendy will be entitled to a deduction of $3,500.

b. The payments are level, with no front loading. They are includible and deductible according to § 71(a) and § 215(a).

c. Yes. There isn't a penalty for end-loading payments. There is no recapture because the payments are even over the first three years. Recapture looks only at the first three years.

d. The whole excess payment problem disappears under § 71(f)(5)(A), and no recapture is necessary. Section 71(f)(5) sets forth exceptions wherein recapture will not apply, *e.g.*, if: (1) either spouse dies before the close of the third year, or the payee spouse remarries before the close of the third year, and (2) the alimony payments cease by reason of such death or remarriage. [Note: For payments to constitute alimony, they do not have to cease on death of payor (they must on death of payee per § 71(b)(1)(D)); however, if they do, there is no recapture problem per § 71(f)(5)(A). If there is not a provision that says payments cease on death of payor, and his estate can continue to pay, then recapture does apply.]

e. Recapture does not apply. Section 71(f)(5)(B) provides that recapture does not apply to temporary orders such as those in § 71(b)(2)(C); there is no front-loading problem until final decrees are entered.

f. Section 71(f)(5)(C) is the final exception to recapture; this provision does not consider any payments made as a continuing liability for more than three years, which are paid as a fixed percentage of income from business, to be alimony. Recapture does not apply.

g. Section 71(f) is intended to prevent property settlements from being characterized as alimony by discouraging "front-loading."

PROBLEM #11 DEDUCTIONS FOR LOSSES AND BUSINESS EXPENSES

1. This is an ordinary and necessary expense in carrying on a trade or business. I.R.C. § 162(a). Since Foulup is a partner and owner, the deduction is probably an "above-the-line" deduction. I.R.C. § 62(a). [Note: If the firm has insurance to replace the money then the deduction is not necessary.]

2. Yes, Foulup can deduct his C.L.E. expenses because the purpose of C.L.E. is to maintain skills and do not qualify him for a new trade or business. As a general rule, education expenses are deductible under § 162 if they are incurred in order to maintain or improve skills in a trade or business in which the taxpayer is already engaged. Treas. Reg. § 1.162-5(a)(1). Education expenses are also deductible under § 162 if they are incurred to meet the requirements of one's employer or of one's profession as a condition to retention of employment. Treas. Reg. § 1.162-5(a)(2). However, education expenses incurred to meet the minimum requirements for qualifying to engage in a trade or business are considered personal and are not deductible under § 162. Treas. Reg. § 1.162-5(b)(2). Nor does § 162 authorize a deduction for education expenses incurred in order to enter a new trade or business. Treas. Reg. § 1.162-5(b)(3). Here, the deduction will be above-the-line because Foulup is partner/owner. If Foulup were an associate, the deduction would be below-the-line unless he were reimbursed by his employer.

3. If Foulup pursued a tax LL.M. degree after practicing as a litigation attorney, he would be able to deduct the LL.M tuition expenses; such expenses will improve skills in his existing trade or business (practicing law) and will not qualify him for a new trade or business. If, however, Foulup had gone straight to the LL.M. program from law school, he would NOT get a deduction because the tuition would not be an ordinary or necessary expense in "carrying on" an existing trade or business. He would need to practice for some time to establish himself in a trade or business. How long? A year should do, but some recommend a shorter period.

4. a. Foulup can take this deduction, but he should be advised against it. Employees should generally take a reimbursement if offered because unreimbursed employee business expenses are considered miscellaneous itemized deductions. Miscellaneous itemized deductions are allowed only to the extent they exceed 2% of adjusted gross income. I.R.C. §§ 62(a), 67(a), (b).

   b. Zero, because he has income for the reimbursement amount, but an above-the-line deduction for the reimbursed expenses. If a taxpayer is reimbursed dollar for dollar for deductible expenses, he need not put anything on the return.

5. Section 162(a)(2) authorizes the deduction of "traveling expenses . . . while away from home in the pursuit of a trade or business." If a taxpayer travels to a destination and while at such destination engages in both business and personal activities, traveling expenses to and from such destination are deductible only if the trip is related primarily to the taxpayer's business. Treas. Reg. § 1.162-2(b)(1). It looks like Foulup is primarily in Hawaii on business—Monday through Wednesday were business; Thursday and Friday were pleasure; and Saturday and the first Sunday were travel days and so are considered business. Therefore his travel expenses (cost of airfare) are deductible because he is there primarily for business. The cost of his meals and hotels are deductible only for business days. If Foulup's trip had been to the Bahamas, we would need to look at § 274(c), which deals with foreign travel. Here, the result would be the same since Foulup did not spend more than a week in the Bahamas. If more than a week was spent then he must allocate travel expenses.

6. Section 62 gets better treatment because $1 of above-the-line deduction offsets gross income of $1. A below-the-line itemized deduction of $1 does not always do that.

7. No. Musky realizes a loss of $4,700 ($5,200 adjusted basis minus $500 amount realized). I.R.C. § 1001(a). Is that loss deductible? Remember, deductions are a matter of legislative grace; Musky must find a Code provision that allows the deduction. Section 165(a) allows a deduction of losses, but § 165(c) provides a limitation. In the case of individuals, only three types of losses are allowed: (1) business; (2) investment; and (3) casualty. I.R.C. § 165(c)(1)-(3). This a non-deductible personal loss.

8. Section 165(c)(3) authorizes the deduction of personal losses "if such losses arise from fire, storm, shipwreck, or other casualty, or from theft." Assuming a taxpayer receives no compensation, the amount of the taxpayer's personal casualty loss is determined by reference to either the property's adjusted basis or to the property's decline in fair market value, whichever is less. I.R.C. § 165(b); Treas. Reg. § 1.165-7(b)(1). [In the case of theft, the fair market value of the property after theft is $0, meaning that the maximum casualty loss for personal use property with a basis greater than its fair market value is its fair market value.] Losses from casualties to personal use property are subject to two main limitations: a $100 threshold, and a 10% of adjusted gross income threshold. Musky's tax consequences are determined as follows:

$10,000	basis of jewelry
$ 800	fair market value of furniture
$ 700	basis of paintings
$11,500	
− $100	§ 165(h)(1) exclusion (applied per casualty, not per property stolen)
$11,400	total loss

Musky gets a deduction only to the extent of the excess of 10% of adjusted gross income. I.R.C. § 165(h)(2). 10% of $110,000 = $11K. So Musky gets a $400 itemized deduction. If he takes the standard deduction instead of itemizing, he does not get anything.

PROBLEM #12 CAPITAL GAINS AND LOSSES

1. Section 1221(a) defines the term "capital asset" as all property held by the taxpayer, except for items described in § 1221(a)(1)-(8). *In the hands of Ms. Inglink*, Darwinacre is a capital asset because it is property and it is not within any of the exclusions of § 1221. *In the hands of Tarzan*, Darwinacre is not a capital asset because it is real property used in Tarzan's trade or business. I.R.C. § 1221(a)(2). Note, however, that if Darwinacre is held by Tarzan for more than one year, it is "section 1231 property" (*i.e.*, a quasi-capital asset) in Tarzan's hands and may still receive capital gain or loss treatment on later disposition. I.R.C. § 1231(b). *In the hands of Cheetah*, Darwinacre is not a capital asset because it is inventory or inventory-like property. I.R.C. § 1221(a)(1) (excluding from the definition of capital asset "property held by the taxpayer primarily for sale to customers in the ordinary course of a trade or business"). [Note that it is often difficult to ascertain whether a landowner has held property primarily for sale (not a capital asset) or primarily for investment (a capital asset). Consider, for example, a landowner who subdivides real property and then recognizes gain on the sale of one of the subdivided tracts. Did the seller hold the tract as a dealer or as an investor? Section 1237 clarifies the character of land when a landowner subdivides real property and sells it. More specifically, section 1237, when applicable, assures a taxpayer who holds property for many years and makes minimal subdivision improvements before selling it will not fall under the "dealer" category so that he can sell a certain number of lots and enjoy capital gains treatment.]

2. a. B. Fuddled's gain realized on the sale is $6K ($20K amount realized minus $14K adjusted basis). I.R.C. § 1001(a). The gain realized is recognized (*i.e.*, reportable on B. Fuddled's 2007 tax return) because there is no applicable non-recognition or exclusion provision (*e.g.*, § 1202 does not apply to exclude half the gain because the stock is not qualified small business stock held for more than five years) . I.R.C. § 1001(c). The character of the gain is "long term capital gain" (gain from the *sale or exchange* of a *capital asset* held for *more than one year*). I.R.C. § 1222(3). Assuming no other capital gain or loss transactions, B. Fuddled has a "net capital gain" in 2007 of $6K, which is entitled to a special capital gains rate of 15%. I.R.C. § 1(h). [Note: If a taxpayer has a "net capital gain," it is necessary to determine the special rate(s) at which that net capital gain is taxed. Part of net capital gain may be made up of "28-percent rate gain" which is taxed at a maximum rate of 28% (*e.g.*, gain from the sale of collectibles). Part of net capital gain may be made up of "unrecaptured section 1250 gain" which is taxed at a maximum rate of 25% (*e.g.*, gain attributable to depreciation allowed with respect to depreciable real estate held for more than one year). Currently, any capital gain that does not fall under one of these two categories is considered "adjusted net capital gain." Adjusted net capital gain is taxed at a rate of 15% if the taxpayer's ordinary marginal tax rate is 25% or higher; adjusted net capital gain is taxed at a rate of 5% if the taxpayer's ordinary marginal tax rate is below 25%. A 0% rate will replace the 5% rate for the tax years 2008, 2009, and 2010.]

   b. Fuddled realizes a loss of $8K on the sale of the stock. The loss is a deductible loss under § 165(a), (c)(2). After determining that the loss is deductible, we must determine the extent to which the loss may be deducted in the current year. Section 165(f) provides that the deduction of capital losses is restricted by §§ 1211 and 1212. Section 1211(b) provides that capital losses (whether long term or short term) may be deducted to the extent of capital gains (whether long term or short term). To the extent capital losses exceed capital gains in a given tax year, up to $3K of the excess can be used to offset ordinary income in that year. Capital losses not allowed because of the § 1211(b) limitation may be carried over into subsequent tax years. I.R.C. § 1212(b)(1). In this problem, B. Fuddled's $8K loss is characterized as a "long term capital loss" (loss from the sale or exchange of a capital asset held for more than one year). I.R.C. § 1222(4). Assuming no capital gains for the year, only $3K of the capital loss is allowed this year. The $5K not allowed this year may be carried over to 2008 and treated as though it arose in that year.

c. B. Fuddled's gain realized and recognized is $9K ($20K amount realized minus $11k adjusted basis). I.R.C. § 1001(a)-(c). The character of the gain is short term capital gain (gain from the sale or exchange of a capital asset held for not more than one year). I.R.C. § 1222(1). The short term capital gain is not eligible for preferential tax treatment and will be taxed as ordinary income. I.R.C. § 1(h); 1222(11).

d. B. Fuddled's gain realized and recognized is $10K ($20K amount realized minus $10K adjusted basis). I.R.C. § 1001(a)-(c). The character of the gain is long term capital gain (gain from the sale or exchange of a capital asset held for more than one year). I.R.C. § 1222(3). Assuming no other capital gain or loss transactions, B. Fuddled has a "net capital gain" in 2007 of $10K, which is entitled to a special capital gains rate of 5%. Recall from the answer to (a) above that for 2007 adjusted net capital gain is taxed at a rate of 5% if the taxpayer's ordinary marginal tax rate is 10% or 15%.

e. If the Confused.Com stock were so-called "qualified small business stock" held for more than five years, B. Fuddled could exclude 50% of gain from the sale of the stock. The remaining gain would be considered "28-percent rate gain" which is taxed at a maximum rate of 28%. I.R.C. § 1(h)(7). Note that the 28% rate applies only if the taxpayer is in a bracket higher than 28% (*e.g.*, 35%). If a taxpayer is in a bracket lower than 28% (*e.g.*, in (d) above), any 28-percent rate gain would be taxed at that lower bracket just as would the taxpayer's ordinary income.

3. The sale of land is a realization event within § 1001(a). Leo's amount realized is $115K, the amount of money received. I.R.C. § 1001(b). Leo's adjusted basis in the land is $100K (§ 1012 cost basis of $100K, with no § 1016 adjustments for improvements or depreciation). Therefore, Leo's gain realized is $15K ($115K AR minus $100K AB). I.R.C. § 1001(a). The next issue is whether the gain realized is recognized. As a general rule, all gains realized must be recognized unless there is an applicable nonrecognition provision. I.R.C. § 1001(c). Assuming the land was not sold under threat of condemnation (so that § 1033 might apply), the $15K gain realized is recognized. The next issue is the character of the gain. Hopefully it is long term capital gain, as such gains are entitled to preferential rate treatment. A long term capital gain is defined as gain from the sale or exchange of a capital asset held for more than one year. I.R.C. § 1222(3). Here, we have gain from the sale of property held for more than one year. But is the land a capital asset in Leo's hands? Section 1221 defines a capital asset as all property held by the taxpayer, subject to certain exceptions. One type of property excluded from the definition of capital asset is real property used in the taxpayer's trade or business. I.R.C. § 1221(a)(2). Because Leo's land is not a capital asset, it would appear that the gain would be characterized as ordinary income. But wait! Section 1231, a

special characterization provision, may help to supply capital gain treatment. Is the $15K gain considered "section 1231 gain"? The first transaction to which section 1231 applies is the sale or exchange of "property used in the trade or business." I.R.C. § 1231(a)(3)(A)(i). The phrase "property used in the trade or business" includes real property used in business that has been held more than one year (commonly referred to as quasi-capital assets). I.R.C. § 1231(b). To determine the ultimate character of the section 1231 gain, Leo must place it in an imaginary basket (the principal hotchpot) for netting with other section 1231 gains and losses. Before we net the principal hotchpot, we must analyze the next transaction that occurred in the current year—the theft of the delivery truck—to see if it also produced a section 1231 gain or loss.

The theft of the delivery truck produced a $10K loss under § 165(a) (providing that a deduction shall be allowed for any loss sustained during the year and not compensated by insurance or otherwise) and § 165(b) (providing that the amount of the loss cannot exceed basis). In the case of individuals, only three types of losses are allowed—business losses, investment losses, and casualty losses. I.R.C. § 165(c)(1)-(3). This is a (c)(1) business loss. We must next determine the extent to which the loss may be deducted in the current year. Section 165(f) provides that the deduction of capital losses is restricted by §§ 1211 and 1212. So, what is the character of the loss? Hopefully it will be characterized as an ordinary loss not subject to the capital loss limitations. A long term capital loss is defined as a deductible loss from the sale or exchange of a capital asset held for more than one year. I.R.C. § 1222(4). Here, two elements are missing; we don't have a "sale or exchange" and we don't have a "capital asset" within the meaning of § 1221. I.R.C. § 1221(a)(2) (excluding depreciable property from the definition of capital asset). While it appears, then, that the loss is characterized as an ordinary loss, we must turn to § 1231, which operates on transactions that are not characterized under general characterization principles. This is a "section 1231 loss" that would seemingly have to be placed in the principal hotchpot to be netted with the section 1231 gain from the sale of land. But, a special rule provides that gains and losses from involuntary conversions (*e.g.*, theft) are not subject to section 1231 if the total involuntary losses exceed the involuntary gains. I.R.C. § 1231(a)(4)(C). To apply the rule, the $10K section 1231 loss arising from the theft must first be placed in a preliminary basket (commonly known as the preliminary hotchpot or fire pot).

Now, we must actually apply § 1231 and do some netting to determine the actual character of the theft loss and land gain. First, we net the preliminary basket to see if the loss will drop down into the principal hotchpot. Since the involuntary losses for the year ($10K) exceed the involuntary gains for the year ($0K), the $10K loss does not drop into the principal hotchpot and is treated as an ordinary loss— deductible in full and not subject to the capital loss limitations of §§ 1211 and 1212. Good! Now, we net the principal hotchpot. Since Leo's section 1231 gains for the year ($15K) exceed section 1231 losses for the year ($0K), then the gain is treated as long term capital gain. Also good! Note that section 1231 is a pro-taxpayer rule, permitting the casualty loss here to remain characterized as ordinary loss while permitting the land gain in the same year to be characterized as long term capital gain.

Assuming no other capital gain or loss transactions for the year, Leo has a net capital gain of $15K entitled to preferential rate treatment.

PROBLEM #13 DEPRECIATION AND RECAPTURE

1. Jasper's shredder is depreciable property—that is, a wasting asset used in a trade or business. I.R.C. § 167(a). Because the shredder is depreciable tangible property acquired after 1980, we turn to § 168 (Accelerated Cost Recovery System) to determine Leo's annual depreciation deductions. Section 168 applies an arbitrary cost recovery system that generally allows a taxpayer to recover his cost in depreciable tangible property well before it ceases to be useful in his business. To prepare a depreciation schedule for the shredder, we must ascertain: (1) the applicable convention; (2) the applicable recovery period; and (3) the applicable depreciation method. I.R.C. § 168(a)(1)-(3).

    Applicable Convention. The applicable convention tells us when an asset is to be treated as placed in service. The half-year convention generally applies. I.R.C. § 168(d)(1). That means, regardless of when Leo purchased the shredder, Leo is treated as having acquired the shredder on July 1st of Year 1. I.R.C. § 168(d)(4). Therefore, Leo will be entitled to a half year's worth of depreciation for the first year even if he purchased it on January 15. [Note: The mid-month convention in § 168(d)(2) does not apply because the shredder is not depreciable real property (*e.g.*, a rental building or a business warehouse), and the mid-quarter convention in § 168(d)(3) does not apply per the facts (*i.e.*, Leo did not acquire a substantial portion of total depreciable assets during the last quarter of the year).] Leo will be entitled to a full-year's depreciation in subsequent years.

    Applicable Recovery Period. Despite what Leo might project to be the useful life of the shredder, § 168 provides arbitrary time periods for recovering the cost of depreciable tangible property. We are told that the shredder has a class life of five years (this was determined under Revenue Procedure 87-56, which prescribes class lives for many categories of tangible property). Section 168(e) tells us that property with a class life of five years is identified as "5-year property." Section 168(c) tells us that 5-year property has an "applicable recovery period" of five years. Brilliant! In short, the cost of the shredder will be recovered over a five-year period even if it has a longer economic life. Actually, to make up for the half year convention, we must extend the depreciation schedule into Year 6. We wouldn't be able to fully recover the cost of the shredder unless we extend the recovery period out one additional year. Nothing in the Code tells us to do this, but one-half a year's depreciation will have to be allowed in Year 6 since only one half is allowed in Year 1. So far, the depreciation schedule looks like this:

Year	HYC	%	Base	Dep. Ded.
1	½			
2	1			
3	1			
4	1			
5	1			
6	½			

    Applicable Depreciation Method. Under § 168(b)(1)(A), the presumption or default method is the 200% declining balance method. This is an accelerated method, which permits Leo to take larger amounts of depreciation deductions in the earlier years of the shredder's life and smaller amounts in later years. However, the aggregate amount Leo can depreciate is still limited to his basis in the property. I.R.C. § 167(c). The 200% declining balance method refers to 200% of the straight line rate. To determine the straight line rate, divide 100% or 1.0 by the applicable recovery period of 5 years. The straight line rate is 20%. Hence, the double declining balance rate is 40%.

To determine the depreciation allowance for Year 1, we multiply Leo's basis in the shredder of $10,000 by our rate of 40% and then multiply that amount by .5 (because, remember, only one-half is allowed in the first year). This yields a depreciation allowance for Year 1 of $2000. The basis in the shredder would be reduced by $2000 allowed in Year 1 per § 1016(a)(2). Thus, the shredder's adjusted basis at the beginning of Year 2 will be $8,000. To determine the depreciation allowance for Year 2, we multiply Leo's adjusted basis at the beginning of Year 2 of $8,000 (notice we're not using the original $10,000 basis, but we're using a declining balance basis which reflects prior years' depreciation allowances) by 40% This yields a depreciation allowance for Year 2 of $3,200. Continuing this method yields a depreciation allowance in Year 3 of $1,920. So far, the schedule looks like this:

Year	×	HYC	×	%	×	Base	=	Dep. Ded.
1	×	½	×	40	×	$10,000	=	$2,000
2	×	1	×	40	×	8,000	=	3,200
3	×	1	×	40	×	4,800	=	1,920
4	×	1						
5	×	1						
6	×	½						

Note that when using the double declining balance method (applying a percentage to a declining amount), we'll never get to $0. At some point down the line, we will have to make some adjustments. Read § 168(b)(1)(A) carefully. We're told that we will use the same double declining balance method (the 40% rate) until the first taxable year where the straight line method would yield a larger depreciation allowance. Would it be better to switch to the straight line method after Year 3 (the beginning of Year 4)? After Year 3, the straight line rate would be 40% (that is, 100% divided by 2.5 years remaining in the original recovery period). Because the straight line rate at the end of Year 3 of 40% is not better than our declining balance rate we've been using of 40%, we will not switch methods in Year 4. The depreciation allowance in Year 4 is $1,152 ($2,880 basis multiplied by our declining balance rate of 40%). Would it be better to switch to the straight line method after Year 4 (the beginning of Year 5)? After Year 4, the straight rate would be 66 ⅔% (that is, 100% divided by 1.5 years remaining in the original recovery period). Because the straight line rate at the end of Year 4 of 66 ⅔% is better than our declining balance rate we've been using of 40%, we will switch to the straight line method in Year 5. Under the straight line method, we take a flat rate (66 ⅔%) and multiply it by the same base ($1,728 adjusted basis at the beginning of Year 5). The depreciation allowance in Year 5 is $1,152 ($1,728 × .666). The depreciation allowance in Year 6 is $576 ($1,728 x .666 x .5). The complete depreciation schedule for the shredder looks like this:

Year	×	HYC	×	%	×	Base	=	Dep. Ded.
1	×	½	×	40	×	$10,000	=	$2,000
2	×	1	×	40	×	8,000	=	3,200
3	×	1	×	40	×	4,800	=	1,920
4	×	1	×	40	×	2,880	=	1,152
5	×	1	×	66 ⅔	×	1,728	=	1,152
6	×	½	×	66 ⅔	×	1,728	=	576

At the end of Year 6, Leo will have fully recovered the cost of the shredder as all yearly depreciation allowances add up to $10,000. His adjusted basis in the shredder at the end of Year 6 will be $0 per § 1016(a)(2). [Note: the basis of property must be reduced to account for amounts "allowed" (actually taken) or "allowable" (which could have been taken) for depreciation deductions. Read § 1016 carefully. If no deduction is taken, basis must, nevertheless be reduced that the amount that could have been taken under the straight line method. The effect of this is to force taxpayers to take depreciation.]

2. The presumptive depreciation method is the 200% declining balance method. There are other options for Leo in § 168(b). For example, if Leo wants to depreciate the shredder using the 150% declining balance method or the straight line method, he can do so if he makes an election. Under the straight line method, depreciation deductions are spaced evenly throughout the asset's recovery period. A straight line depreciation schedule for the shredder would look like this:

Year	×	HYC	×	%	×	Base	=	Dep. Ded.
1	×	½	×	20	×	$10,000	=	$1,000
2	×	1	×	20	×	10,000	=	2,000
3	×	1	×	20	×	10,000	=	2,000
4	×	1	×	20	×	10,000	=	2,200
5	×	1	×	20	×	10,000	=	2,000
6	×	½	×	20	×	10,000	=	1,000

Another option for Leo is found in § 179. It allows one to elect to write off the cost of acquisition of "section 179 property" as an expense "not chargeable to a capital account." I.R.C. § 179(a). Section 179 property is defined as tangible property which is "section 1245 property" and which is purchased for the active conduct of a trade or business. I.R.C. § 179(d)(1). Section 1245 property is generally depreciable personal property. Skim I.R.C. § 1245(a)(3). In this problem, Leo's shredder qualifies as "section 179 property." There are limits on the amount that can be expensed in any given year. First, the maximum allowable deduction for all qualifying property placed in service is currently $100K (for taxable years beginning after 2002 and before 2010). I.R.C. § 179(b)(1). The $100K amount is reduced dollar-for-dollar (but not below zero) by the amount by which the cost of qualifying property placed in service during the tax year exceeds $400K (in the case of taxable years beginning after 2002 and before 2010). I.R.C. § 179(b)(2). Second, the amount eligible to be expenses cannot exceed the taxable income derived by Leo from the active conduct of his trade or business, with any disallowed deductions due to this limitation permitted to be carried forward. I.R.C. § 179(b)(3). [NOTE: The $100K limit and the $400K limit are adjusted for inflation. I.R.C. § 179(b)(5)(A).] In this problem, assuming Leo has not purchased $500K of section 179 property in 2008, and assuming sufficient taxable income, Leo may elect to deduct immediately the $10,000 cost of the shredder. His basis would be reduced to zero per § 1016(a)(2), leaving nothing left to depreciate under § 168.

3. a. Although the radio transmitter has declined in value, Rush will realize gain on its sale due to the fact that § 168 permitted Leo to claim $80K in accelerated depreciation deductions. Rush's gain realized on the sale is $5K-that is, $25K amount realized minus $20K adjusted basis ($100K cost basis under § 1012 reduced by $80K depreciation deductions per § 1016(a)(2)). The gain realized is recognized per § 1001(c). The next issue is the character of the recognized gain. Rush would like the gain to be characterized as long term capital gain to receive preferential rate treatment. A long term capital gain is defined as *gain* from the *sale or exchange* of a *capital asset* held for *more than one year*. I.R.C. § 1222(3). The radio transmitter is not a capital asset within the

meaning of § 1221, because it is depreciable property. It is, however, "section 1231 property" (*i.e.*, a quasi-capital asset); the gain is placed in the § 1231 principal hotchpot to be netted with other § 1231 gains and losses to determine the gain's ultimate character. Before we actually apply § 1231 and perform any netting, we must turn to § 1245 to see whether it applies. Section 1245 is an overriding provision that prevents taxpayers from receiving a windfall with respect to depreciable property—that is, taking ordinary depreciation deductions in early years (in most cases accelerated deductions producing large tax benefits for the taxpayer), and then claiming preferential capital gains treatment on later sale of the property. I.R.C. § 1245(d). Section 1245 recapture comes into play whenever "section 1245 property" is "disposed of." I.R.C. § 1245(a)(1). The radio transmitter is § 1245 property because it is depreciable tangible personal property, and it is disposed of in a sale. I.R.C. § 1245(a)(3). Accordingly, § 1245 will reach into our § 1231 principal hotchpot and pull out part or all of the § 1231 gain and characterize it as ordinary income. The amount treated as ordinary income under § 1245 is the lower of: (1) "recomputed basis" minus adjusted basis; or (2) amount realized minus adjusted basis. I.R.C. § 1245(a)(1). Recomputed basis is simply the property's adjusted basis recomputed by adding back all the depreciation adjustments reflect in the adjusted basis; in most cases, recomputed basis is simply the property's original basis. I.R.C. § 1245(a)(1)(A). Here, recomputed basis of $100K (that is, adjusted basis of $20K plus depreciation deductions of $80K) exceeds adjusted basis of $20K, by $80K (the amount of depreciation deductions claimed). Amount realized of $25K exceeds adjusted basis of $20K, by $5K (the amount of gain realized). The lower of the two figures ($5K) is the amount to be recaptured as ordinary income (the amount attributable to previous depreciation deductions). In conclusion, § 1245 will reach into the § 1231 hotchpot and pull out all $5K as ordinary income. No part of the gain remains in the pot to receive capital gains treatment. This makes sense because the gain was attributable to depreciation deductions taken and not to economic appreciation in value.

b. If Rush made the § 179 election in 2008, he would have expensed the full $100K cost of the transmitter in 2008 and his basis would have been reduced to zero. I.R.C. § 1016(a)(2). On later sale in 2011, Rush would have gain realized and recognized of $25K ($25K amount realized minus $0K adjusted basis). Does § 1245 apply? Yes, because the transmitter is considered "section 1245 property." The amount treated as ordinary income under § 1245 is the lower of: (1) recomputed basis minus adjusted basis; or (2) amount realized minus adjusted basis. I.R.C. § 1245(a)(1). In determining recomputed basis, a taxpayer must add back not only depreciation deductions under § 167, but also amounts expensed under § 179. I.R.C. § 1245(a)(2)(C). In this problem, recomputed basis of $100K (that is, adjusted basis of $0K plus the § 179 expensed amount of $100K) exceeds adjusted basis of $0K, by $100K. Amount realized of $25K exceeds adjusted basis of $0K, by $25K (the amount of gain realized). The lower of the two figures ($25K) is the amount to be recaptured and treated as ordinary income. As with (a) above, the entire gain is characterized as ordinary income; nothing is characterized as § 1231 gain.

c. Although the radio transmitter increased in value by only $25K, Rush will realize $105K of gain due to the fact that he took ordinary depreciation deductions with respect to the property ($125K amount realized minus $20K adjusted basis). The gain is recognized as there are no applicable nonrecognition provisions. I.R.C. § 1001(c). The gain is considered § 1231 gain—gain recognized from the sale or exchange of property used in a trade or business. I.R.C. § 1231(a)(3), (b). It is placed in the principal hotchpot to be netted with other § 1231 gains and losses, if any, that occurred during the year. Before actually applying § 1231, however, we must turn to § 1245, an overriding characterization provision. I.R.C. § 1245(d). The amount treated as ordinary income under § 1245 is the lower of: (1) "recomputed basis" minus adjusted basis; or (2) amount realized minus adjusted basis. I.R.C. § 1245(a)(1). Recomputed basis is simply the property's adjusted basis recomputed by adding back all the depreciation adjustments reflect in the adjusted basis; in most cases, recomputed basis is simply the property's original basis. I.R.C. § 1245(a)(1)(A). Here, recomputed basis of $100K (that is, adjusted basis of $20K plus depreciation deductions of $80K) exceeds adjusted basis of $20K, by $80K (the amount of depreciation deductions claimed). Amount realized of $125K exceeds adjusted basis of $20K, by $105K (the amount of gain realized). The lower of the two figures ($80K) is the amount to be recaptured as ordinary income (the amount attributable to previous depreciation deductions). In conclusion, § 1245 will reach into the § 1231 hotchpot and pull out $80K as ordinary income. The remaining $25K of gain remains in the principal pot to be netted with other § 1231 gains and losses. Assuming no other § 1231 transactions, the $25K § 1231 gain would be characterized as long term capital gain, as § 1231 gains for the year ($25k) exceed § 1231 losses for the year ($0K). Note that gain attributable to ordinary depreciation deductions ($80K) is characterized as ordinary income under § 1245, and gain attributable to economic appreciation in value ($25K) is characterized as long term capital gain under § 1231.

d. Section 1245 comes into play only when § 1245 property is "disposed of," a sufficiently broad term that encompasses many transactions. However, certain transactions are excluded. For example, § 1245 does not apply to dispositions by gift. I.R.C. § 1245(b). If Rush did not sell the radio transmitter, but instead gave it to Sinead, § 1245 would not apply to Rush. However, when Sinead later sells the transmitter, she will be required to recapture as ordinary income any gain attributable to the depreciation deductions claimed by Rush. This is because "recomputed basis" is Sinead's adjusted basis (same adjusted basis Rush had at the time of gift per § 1015) plus "*all* adjustments reflected in such basis on account of deductions," including adjustments made by Rush. I.R.C. § 1245(a)(2)(A). In short, Sinead will have $105K gain realized and recognized ($125K amount realized minus $20K adjusted basis). I.R.C. § 1001. $80K of the gain will be recaptured and characterized as ordinary income under § 1245. $25K of the gain will be characterized as long term capital gain under § 1222(3). [Note that the transmitter in Sinead's hands is most likely a capital asset within the meaning of § 1221. In addition, the requisite holding period of "more than one year" is met since Sinead can tack on to her actual holding period Rush's holding period per § 1223(2).]

e. When Rush bequeaths the radio transmitter to Sinead, § 1245 does not apply to Rush or Rush's estate. I.R.C. § 1245(b)(2). Sinead's basis in the transmitter is $125K per § 1014. When she sells the transmitter for $125K, she realizes no gain or loss.

f. While § 1245 generally applies to depreciable personal property, § 1250 generally applies to depreciable real property, such as residential rental property (apartment buildings) and non-residential real property (office buildings and warehouses). I.R.C. § 1250(c). The amount treated as ordinary income under § 1250 is the "applicable percentage" (typically 100%) of the lower of: (1) "additional depreciation" or (2) gain realized. I.R.C. § 1250(a). Additional depreciation, in the case of property held for more than a year, is defined as depreciation adjustments in excess of what would be allowed under the straight line method. I.R.C. § 1250(b)(1). Interestingly, for depreciable real property acquired after 1986, the straight line method must be used. Hence, for real property acquired after 1986, there will be no "additional depreciation" and hence, no amount recaptured as ordinary income. However, "unrecaptured section 1250 gains" are taxed at a maximum rate of 25%, much higher than the 15% maximum rate applicable to other long term capital gains. The term "unrecaptured section 1250 gain" means long term capital gain from the sale of depreciable real property attributable to depreciation deductions taken that are not recaptured as ordinary income. I.R.C. § 1(h)(7). Thus, gain attributable to depreciation deductions, while not taxed at ordinary income rates, are taxed at higher capital gains rates.

In this problem, Rush's gain on the sale of the rental property is $550K ($600K amount realized minus $50K adjusted basis). What is the character of the gain? The rental building is § 1250 property. The amount recaptured as ordinary income is the applicable percentage (assume 100%) of the lower of additional depreciation or gain realized. Additional depreciation is zero since Rush did not take depreciation adjustments in excess of straight line. Applying the lower of rule, the amount recaptured is 100% of $0, or $0. Assuming no other § 1231 transactions, the entire $550K gain comes out of the § 1231 hotchpot as long term capital gain. However, $15K of the gain is "unrecaptured section 1250 gain" (*i.e.*, gain attributable to depreciation not recaptured as ordinary income) and is taxed at a maximum rate of 25%. The remaining $535K of the gain is long term capital gain taxed at a maximum rate of 15%.

4. Section 197, enacted in 1993, dramatically changed the tax treatment of intangible assets, including goodwill. Prior to 1993, the capitalized costs of acquiring intangible assets could be depreciated (or "amortized") only if the intangible asset had a useful life that could be determined with reasonable accuracy. This seemingly simple rule meant that taxpayers could not depreciate or amortize the capitalized costs of many intangibles, such as trade secrets, trademarks, trade names, and goodwill. In a major shift in tax policy, § 197 created an arbitrary fifteen-year recovery period for many types of intangible property. I.R.C. § 197(a). More specifically, § 197 allows an amortization deduction for the capitalized costs of an "amortizable section 197 intangible" and prohibits any other depreciation or amortization with respect to that property. I.R.C. § 197(a), (b). An "amortizable section 197 intangible" is any "section 197 intangible" acquired after August 10, 1993 and held in connection with the conduct of a trade or business or an activity described in § 212. I.R.C. § 197(c)(1). A "section 197 intangible" generally includes goodwill, going concern value, customer and supplier lists, patents, copyrights, trademarks, trade names, licenses, covenants not to compete, and a few other intangibles. I.R.C. § 197(d)(1). There are several important exceptions. For example, § 197 does not apply to certain intangibles acquired separately (*i.e.*, that are *not* acquired in a transaction involving the acquisition of assets constituting a trade or business). I.R.C. § 197(e)(4). In addition, a § 197 intangible does not include off-the-shelf software (*i.e.*, software that is readily available to the general public

on similar terms, is subject to a nonexclusive license, and has not been substantially modified). In this problem, Best Cleaners will be acquiring several intangibles. All of the listed intangibles appear to constitute § 197 intangibles that do not fall within any exception. The amount of the § 197 amortization deduction is determined by amortizing the adjusted basis of each § 197 intangible ratably over a fifteen-year period. The fifteen-year period begins on the first day of the month in which the intangible is acquired and held in connection with the trade or business. [Note: Section 1245 recapture will apply if and when Best Cleaners sells the § 197 intangibles. Section 1245 property is defined as depreciable personal property, which includes both tangible property and intangible personal property. I.R.C. § 1245(a)(3); Treas. Reg. § 1.1245-3(b).]

PROBLEM #14 THE CHARITABLE DEDUCTION

1. a. All of the requirements for a charitable contribution deduction under § 170 are met (*e.g.*, Al transferred money with no expectation of a return benefit and the school is a qualified recipient under § 170(c)). The amount of the contribution is the amount of the donated money, $55K. The total amount deductible in the current year, however, is limited to 50% of Al's contribution base for the year. I.R.C. § 170(b)(1). Al's contribution based is $100K (generally defined as his adjusted gross income). I.R.C. § 170(b)(1)(G). Thus, Al may currently deduct only $50K of the $55K he gave to the school. He may carryover the remaining $5K to the next year (the next five years if necessary).

    b. Again, all the requirements for a charitable contribution deduction are met (*e.g.*, Al transferred unencumbered property with no expectation of a return benefit and the school is a qualified recipient under § 170(c)). The potential amount of the charitable contribution is $100K, the fair market value of the donated land. Treas. Reg. § 1.170A-1(c)(1). However, when appreciated property is donated, the amount of the contribution may be reduced by some or all of the amount of the built in gain. To determine whether a reduction occurs here, it is necessary to determine the character of the gain that would be recognized if the property were sold by Al in a hypothetical sale. If the gain would be other than long term capital gain (*i.e.*, characterized as ordinary income or short term capital gain), the amount of the contribution is reduced by the total amount of the hypothetical ordinary income or short term capital gain. Because Al held the land for only three months, he would realized a $50K short term capital gain in a hypothetical sale of the land. Accordingly, the amount of Al's contribution is reduced by the amount of that hypothetical $50K STCG, from $100K (fair market value) to $50K (adjusted basis). That amount is deductible in the current year only to the extent of 50% of his contribution base. Al's contribution base is $100K; thus Al may currently deduct the full $50K contribution.

    c. If Al gives the $55K cash to the Sound Foundation, § 170(b)(1)(B) will limit deductibility in the current year to the lesser of (1) 30% of Al's contribution base or (2) the excess of 50% of Al's contribution base over the amount allowable under the 50% limitation rule. I.R.C. § 170(b)(1)(B). Assuming Al made no other charitable gifts during the year, he can deduct currently $30K (30% of his $100K contribution base) of the $55K which he gave to Sound Foundation. The remaining $25K can be carried over to the following year (or for the following five years if necessary). I.R.C. § 170(b)(1)(B).

2. a. All of the requirements for a charitable contribution deduction under § 170 are met (*e.g.*, Martindale transferred his entire interest in the paintings with no expectation of a return benefit, and the museum is a qualified charitable recipient under § 170(c)). The potential amount of the contribution is $50K, the fair market value of the Picasso paintings. Treas. Reg. § 1.170A-1(c)(1). Because the paintings are appreciated property, we must determine whether § 170(e) will reduce the amount of the contribution by the amount of built in gain. Because gain on a hypothetical sale of the paintings would produce long term capital gain under § 1222(3) (gain from the sale or exchange of a capital asset held for more than one year), the gain wring out rule of § 170(e)(1)(A) does not apply to reduce the amount of the contribution. Further, because the paintings (tangible personal property) are being donated to an art museum and

the use of the paintings is presumably related to the charity's function, the gain wring out rule of § 170(e)(1)(B)(i) does not apply to reduce the amount of the contribution. Accordingly, the amount of the contribution remains $50K, the paintings' fair market value. The next issue whether the total amount of the contribution is deductible in the current year. Congress imposes various limits on the total amount that may be deducted in any taxable year. Contributions to § 170(b)(1)(A) organizations are generally deductible to the extent that such contributions do not exceed 50% of the contribution base. It would appear that Martindale could deduct his entire contribution under the 50% ceiling. However, there is a further ceiling on gifts of appreciated long term capital gain property. More specifically, a contribution to a public charity of long term capital gain property which does not have its long term capital gain wrung out because it is not unrelated to the charitable function is subject to a further ceiling—30% of contribution base. I.R.C. § 170(b)(1)(C)(i). As a result of the 30% ceiling rule, Martindale can deduct currently only $30K of the $50K contribution (30% of the $100K contribution base). [Note that Martindale may elect to reduce the amount of the contribution by the long term capital gain lurking in the paintings ($25K) so that the contribution is then subject to only the 50% ceiling. I.R.C. § 170(b)(1)(C)(iii). This would not be wise, as such election would yield a current deduction of only $25K.]

b. Because the paintings (tangible personal property) are donated to a church and the use of the paintings by the church is presumably unrelated to the church's function, the amount of the contribution must be reduced by the amount of the lurking long term capital gain (character of gain on a hypothetical sale of the paintings by the Mardindale). I.R.C. § 170(e)(1)(B). *See* Treas. Reg. § 1.170A-4(b)(3) (defining unrelated use). Thus, the amount of the Martindale's contribution is $25K. It would be deductible in full in the current year under the 50% ceiling rule. I.R.C. § 170(b)(1)(A).

3. a. For charitable contributions of most forms of intellectual property made after June 3, 2004, new § 170(e)(1)(B)(iii) broadly denies a deduction for the long term capital gain inherent in such property. In this problem, Dweeb must reduce the potential amount of the contribution ($200K fair market value) by the amount of long term capital gain Dweeb would realize on a hypothetical sale of the patent ($200K), resulting in a contribution of $0. Although the gain wring out rule under § 170(e)(1)(B)(iii) prevents Dweeb from receiving any initial charitable deduction, new § 170(m) permits Dweeb to receive future charitable deductions (for up to ten years). The amount of future deductions is a percentage of "qualified donee income" received or accrued by the charity from the donated patent itself, rather than income stemming from the activity in which the donated patent is sued. I.R.C. § 170(m)(1), (3), (7). The percentage decreases each year (*e.g.*, in the first and second years after the contribution, Dweeb can deduct 100% of the qualified donee income; in year three, Dweeb may deduct 90% of the qualified donee income; in year ten, only 20% of the qualified donee income is deductible). The deduction under § 170(m) is subject to the percentage limits in § 170(b)(1)(A), and is reduced by the amount of the deduction allowed in the year of gift. I.R.C. § 170(m)(2), (m)(10)(A).

b. Section 170(e)(1)(B)(iii) applies to wring out the built-in gain. The deduction is $50K. As in (a) above, § 170(m) will apply but only to the royalties in excess of the $50K already deducted. I.R.C. § 170(m)(2).

PROBLEM #15 NONRECOGNITION PROVISIONS

1. a. In regards to Paul, the exchange of the boat for the land is a realization event within the meaning of § 1001. Paul's gain realized is equal to "amount realized" minus "adjusted basis." I.R.C. § 1001(a). Paul's amount realized on the exchange is the amount of money received ($0), plus the fair market value received ($20K FMV of the land), plus relief of liabilities per *Crane* ($0). I.R.C. § 1001(b); Treas. Reg. § 1001-2; *Crane*. Paul was not relieved of any liabilities, but he did take on Terry's $5K liability; under reverse-*Crane* notions, such assumption should reduce Paul's amount realized. Therefore, Paul's amount realized on the exchange is $15K. Paul's adjusted basis in the boat exchanged is $8K. Accordingly, Paul's gain realized is $7K ($15K AR minus $8K AB). [Note that the same result would occur if you increased Paul's adjusted basis by the assumption of Terry's liability instead of decreasing Paul's amount realized (*e.g.*, $20K AR minus $13K AB equals $7K gain realized).] The next issue is whether the gain realized is recognized. As a general rule, all gains realized are recognized unless otherwise provided in the Code. I.R.C. § 1001(c). Here, Paul's gain is recognized because the facts state that the exchange does not qualify for any provision relating to nonrecognition of gain. What is Paul's adjusted basis in the land received? Under the *Philadelphia Park Amusement Co.* case, the basis of property received in a taxable exchange is the fair market value of the property received. Paul's basis in the land is its fair market value at the time of exchange, or $20K. This makes sense. First, Paul's entire gain realized on the exchange was recognized—If Paul were to sell the land soon after the exchange for its value of $20K, Paul should not have any additional gain to report. Second, "tax cost basis" notions support a $20K basis—Paul had a basis of $8K in his boat, plus he assumed a $5K liability, plus he recognized $7K of gain on receipt of the land. $8K + $5K + $7K = $20K basis in the land.

     b. In regards to Terry, the exchange of the land for the boat is also a sale or other disposition within the meaning of § 1001. Terry's amount realized is $20K—the amount of money received ($0) plus the fair market value of the boat received ($15K) plus relief of liabilities per *Crane* ($5K). I.R.C. § 1001(b). Terry's gain realized is $5K—$20K amount realized minus $15K adjusted basis. I.R.C. § 1001(a). The $5K gain realized is recognized because the exchange does not qualify for nonrecognition under any provision in the Code. I.R.C. § 1001(c). Because this was a taxable exchange, Terry's basis in the boat is $15K-the fair market value of the boat at the time of the exchange. *Philadelphia Park Amusement Co.*

2. a. In regards to Thomas, the exchange of his apartment building for Tim's apartment building is a realization event within the meaning of § 1001. Thomas' gain realized on the exchange is $50K-the fair market value of Tim's property received ($100K) minus Thomas' adjusted basis in his property exchanged ($50K). The gain realized is not recognized because the exchange qualifies under § 1031 for nonrecognition. Because § 1031 applies, Thomas' basis in the property received is determined under § 1031(d)—not the *Philadelphia Park Amusement Co.* case as in problem 1 above. Thomas' basis in the property received is $50K—the basis of the property given up ($50) minus money received ($0) plus gain recognized ($0). [Note that by giving Thomas an exchange basis in the land received, § 1031 grants deferral of gain recognition rather than complete forgiveness. Deferral derives from the basis rules.

If Thomas were to turn around and sell the new property for its value of $100K, Thomas would realize and recognize $50K of gain—the amount of gain that went unrecognized on the initial exchange.] Under the holding period rule of § 1222(1), Thomas can tack on to the holding period of the property received the holding period of the property given up, provided the old property was a capital asset or § 1231 property in Thomas' hands.

In regards to Tim, the exchange is an "other disposition" within the meaning of § 1001. Tim's loss realized on the exchange is $5K—$110 adjusted basis in the property given up minus $100 fair market value of the property received. The loss realized is not recognized because the exchange qualifies for nonrecognition under § 1031. [Note that § 1031 is *not* elective. When it applies, it applies mandatorily.] Tim's basis in the property received is $110K under § 1031(d). Tim's holding period in the property received includes the holding period of the property given up, provided the property given up was a capital asset or § 1231 property in Tim's hands.

[Recall that § 1250, the depreciation recapture rule, overrides all other Code sections. This means that it will trump nonrecognition rules. However, § 1250 has a cutback rule applicable to like-kind exchanges. Section 1250(d)(4) essentially provides that § 1250 will not override § 1031 as long as the property received in the exchange is also § 1250 property.]

   b. There are certain categories of property to which § 1031 does not apply, such as business inventory. I.R.C. § 1031(a)(2). If Tim were a professional "dealer" in apartment buildings, he would not qualify for nonrecognition under § 1031. Accordingly, Tim would get to recognize his $5K loss realized! I.R.C. § 1001(c). Tim's basis in the property received would be $100K, its fair market value at the time of the exchange. His holding period in the property received would begin the day after the exchange.

The fact that Tim does not qualify for nonrecognition does not affect Thomas. In other words, Tim's use of property is irrelevant in determining whether Thomas qualifies for non-recognition under § 1001. Thomas is within § 1031 if he intends to hold the new property for investment or use in a trade or business. Treas. Reg. § 1.1031(a)-1(a).

   c. The sale and subsequent purchase does not qualify for non-recognition under § 1031. As a general rule, receipt of cash is fatal. Thomas will recognize $50K gain and will have a § 1012 cost basis in Tim's apartment building.

3. a. In regards to Woody, the exchange is a realization event within the meaning of § 1001. Woody has a gain realized of $20K determined as follows:

> $70K FMV of property received I.R.C. § 1001(b)
>
> + $40K Mortgage transferred (*Crane*)
>
> − $40K Mortgage assumed (reverse *Crane* notions)
>
> $70K Amount realized
>
> − $50K Adjusted basis of property given up
>
> $20K Gain realized I.R.C. § 1001(a)

The $20K gain realized is recognized unless § 1031 applies. I.R.C. § 1001(c). The properties exchanged are considered like kind. Treas. Reg. § 1.1031(a)-1(b). Woody held the old property for business or investment purposes and presumably intends to hold the new property for either business or investment

ANSWERS TO CHAPTER 9 PROBLEMS

purposes. Treas. Reg. § 1.1031(a)-1(a). Woody, however, is being relieved of a $40K liability, which is treated as the equivalent of cash boot. *See* I.R.C. § 1031(d) (last sentence). [This has significance for both gain recognition under subsection 1031(b) and for the basis calculation under subsection 1031(d).] Section 1031(b) provides that the recipient of boot must recognize gain to the extent of the *lesser* of gain realized or the value of the boot received. Here, is the amount of boot really $40K, the relief of liability? What about the $40K liability Woody is taking on? The Code doesn't tells us what to do when liabilities pass in both directions, as when each property is subject to a mortgage. Fortunately, the regulations fill in the gaps and provide that the assumptions of liability are netted for boot purposes. Treas. Reg. § 1.1031(d)-2, ex. 2(c). Thus only the transferor of the property subject to the greater liability is deemed to have boot for gain recognition purposes. Here, Woody has no net liability relief. Hence, Woody has no boot for gain recognition purposes. None of the $20K gain realized is recognized by Woody. Woody's basis in the new property is $50K determined as follows:

> $50K Old basis
>
> − $0K Money received (net liability relief on mortgages)
>
> + $0K Gain recognized
>
> $50K New basis. *See* Treas. Reg. § 1.1031(d)-2, Ex. 2(c)

Woody's holding period for the new property includes the holding period of his old property, assuming it was a capital asset or § 1231 property in Woody's hands. I.R.C. § 1223(1).

In regards to Ron, the analysis is the same. Ron's gain realized is $40K. Because Ron has no net liability relief, he has no boot for gain recognition purposes. Therefore, none of the $40K gain realized is recognized by Ron. Ron's basis in the new property is $30K. And, "tacking" of holding period applies, assuming Ron's property given up was a capital asset or § 1231 property in Ron's hands.

b.   Woody has a gain realized of $30K determined as follows:

> $70K FMV of property received I.R.C. § 1001(b)
>
> + $50K Mortgage transferred (*Crane*)
>
> − $40K Mortgage assumed (reverse *Crane* notions)
>
> $80K Amount realized
>
> − $50K Adjusted basis of property given up
>
> $30K Gain realized I.R.C. § 1001(a)

The $30K gain realized is recognized unless § 1031 applies. I.R.C. § 1001(c). The exchange seems to be within § 1031 but for the relief of liabilities. *See* I.R.C. § 1031(d) (last sentence). The regulations provide that the assumptions of liability are netted for boot purposes. Treas. Reg. § 1.1031(d)-2, ex. 2(c). Here, Woody has $10K net liability relief. Hence, Woody has $10K boot for gain recognition purposes. Section 1031(b) provides that the recipient of boot must recognize gain to the extent of the *lesser* of gain realized ($30K) or the boot received ($10K). In sum, Woody must recognize $10K of gain. Woody's basis in the new property is $50K determined as follows:

$50K Old basis

— $10K Money received (net liability relief on mortgages)

+ $10K Gain recognized

$50K New basis. *See* Treas. Reg. § 1.1031(d)-2, Ex. 2(c)

Woody's holding period for the new property includes the holding period of his old property, assuming it was a capital asset or § 1231 property in Woody's hands. I.R.C. § 1223(1).

Ron's gain realized is $40K ($70K amount realized minus $30K adjusted basis). Because Ron has no net liability relief, he has no boot for gain recognition purposes. Therefore, none of the $40K gain realized is recognized by Ron. Ron's basis in the new property is $40K—$30K old basis, plus $50K mortgage assumed (treated as cash paid), minus $40K mortgage transferred (treated as cash received), plus $0 gain recognized. And, "tacking" of holding period applies, assuming Ron's property given up was a capital asset or § 1231 property in Ron's hands.

c. Woody has a gain realized of $30K determined as follows:

$70K FMV of property received I.R.C. § 1001(b)

+ $10K Cash received

+ $30K Mortgage transferred (*Crane*)

— $40K Mortgage assumed (reverse *Crane* notions)

$70K Amount realized

— $50K Adjusted basis of property given up

$20K Gain realized I.R.C. § 1001(a)

Is this gain recognized? I.R.C. § 1001(c). The exchange seems to be within § 1031 but for potential boot. Woody receives $10K of cash-clearly boot. But Woody also is assuming an extra $10K of liabilities. Can the assumption of liability offset cash received for boot purposes? The regulations say NO! Treas. Reg. § 1.1031(d)-2, ex. 2(c). Woody's recognized gain is $10K. Woody's basis in the new property is $50K determined as follows:

$50K Old basis

— $10K Cash received

+ $40K Mortgage assumed (treated as cash paid)

— $30K Mortgage transferred (treated as cash received)

+ $10K Gain recognized

$60K New basis. *See* Treas. Reg. § 1.1031(d)-2, Ex. 2(c)

Woody's holding period for the new property includes the holding period of his old property, assuming it was a capital asset or § 1231 property in Woody's hands. I.R.C. § 1223(1).

Ron has a gain realized of $40K determined as follows:

$70K FMV of property received I.R.C. § 1001(b)

+ $40K Mortgage transferred (*Crane*)

− $30K Mortgage assumed (reverse *Crane* notions)

$80K Amount realized

− $30K Adjusted basis of property given up

− $10K Adjusted basis of cash given up

$40K Gain realized I.R.C. § 1001(a)

Is this gain recognized? I.R.C. § 1001(c). The exchange seems to be within § 1031 but for potential boot. Ron has a net liability relief of $10K, which is generally treated as boot. But Ron also is kicking in $10K of cash. Can the cash contribution offset the net liability relief for boot purposes? The regulations say YES! Treas. Reg. § 1.1031(d)-2, ex. 2(c). Ron's recognized gain, therefore, is $0. Ron's basis in the new property is $30K determined as follows:

$40K Old basis (in both the building and the cash)

+ $30K Mortgage assumed (treated as cash paid)

− $40K Mortgage transferred (treated as cash received)

+ $0K Gain recognized

$30K New basis. *See* Treas. Reg. § 1.1031(d)-2, Ex. 2(c)

Ron's holding period for the new property includes the holding period of his old property, assuming it was a capital asset or § 1231 property. I.R.C. § 1223(1).

4. One possibility is a *three cornered exchange*. This would involve Goodman purchasing Bryan's property and then engaging in a § 1031 exchange with Peacock. As can be seen, although it may take two to tango, it often takes three to do a like kind exchange. A three cornered exchange has some tricky aspects. For example, Peacock will want to be certain that Goodman will obtain the right exchange property. Goodman will want to be certain that Peacock will not back out of the deal after Goodman has bound himself to purchase the exchange property. These objectives are typically accomplished through the use of a contract that includes an escrow arrangement. Goodman may deposit some funds with an escrow agent. Those funds may be forfeitable by Goodman if he fails to perform. A concern for Peacock is whether the doctrine of constructive receipt could cause the money placed in escrow to be treated as boot, or, even worse, as an outright cash sale. The regulations provide that cash held in escrow is not constructively received by Peacock as long as Peacock's right to control receipt is subject to substantial restrictions. Treas. Reg. § 1.1031(k)-1(f).

5. a. The condemnation is a realization event (sale or other disposition) within the meaning of § 1001(a). Charles' gain realized on the condemnation is $60K ($180K amount realized minus $120K adjusted basis).

b. The $60K gain realized will be recognized unless a non-recognition provision applies. I.R.C. § 1001(c). Under § 1033(a)(2), if property is involuntarily converted into money (*e.g.*, a condemnation award), gain realized, if any, will be recognized unless the taxpayer elects non-recognition treatment by purchasing similar-use property within a prescribed time period. [Note gain is recognized to the extent that the conversion proceeds exceed the cost of the qualified replacement property.] The "similar or related in service or use" standard of § 1033 is more stringent than the like-kind standard of § 1031. To achieve a better parity between the replacement requirements in §§ 1031 and 1033, Congress enacted § 1033(g), which allows certain converted real property, such as Charles' building, to be replaced by like-kind property. What is the latest date Charles has to purchase qualified replacement property to recognize any gain? As a general rule, the replacement period begins on the date of involuntary conversion and ends two years after the close of the taxable in which gain is first realized (*i.e.*, when proceeds in excess of basis become available to the taxpayer). I.R.C. § 1033(a)(2)(B). A special three-year replacement period applies to condemnations of business or investment real property described in § 1033(g). Therefore, Charles has until December 31, 2011 (three years after the close of the 2008-the year in which gain was realized.

c. Section 1033 does not permanently exclude gain, instead, it defers gain until disposition of the replacement property. As with § 1031, deferral of gain is achieved through the mechanism of basis. If property is involuntarily converted into money and the taxpayer elects not to recognize gain pursuant to § 1033(a)(2), then the basis of the replacement property is the cost of the replacement property minus the amount of unrecognized gain on the conversion. I.R.C. § 1033(b)(2). Charles' basis in the replacement property is $140K ($200K cost minus $60K unrecognized gain on the conversion).

6. a. Leon has a gain of $300K on the sale of his Charleston residence. Under § 121, a taxpayer may exclude from gross income up to $250K ($500K with respect to certain married couples filing jointly) of gain realized on the sale of a principal residence. To be eligible for the exclusion: (1) the taxpayer must have *owned* the residence and *used* it as a *principal residence* for at least two of the five years before the sale, and (2) the taxpayer must not have claimed the exclusion for another sale within the immediately preceding two year period. Assuming Leon used the Charleston residence as his "principal residence" for two out of the four years he owned it, and assuming Leon did not claim the benefits of § 121 with respect to another residence during the past two years, Leon may exclude $250K of gain

b. Section 121(c) provides a reduced maximum exclusion for taxpayers who sell a principal residence, but who fail to satisfy the ownership and use requirements or the one-sale-every-two years rule. In order to claim a reduced exclusion, the sale must be because of a change in place of employment, health, or unforeseen circumstances. The amount of the reduced maximum exclusion is a portion of the general $250K (or $500K) exclusion amount that would otherwise apply if the taxpayer satisfied the ownership and use requirements. The portion is determined by the following formula:

$$\text{Reduced Maximum Exclusion} = \text{Normal Exclusion Amount} \times \frac{\text{Shorter of (1) period owned and used as a principal residence or (2) period between prior sale for which gain was excluded and current sale}}{\text{24 Months or 730 Days}}$$

Since Leon failed to meet the two-year ownership and use requirements for the exclusion by reason of a change in place of employment, he is eligible to exclude up to $125K of gain ($250K x $\frac{12}{24}$).

c. A husband and wife may exclude up to $500K of gain if: (1) the spouses file a joint return for the year of sale; (2) either spouse meets the two-year ownership requirement with respect to the property; (3) both spouses meet the use requirement with respect to the property; and (4) neither spouse used the exclusion within the last two years. I.R.C. § 121(b)(2)(A). Here, Leslie did not meet the "use" requirement with respect to the property. Accordingly, the requirements for a maximum exclusion of $500K are not met. All is not lost. The § 121 exclusion is determined on an individual basis—$250K of gain is excludable because that is what Leon could have excluded if he had filed a separate return.

d. Now, Leslie does meet the "use" requirement with respect to Leon's property. If they file a joint return, the $300K of gain is excludable. Note: This assumes that Leslie has not used the exclusion within the last two years with respect to any of her property. If so, Leon would be entitled to a maximum exclusion of $250K. In other words, nothing prevents a taxpayer from claiming the exclusion he or she would otherwise be entitled to. I.R.C. § 121(b)(2)(B).

PROBLEM #16 LIMITATIONS ON DEDUCTIONS: "AT RISK" AND "PASSIVE LOSS" RULES

1. a. *1st Year of Operation:* Risky's beginning at risk amount is $75K, the sum of the cash and the basis in the contributed property. I.R.C. § 165(b)(1)(A). Thus, only $75K of the loss is currently deductible. The loan is clearly not qualified non-recourse financing since it is not for a real estate holding activity. I.R.C. § 465(b)(6)(B). The remaining $50K of losses carry over as a deduction next year. I.R.C. § 465(a)(2). Risky's at risk amount falls to zero. I.R.C. § 465(b)(5).

   2nd Year of Operation: The $50K of suspended losses from Year 1 can be deducted from the second year's earnings. I.R.C. § 465(a)(2).

   b. *1st Year of Operation:* Risky's beginning at risk amount is $375K, the sum of the cash, the basis in the contributed property, and the debt. I.R.C. § 465(b)(1)(A) & (B). Thus, all $125K of the loss is currently deductible. Risky's at risk amount falls to $250K. I.R.C. § 465(b)(5).

2. a. A net loss from passive activities is not permitted to offset income from non-passive activities. I.R.C. § 469(a)(1). A passive activity is a trade or business in which the taxpayer does *not* "materially participate." I.R.C. § 469(c)(1). Material participation is participation in the activity on a "regular," "continuous," and "substantial" basis. I.R.C. § 469(h)(1). The regulations set out detailed criteria for meeting the material participation standard, including some bright line tests. A limited partner is automatically deemed *not* a material participant unless the limited partner is also a general partner or meets other requirements. I.R.C. § 469(h)(2); Treas. Reg. § 1.469-5T(e)(1), (2), (3)(ii). In this problem, Passive A. Gressive is a limited partner and not a general partner. Accordingly, he will not be able to offset his law firm earnings with the losses from the limited partnership, unless he meets one of the following three exception to the limited partner passive taint: (1) he works 500 hours or more in the partnership activity; (2) he materially participated in the partnership activity in any 5 of the prior 10 years; or (3) the activity is a personal service activity and he materially participated in that activity in any 3 prior years. Treas. Reg. § 1.469-5T(e)(2) (referring to the three material participation tests in Treas. Reg. § 1.469-5T(a)(1), (5), or (6)).

   b. In contrast to (a) above, it less likely in part b. that Mr. Gressive could meet any of the three exceptions to the limited partner passive taint contained in Treas. Reg. § 1.469-5T(e)(2). His share of the partnership loss ($55) will be disallowed and carries over as a deduction for the next year where it can be used to offset passive income. I.R.C. § 469(b), (d)(1). [NOTE: Portfolio income such as stock dividends, which seems passive, are not deemed passive for purposes of § 469. I.R.C. § 469(e)(1). Thus, passive losses cannot offset portfolio income.]

   c. If Mr. Gressive holds a general partnership interest, as opposed to a limited partnership interest, he may use any one of the seven tests in Treas. Reg. § 1.469-5T(a)(1)-(7) to qualify for material participation. He most likely could meet one and, thus, offset his earnings from law practice with the losses from the partnership.

3. There is a limited exception to the loss disallowance rule for losses from rental real estate activities in which the taxpayer who is at least a 10% owner "actively participates." I.R.C. § 469(i). If the exception applies, the losses are treated as non-passive up to $25K. I.R.C. § 469(i)(1) & (2). However, this amount is reduced by

one dollar for every two dollars by which the taxpayer's adjusted gross income (determined without regard to passive losses) exceeds $100K. I.R.C. § 469(i)(3)(A).

a. If Ma does not "actively participate" as stated in the facts, then she cannot benefit from § 469(i). She will not be able to offset her grocery store income by the losses generated by the apartments.

b. If Ma spends 10 hours per week managing the apartments, the issue is whether she meets the "active participation" requirement. The active participation requirement is not as stringent as the material participation rule. It can be satisfied without regular, continuous, and substantial involvement in operations if the taxpayer participates in the making of significant management decisions. The time spent by Ma each week relates to management of the apartments (most likely approving new tenants, deciding on rental terms, approving repairs and capital improvements). She should be deemed to actively participate and, thus, $25K of the $40K loss can offset income from non-passive activities.

c. The $25K limit is reduced by one dollar for every two dollars by which the taxpayer's adjusted gross income (determined without regard to passive losses) exceeds $100K. I.R.C. § 469(i)(3)(A). Here, Ma Kettle's has adjusted gross income of $150K. As a result, she gets no benefit from the exception. She will not be able to offset her grocery store income by the losses generated by the apartments. [NOTE: If § 467(c)(7) applies to the rental real estate, no assistance is needed from § 469(i). Under this special rule, a rental real property trade or business of a taxpayer is treated as "active" as opposed to a "passive" activity (and, hence, not subject to the passive activity rules). To qualify, however, more than half of the personal services performed by the taxpayer in all trades or business during the year must be performed in real property trades or businesses in which the taxpayer materially participates.]

d. Ma's grocery store income would be passive and could absorb the passive rental losses. Most taxpayers attempt to convert passive losses into active losses to deduct such losses. Ma achieved the same result by instead converting active income into passive income.

e. Dispositions of passive activities by sale can serve to release some or all of the previously disallowed losses for deduction against non-passive income. In the case of an outright sale of a passive activity to an unrelated person, the carried losses are first used for offsetting income from the activity in the year of the sale, then against all other passive income for the year, and then are released for use against the gain on the sale or even against non-passive income. I.R.C. § 469(g)(1)(A). In the case of a sale of a passive activity to a related person, the suspended losses are not released until the related person sells the interest. In the meantime, they remain with the original owner. I.R.C. § 469(g)(1)(B). A taxable installment sale releases the losses in installments in the same proportion as gain recognized in the current year bears to gross profit on the sale. I.R.C. § 469(g)(3). A gift of the activity does not release the carried over losses but the donee's basis in the activity may be stepped up by the amount of the carried over loss (not to exceed fair market value of the activity for loss purposes). I.R.C. § 469(j)(6). See I.R.C. § 1015(a).

Appendix IV

ANSWERS TO CHAPTER 10 PRACTICE EXAMS

(Answers are included for Practice Exams #1, #2, and #3. For answers to Practice Exams #4 and #5, email us your answers at rgershon@charlestonlaw.org or jmaine@usm.maine.edu, and we will critique them!)

SAMPLE ANSWER TO PRACTICE EXAM #1

PROBLEM I

The first thing you need to address in the problem is the paragraph relating to your successful law practice. Under § 61, the $400K in legal fees you earned during 2007 will be included in gross income as compensation for services. The free advice you give to your friends will be gross income to them under § 61, unless they can establish that you intended the free advice to be a gift under § 102. Gifts under § 102 are excluded from gross income. In order to prove that the free advice was intended as a gift, your friends must each show that you performed the services with a detached and disinterested generosity, as required by *C.I.R. v. Duberstein,* 363 U.S. 278 (1960). In order to determine whether, in fact, there is a detached and disinterested generosity, your friends must establish that you did not expect to receive anything in return for the services. In Zsa Zsa's case, for example, the $100K of free tax advice she received will be presumptively income under § 61. If Zsa Zsa can show that the relationship is one of friendship, as opposed a business relationship, she may be able to establish that she has received a gift which will be excluded under § 102.

The amounts you will receive from the "Tax Hotline," will all be gross income under § 61. Specifically, they will be income from the active conduct of a trade or business under § 61(a)(2). The payments that you made to the phone company might be deductions under § 162, or they may be capital expenditures, which are not deductible under § 263. They will qualify as deductible expenses only if they are "ordinary and necessary" expenses incurred in carrying on a trade or business. *Welch v. Helvering,* 290 U.S.111 (1933), refused to give a "black-letter" definition of "ordinary and necessary," saying that life in all its fullness must supply the answer to the riddle. Thus the question of deductibility is a fact question which must be determined on a case by case basis. A business phone line will most likely be ordinary and necessary to the business. To be deductible immediately, however, the payment must be an expense as opposed to a capital expenditure under § 263. An item is an expense if it does not purchase an asset that will last more than one taxable year. Meals, rents and salaries are examples of expenses. On the other hand, the purchase of a computer, a building or an education are capital expenditures, because they provide the taxpayer with an asset lasting more than one taxable year. These payments are deductible, if at all, over the lifetime of the asset rather than in the year of purchase. (See § 179 for an exception which allows for capital expenditures to be deductible in the year of purchase.) Anything having a basis is a capital expenditure.

Whenever you deal with payments surrounding either divorce or separation, you must first address whether these payments meet the requirements of being alimony or separate maintenance payments under § 71(b). Accordingly, you should not discuss recapture of excess alimony until you have discussed the elements of alimony. Section 71(b) requires that payments will only be includable in the recipient's gross income as alimony if they are in cash, they are made to or on behalf of the spouse or ex-spouse, the parties are not living in the same household, and the payments cease upon the death of the recipient spouse. Furthermore, the payments must be pursuant to a decree or a written instrument and there must be nothing in that decree or written instrument that states that the payments will not be treated as alimony.

In the case at hand, Woody will be making cash payments pursuant to a written decree, Woody and Mia will be living in separate households, and the payments will cease upon Mia's death. Furthermore, Woody and Mia have not specified that the payments will be treated as something other than alimony. Consequently, Mia will have gross income of $100K in 2007, $90K in 2008, $70K in 2009 and $20K in 2010. Woody will have an above-the-line deduction of those same amounts pursuant to § 215 and § 62. The $20K per year for child support that Woody will pay Mia will not be included in her gross income and will not be deductible by Woody according to § 71(c).

Since the payments decline in value over the first three years, we must next discuss potential recapture of excess alimony payments. The first thing we must address will be whether there is any excess alimony paid in the second year. Since the $90K payment made in 2008 exceeds the $70K payment made in 2009 by more than $15K, there will be a second year excess. That excess will be $5K, which is determined by subtracting $70K (the third year payment) plus $15K from $90K, or $90K minus $85K, and equals $5K. Next, we must determine the first year excess. The first year excess will be the amount by which the first year payment exceeds the sum of the average of the second year payment minus the second year excess plus the third year payment increased by $15K. In this case, we will be subtracting from the first year payment of $100K, the average of ($90K minus $5K) plus $70K, or $77.5K plus $15K, which equals $92.5K. $100K minus $92.5K gives us an excess first year payment of $7.5K. We add the first year excess to the second year excess to get a total of $12.5K in excess alimony payments. Under § 71(f), Woody will be required to include the $12.5K in his gross income for the third post-separation year. On the other hand, Mia will be entitled to a deduction of $12.5K for that same year.

The illegal kick-backs received by your old army buddy will be gross income under § 61. Specifically, § 1.61-14 of the regulations states that "income" includes income from whatever source derived, including illegal source income. When she gives the money to her son Minor, the 12-year-old, the son will have no gross income, because the amount will be excluded as a gift under § 102. Transactions between family members are presumed to be made out of disinterested generosity. Notice that Minor could not be taxed on the income earned by Major, because that was service income, and the incidence of taxation from service income cannot be shifted gratuitously by assignment from the taxpayer who earned it (*Lucas v. Earl*, 281 U.S. 111 (1930)). When Minor purchased the Blockbuster Video stock for $300K, he had a § 1012 cost basis of $300K. (On the exam, many people forgot to mention Minor's basis in answering this question.) The dividends that Minor received from stock will be gross income to Minor because they were produced by property owned by Minor. The rents generated by the apartments owned by his aunt, however, will be gross income to the aunt because she still owns the underlying property interest. When Minor received the $4,500 in rents, they will be excluded from gross income as a gift under § 102. Thus Minor will be taxed only on the $1,400 he receives as a dividend from Blockbuster. Remember, however, that since Minor is under 14 years old at the end of the taxable year, and since he had dividend income which is unearned income in excess of $1,000, he will be subject to the "Kiddie Tax" under § 1(g). That is, to the extent that his unearned income exceeds $1,000, in this case $400, he will be taxed at his parents' rates. Since I have told you that his mother is alive, you know that one parent is, in fact, alive, which is one of the requirements for the application of the "Kiddie Tax."

At first glance, it would appear that Queenie suffered a loss on the destruction of her business building, because it was worth $200K but she received only $120K from her insurance company. Section 1001, however, tells us that Queenie actually experienced a gain from this transaction since her amount realized (the insurance proceeds of $120K) exceeded her adjusted basis of $50K. Consequently, she had a $70K gain realized on this transaction. Under § 1001(c), all gains realized must be recognized, unless otherwise proved by the Internal Revenue Code. In the case of property destroyed by involuntary conversion such as fire, storm, or other casualty, § 1033 provides that no gain shall be recognized if proceeds, such as insurance, from the involuntary conversion are reinvested in property similar or related in service and use within two years. Accordingly, if Queenie reinvests the insurance proceeds from her tragedy in a new building within two years of the close of the year in which gain is realized, she will not have to report the gain. If she elects to avoid gain recognition, she will have a basis in the new building equal to the basis of the old building. If, on the other hand, she elects to recognize the gain, the character of the gain will be determined under § 1231, because the property was real property used in a trade or business. Subject to the recapture provisions of §§ 1245 and 1250, § 1231 would give Queenie either capital or ordinary treatment, depending upon her other § 1231 transactions for the year. (You really do not have the necessary information in this problem to discuss the § 1231 and §§ 1245/1250 issues fully, but it can't hurt to mention them.)

Queenie's family jewels, on the other hand, do involve an actual tax loss under § 165(c)(3). Her loss, determined under § 1001 was $14K, which was the extent to which her adjusted basis of $14K exceeded her amount realized of 0. Thus, even though her economic loss was $65K, her maximum tax loss is her basis. Section 165 allows for losses to be deductible if they involve property used in the taxpayers trade or business (§ 165(c)(1)), or property used in a transaction entered into for profit (§ 165(c)(2)). Unfortunately, Queenie's jewels do not fall into either of those categories. Fortunately, there is a limited allowance of a deduction for personal losses, if those losses arose from fire, storm, shipwreck, or other casualty, or from theft (§ 165(c)(3)). Queenie's stolen jewels qualify for the deduction under § 165(c)(3) because they resulted from theft and she was not compensated by insurance. Since the government does not wish to be an insurer, however, Queenie's casualty loss will be limited by § 165(h). Section 165(h)(1) limits her loss to the extent that each casualty exceeds $100 (basically, a $100 deductible, much like the deductible under an insurance policy).

Here, Queenie's $14K loss exceeds $100 by $13,900. This loss is further limited by § 165(h)(2) which states that personal casualty losses are deductible only to the extent that the net casualty loss of a taxpayer for a taxable year exceeds 10% of the taxpayer's adjusted gross income. Assuming that Queenie does not have any more casualties this year, she will have a net loss of $13,900. The problem tells us that her adjusted gross income for the year is $130K. Thus, her loss exceeds 10% of her adjusted gross income ($13K), by only $900.

Accordingly, her loss deduction is only $900, even though the property destroyed was worth $65K. To make matters worse, she must itemize this deduction. Thus, if her standard deduction under § 63 exceeds her itemized deductions, she will not be able to deduct her casualty loss at all!

When Lizzie Borden receives $300K in life insurance proceeds, § 101(a) presumes that those proceeds are excluded from gross income because she received them from an insurance company due to the death of an insured. Section 101(a)(2), however, states that when a beneficiary has paid valuable consideration for an insurance policy, the amount excluded will only be the amount of valuable consideration paid by the beneficiary. Accordingly, it might appear that Lizzie will be able to exclude only the $10K she paid for the policy when she purchased it from her parents. There are exceptions under § 101(a)(2) when valuable consideration is paid in a situation involving a partnership or corporation, but this is not the case here. Another exception applies when the purchaser's basis is determined with reference to the basis of the insurance policy in the hands of the insured. For example, if a purchaser acquired the property from a spouse under § 1041, or by gift under § 1015, the basis will be the same as the basis of the insured. In this problem, Lizzie purchased the policy from her parents for $10K when the policy was worth $15K. Accordingly, this was part sale/part gift, because the property was purchased from a family member for less than fair market value. Consequently, under § 1.1015-4 of the regulations, Lizzie's basis in the insurance policy will be determined with reference to her parents' basis, because that regulation states that the donee's basis in a part sale/part gift transaction will be the greater of the donor's basis or the amount paid by the donee. Therefore, Lizzie will be able to exclude the entire $300K from gross income.

Up until 1996, Lizzie could have excluded $5K of the $11K payment from her mother's employer under § 101(b). Section 101(b) provided for an exclusion to employee death benefits. That section was repealed by § 1402(a) of the Small Business Job Protection Act of 1996. After 1996, the entire $11K payment to Lizzie will be income under § 61 because there is no express exclusion provision in the Code for such a payment. The employer might be able to argue that this is an ordinary and necessary expense incurred in carrying on a trade or business, which is deductible under § 162.

Finally, the problem dealing with Ross Parrot is one of my favorite types of problems to give on an exam. It involves a transfer of property in exchange for services. Anytime I give you an exchange of property for services, you need to say that the employee will have income to the extent of the fair market value of the property received, and a basis in the property equal to its fair market value. Both of these results are due to § 1.61-2(d)(2)(i). On the employer's side, you must address potential gain to the employer from using appreciated property to satisfy an obligation, and you must address the employer's potential deduction. Thus, in the problem from this exam, Ross Parrot will have a $50K gain because he used property worth $75K that had only a $25K basis to pay for your services. Ross might be entitled to a $75K deduction under § 162. You, on the other hand, will have $75K of gross income under § 61, and you will have a basis of $75K in the property.

PROBLEM II

Part A.

Even though each of these questions deal with basis, you must not forget to discuss income inclusions and exclusions where applicable. In this case, Henry will have an amount realized of $300 and he has an adjusted basis of $500. Accordingly, he has a realized loss of $200. Section 1041, however, tells us that on transactions between spouses or former spouses incident to a divorce, no gain or loss will be recognized. Consequently, Henry will not be able to recognize the $200 loss. Ann will not have any income on this transaction either, as § 1041 tells us to treat all transactions between spouses as if they were gifts. Ann's basis in the bowling ball will be $500, according to § 1041(b), because she will take Henry's basis in the ball. Additionally, Ann will have a $50 basis in the bowling shoes and she will not have any income, again due to § 1041. Henry, likewise, will not have income on the transfer of the shoes. When Ann sells the ball to King Burger for $300, she will have a loss realized of $200. This is not a part sale/part gift transaction because King Burger is paying the fair market value for the property and not less than the fair market value. I did accept answers calling this a part sale/part gift if the student explained that they assumed that the fair market value had gone up between the time of the receipt of the property and the sale of the property. Furthermore, there is no split basis problem here, even though the fair market value of the property was less than its adjusted basis at the time of the transfer. Section 1015(e) tells us that all transactions involving spouses are governed by § 1041. Section 1041 does not provide for split basis where fair market value is less than the adjusted basis at the time of the transfer. Finally, don't forget to state that King Burger's basis in the ball is $300 under § 1012.

Part B.

The first thing to discuss in dealing with this problem is that Baked and Fried will not have gross income on the receipt of their interest in the property because they have received an inheritance under § 102 of the Code. Furthermore, the basis in the property as a whole will be $100K under § 1014, which governs property acquired from a decedent. When Baked sold her interest to Big Mac for $80K, she will have $80K realized but her basis for determining gain will be disregarded under § 1001(e), which states that whenever someone sells a term interest acquired by gift, inheritance, or from a spouse, the basis for determining gain on the sale of that term interest will be disregarded. Baked's life estate is such a term interest. Accordingly, Baked will have $80K of gain on the sale of the property to Big Mac. Big Mac will have a cost basis in the property of $80K.

If, on the other hand, Baked sold the life estate to Fried, one could argue that the exception under § 1001(e)(3) applies. That exception states that the basis of the term interest will not be disregarded if there is a transaction in which the entire interest in the property is transferred to one person. Even though both parties have not transferred their interest, I think there is a good argument that the property doctrine of merger, which gives rise to a fee simple interest in Fried's hands, should be considered a transfer of the entire property to one person. If that is the case, then Baked will be able to use her basis for determining gain. Assuming that the basis is $80K and she receives $80K, she will have no gain or loss on the transaction.

Part C.

Mat Robertson's sale of his albums to his son, Cliff, will be considered a part sale/part gift because he sold the albums to a family member for less than their fair market value. Cliff will not have income under § 102. Furthermore, Cliff will have a basis in the property equal to the greater of his father's $2K basis or the $25K he paid for the albums. Since the $25K Cliff paid is the greater amount, Cliff's basis will be $25K.

Section 1015(d)(6) allows Cliff to add a portion of the gift tax paid by Mat to Cliff's basis. The amount of increase is determined by using the formula: **increase = net appreciation/ total gift x gift tax paid.** In this case, the formula would be: **increase = $48K/$25K x gift tax paid of $4K.** This is because there is $48K of net appreciation on this gift (50 minus 2) and the total gift is $25K which represents the $25K worth of consideration paid by Cliff subtracted from the fair market value of the gift. Accordingly, Cliff can increase his basis by the entire $4K of gift tax paid. Of course, any time the donee pays more for the property than the donor's adjusted basis, the donee will be able to increase his basis by the entire amount of the gift tax paid. Finally, Mat will have a gain of $23K on the sale of these albums. This is because his basis was $2K, and he sold the property for $25K. This result is dictated by § 1.1001-1(e) of the regulations.

END

SAMPLE ANSWER TO PRACTICE EXAM #2

PROBLEM I

1. The computers sold by the airline are not capital assets because they are depreciable property used in a trade or business. Section 1221 specifically states that such assets are not capital assets. Assuming, however, that the computers have been held by the company for more than one year, they will be § 1231 trade or business assets. When the computers are sold for $1,200 each, having an adjusted basis of $1,100 each, they will give rise to a realized gain of $100 per computer, for a total of $1,000 of gain realized. Section 1231 treats net gains from the sale or exchange of trade or business assets as capital gains, but § 1245, which deals with depreciation recapture, overrides § 1231 to the extent that the gain was derived not from an increase in the value of the property, but rather from a decrease in the basis due to depreciation. In this case, therefore, § 1245 would dictate that the $100 gain on each computer be ordinary income representing recaptured depreciation. Depreciation recapture is determined under § 1245 by taking the lesser of gain realized (amount realized minus adjusted basis), or depreciation taken (original basis minus recomputed basis). In this case, the $100 of gain realized on each computer is less than the $400 of depreciation taken on each computer. Consequently, the entire $100 of gain realized will be deprecation recapture. Furthermore, because all of the gain has been recaptured under § 1245, there is no gain left to go into the § 1231 hotch-pot.

2. When the airline sells 1,000 of its questionably delicious meals, it will realize a gain of $7,500 because it sold the meals for a total of $8,000 and it had a basis of $500. The character of the gain derived from these meals is somewhat questionable. First, one might argue that the meals are normally sold to air travelers in the ordinary course of the airline's trade or business. The cost of the meals is simply included in the traveler's ticket. Accordingly, if the meals are sold to customers in the ordinary course of the airline's trade or business, they are not capital assets under § 1221, and they are not trade or business assets under § 1231. Rather, they are inventory, and their sale will give rise to ordinary income treatment. On the other hand, one might argue that the meals are not normally sold separately to travelers in the ordinary course of the airline's trade or business. If the meals are not inventory, then they would probably be a capital asset, because § 1221 defines capital assets as the whole world except for inventory, depreciable assets used in a trade or business or real property used in a trade or business, accounts receivable derived from either services or sales of inventory, or artwork created by the artist. Since it is doubtful that airline meals would be considered artwork created by an artist, maybe the meals could be capital assets, in which case they would give rise to $7,500 of capital gain which would be characterized as short-term capital gain, if the meals were held for one year or less, or, as it most likely the case based on most airline meals I've had, long term capital gain if the meals have been held for more than one year. Honestly, I think that the best argument is that the meals are part of the airline's inventory and would probably give rise to an ordinary gain, but I would accept an argument to the contrary provided that such argument was well-reasoned. In any event, if you are not certain, simply present both sides and let me know which you think is the best position.

3. The wrecked airplane presents many interesting issues. But don't tell me that on an exam. Too many times, students waste time telling me that a problem presents "many interesting issues" or "I will begin this problem at the beginning and end it at the end." In this case, the airplane is again a depreciable asset used in a trade or business and is, therefore, a § 1231 asset, provided that it has been owned by the airline for more than a year. If the airline did not have insurance, § 1231 would dictate that whenever an asset

used in a trade or business is destroyed by fire, storm, shipwreck, or other casualty, and that destruction results in a loss, the loss will be netted against any casualty gains derived from the destruction of § 1231 assets. If losses exceed gains, the loss will be an ordinary loss. If gains exceed losses, the gain will be thrown in with the sales and exchanges and the condemnations of § 1231 assets. In this case, however, the airline had $4 million of insurance. If it receives that $4 million, it will have an amount realized of $4 million, an adjusted basis of $1 million, and a gain realized of $3 million. That gain realized will be all ordinary income since the $3 million gain realized is less than the $9 million of depreciation taken on the airplane. If, however, the airline opts to reinvest the proceeds from the insurance in a new airplane, it can avoid gain recognition under § 1033. In this case, the airline would have two years to reinvest the proceeds. Note that §§ 1031 and 1033 override the recapture provisions of §§ 1245 and 1250. Accordingly, the airline may wish to reinvest the proceeds in a new airplane in order to avoid recognizing $3 million of ordinary income.

4. The condemnation of the building will give rise to an amount realized of $150K and a gain realized of $50K, since the airline had an adjusted basis of $100K in the building. The building is not a capital asset because it is real property used in a trade or business. Note that even if the real property was not depreciable, it would be excluded from the coverage of § 1221, because § 1221 says that capital assets do not include *any* real property used in a trade or business. Real property used in a trade or business, however, will meet the definition of § 1231, again assuming that the property has been held by the company for more than one year. Normally, in order to get capital gain treatment, we must have the sale or exchange of a capital asset. Section 1231, however, gives potential capital gain treatment even when there is no sale or exchange and the asset involved is not a capital asset. Such will be the case in the condemnation of the airline's building. Consequently, the $50K gain derived on the condemnation of the building will be considered a capital gain if the airline's net § 1231 transactions for the year result in a gain. Once again, however, the airline could avoid gain recognition this year if it chooses to reinvest the proceeds in another piece of real estate under § 1033. In order to meet the provision of § 1033, the airline would need to make this reinvestment within three years. The airline's basis in the building it acquires in such a nonrecognition transaction will be $100K, which was the basis it had in its old building. If the airline invested more than $100K in a replacement building, but less than $150K, it would have to recognize gain to the extent that it did not reinvest the entire amount of the proceeds it received from the government.

PROBLEM II

Assuming that Homer is not a stock broker, the shares of stock that he sells will be capital assets. Since Homer has sold or exchanged a capital asset, the result will be either capital gain or loss, as the case may be. When Homer sold the Questionable, Inc. stock for $500, he has an amount realized of $500, an adjusted basis of $10K and, therefore, he has a loss realized of $9,500. This loss will be a short-term capital loss, because Homer has held the stock for one year or less. Homer will recognize this loss because there are no provisions in the code allowing for nonrecognition on the sale of stock.

As to the sale of the Prosperous, Inc. stock, Homer will have a $750 gain. His amount realized was $1,000, his adjusted basis was $250 and, therefore, the gain was $750. This will be a long-term capital gain, because Homer has sold a capital asset which he held for more than a year. Thus, for the year, Homer has a net short-term loss of $9,500 and a net long-term gain of $750. Sections 1211 and 1212 of the Internal Revenue Code tell us that Homer will be able to take his short-term loss to the extent of net long-term gain.

Consequently, the $750 of long-term gain will be offset by his short-term loss. Furthermore, Homer will have an excess loss of $8,750. Section 1211 tells us that Homer will be able to use $3,000 of this loss to offset his ordinary income. The remaining $5,750 of short-term loss will be carried over to the next year as a short-term loss for 2008.

As to the charitable contribution planning portion of this problem, it is important to discuss ways in which Homer will be able to maximize his tax benefit while minimizing his cost. The best way to do that is simply to assess the cost versus benefit of a contribution of each of the possible pieces of property that Homer has. Since Homer has $100K of adjusted gross income, which will be his contribution base as defined by § 170, Homer will be able to make a maximum deductible contribution of $50K for this year. That is because, under § 170(b)(1)(A), the greatest amount of contribution which is deductible for a year will be fifty percent of the taxpayer's contribution base. Furthermore, in a planning question, it is easy to eliminate contributions to institutions like the Save the Cockroach Foundation because they are § 170(b)(1)(B) private foundations. Therefore, you can simply tell me that contributions to § 170(b)(1)(B) charities are limited to a much greater degree that contributions to § 170(b)(1)(A) charities, and that the potential for using unrealized appreciation as part of a contribution is available only when applied to contributions to § 170(b)(1)(A) charities. Thus, you need not really even discuss specific contributions to the § 170(b)(1)(B) charity after giving me that explanation.

If Homer gives $50K in cash to the good charity, he will be able to take a $50K current deduction. However, his cost in making that contribution will be greater than his tax benefit. That is, if Homer is in the thirty-three percent tax bracket, he will save $16,500 in taxes by making this contribution. But, he will also be giving the charity $33,500 that he could have kept had he simply paid his taxes and not made the contribution. The reason that Homer can deduct the entire $50K if he makes just the cash contribution is that § 170(b)(1)(A) allows him to deduct up to fifty percent of his adjusted gross income for the year. If Homer decides to give the cash, which he probably should not, he certainly would not want to give any other contributions for the year, because they would yield no deduction for him in the current year.

The land held for investment has promise. It is a long-term capital gain asset because it was held by Homer for more than one year and it does not fall under any of the exceptions under §§ 1221 or 1231. Remember that § 1231 property is considered to be capital gain property for purposes of planning under § 170. If Homer gives the land to a § 170(b)(1)(A) charity, his contribution amount will be its fair market value of $40K. This is because § 170(e) requires a reduction in a taxpayer's contribution to the extent that a sale of the property would have yielded a gain other than a long-term capital gain. Since this is long-term capital gain property, that is not the case here. Furthermore, § 170(e)(1)(B) requires a reduction of the amount that would have been long-term capital gain in cases of contributions of capital gain property to a bad charity, or in cases of contributions of tangible personal property unrelated to the function of the charity. If Homer gives the land to a good charity, he will not have to reduce the amount of his contribution because land is not tangible personal property. Thus, Homer's contribution would be $40K even though the cost of the land was only $10K. If Homer decided to give the land and no other property, he would be able to take a deduction of $30K for the current year. This is because when a taxpayer contributes long-term capital gain property, and that taxpayer is allowed to use the fair market value as the amount of the contribution for that property, there is lower deduction limit under § 170(b)(1)(C). That limit is thirty percent of the taxpayer's adjusted gross income. In Homer's case, he would be allowed to take a $30K current deduction, and under the parameters set forth by § 170(d), he would be allowed to carry over the remaining $10K of contribution as a long-term capital gain contribution applicable for 2008. He would want to make sure he could use this contribution in 2008, because carry-overs can only be taken for a five year period, and carry-overs from earlier years are always taken into account after carry-overs from more recent years. Should Homer decide to contribute the land, his cost will be less than the overall benefit. He has invested $10K after tax dollars in the property. He will be entitled to a tax savings (again assuming a thirty-three percent bracket) of $13,200 if he assures that he will use the $10K carry-over that is not deductible this year. In the current year, Homer's deduction will save him $9,900 in taxes. By comparison, therefore, this is clearly a better choice than a gift of cash.

The stock purchased by Homer in 1950 is not a good candidate for contribution to charity. In fact, depreciated property is never a good item to give to charity because § 170(e) requires a reduction in a contribution's amount to the extent that there would have been gain had the asset been sold. Therefore, in any case where the property has declined in value, the lower fair market value will be the amount of the contribution. Homer would be better off selling the stock for $40K and taking a loss of $5K. If he did sell the stock for a loss, it would be a long-term capital loss which would be carried over to the next year as a long-term capital loss because Homer would have already exceeded the limit set by § 1211 when he sold his shares of stock in the first part of the question.

If Homer decided to give the stock to charity, he would have a contribution of $40K, even though he had $45K after taxes invested in the property. From a cost benefit point of view, this is not a very wise choice. The contribution of the stock would yield a deduction of $40K for the year because, since this is not long-term capital gain property, the contribution would fall under the fifty percent limitation of § 170(b)(1)(A).

The contribution amount for the inventory will be only $1,000. This is because § 170(e)(1)(A) requires us to reduce the amount of contribution by an amount which would not have been long-term capital gain had the property been sold rather than given to charity. Consequently, Homer would have to reduce the $6K fair market value of the property by the $5K which would have been gained had he sold the property.

In fact, any time one makes a contribution of inventory like the property Homer is giving here, the basis will be the amount of the contribution. Inventory is not a capital asset because § 1221 states that capital assets do not include amounts which would properly be considered inventory. Should Homer decide to give the inventory to the charity, the entire $1,000 will be deductible, but once again, Homer's out-of-pocket cost will be greater than his tax savings. That is, he has $1,000 after taxes invested in the inventory which he could have gotten back tax-free had he sold the inventory. His tax savings generated by contributing the inventory will be only $330.

The personal furniture is a long-term capital asset because it does not fall under any of the exceptions under § 1221, and because Homer has held the property for more than one year. Section 170(e)(1)(B) requires a reduction in the amount of a contribution of long-term capital gain property that is tangible personal property if the property is unrelated to the purpose of the charity. This is an important planning consideration for Homer because, if the property is related to the charity's exempt function, his contribution amount will be $32K. If the contribution is not related to the charity's exempt function, the amount of the contribution will only be $7K, which will represent a reduction in the contribution by the amount which would have been capital gain had Homer sold the property instead of giving it. Homer will want to establish that the charity will, in fact, use the furniture, and he will want to stress that he expects the charity to, in fact, use the furniture for several years. See I.R.C. §§ 170(e)(1)(B)(i)(II), (e)(7). If Homer can establish that the furniture will be used by the charity, his contribution will be $32K. He will be able to deduct $30K of that $32K currently. This is because the contribution would fall under § 170(b)(1)(C) and be subject to the limitation equal to thirty percent of his adjusted gross income. The remaining $2,000 would be carried over as a contribution for the next year.

From a planning perspective, the best property for Homer to give from a cost benefit analysis would be the land. The cash and the inventory will give rise to cost greater than Homer's tax benefit. The stock, as was stated before, is not a good item to contribute, but would be a good item to sell. This leaves the land and the furniture as the prime candidates for contribution. (Anytime you can take advantage of appreciation in property as part of a contribution, you should try to do so.)

I would accept an answer that gave rise to a contribution of either the land or the furniture. The land will give a current deduction of $30K, which is a current tax savings of $9,900. The cost of this tax savings is $10K, but there would be a $10K carry-over to 2008 which would give rise to another potential $3,300 in tax savings. The overall tax savings would therefore be in excess of $13K, even though Homer's cost was $10K.

In the current year, the contribution of the furniture would cost Homer only $7K and he would derive a benefit of $9,900, which is the same benefit he could derive currently by contributing the land. The $2K carried over to 2008 would give rise to another $660 in savings. Accordingly, a contribution of the furniture would cost Homer $7K and give rise to a total of $10,560 of savings total over the two years, assuming that Homer, in fact, used the $2K carry-over in the next year. The land would give rise to a $12K plus tax savings for a cost of $10K. Both of these are acceptable schemes. Of course, all of these answers assume that Homer, in fact, wants to give something away because he will always be better off selling the property and keeping the proceeds than he would be giving it away.

PROBLEM III

The first thing we need to address whenever we deal with several activities, one of which is a loss activity, will be the at-risk rules under § 465. In this case, Mr. Head will have $500K at risk because § 465 will not consider the $1 million of non-recourse indebtedness as an at-risk amount. Accordingly, when his deductible expenditures exceeded his income by $520K, he would have a $520K loss under § 465(d). Section 465(a) tells us that he will not get a current deduction to the extent that he is not at risk. Thus, in this case, he will only be able to take a $500K deduction against other activities for the current year. The other $20K, the amount by which he was not at risk, will be carried over as a deduction attributable to the boat rental business for the year 2008.

Head would love to be able to take the full $500K of deductions against his income from other sources. Unfortunately, § 469 states that to the extent Head has net passive losses, they will not be deductible in the current year. Consequently, it is important to determine whether his yacht rental business is, in fact, a passive activity. Section 469(c)(2) states that passive activity includes any rental activity. Therefore, the yacht rental business is a passive activity. Since it is a passive activity, the $500K of losses can only be used to offset passive income. Clearly, the $200K he made from his lawn mower rental business will be passive income. This is because § 469(c)(2) treats all rental activities as passive activities. This will leave Head with $300K of losses from passive activities. He will be able to offset the income from his college book store only if that income is passive source income. Since Head works 10 hours a week in the book store, which will add up to 500 hours per year, he will be considered to materially participate in the book store under § 1.469-5T of the regulations. When a taxpayer materially participates in any activity other than a rental activity, that activity is not a passive activity. Hence, the remaining $300K of loss will be a net passive loss that will not be deductible in 2007. Instead, Head must carry that loss over as a deduction attributable to the yacht rental business for the year 2008.

What would happen to your answer in #1 if the liability had been a recourse debt in 2007 which had been switched to non-recourse in 2008? If that were the case, Head would have been at risk to the full extent of the $520K net loss he incurred in 2007. He would have been able to offset the $200K from his lawn mower rental business, but would have a carry-over loss of $320K under § 469. If Head switched his liability from recourse to non-recourse in 2008, he would have a negative at-risk amount in 2008. This would occur because his at-risk amount was $1.5 million for 2007. He took $520K of losses in 2007, leaving him with $980K at risk at the end of 2007. When he switched the $1 million recourse liability to non-recourse in 2008, he reduced his amount at-risk by $1 million. Accordingly, when he subtracted $1 million from $980K he was in a situation of being negative at-risk by $20K. Section 465 states that whenever a taxpayer's amount at-risk goes below zero, the taxpayer will have gross income to the extent the amount at-risk is below zero. Thus, in this case, Head would have $20K of gross income in 2008. Furthermore, § 465 tells us to treat the amount included in gross income as a deduction attributable to the next year. In this case, Head will have a $20K deduction attributable to the yacht rental business for the year 2009.

None of the above transactions would be affected by the exchange Head made trading his yacht for a yacht owned by another taxpayer. Such a change would only occur if Head had died, or if this had been a fully taxable transaction under § 469(g). Thus, this problem should focus on the § 1031 consequences of the exchange. The first thing you should do in any transaction involving exchanges of property would be to look to see if there is any gain or loss realized under § 1001. In this case, Head has $600K of gain realized. This answer would be based on the fact that he had an amount realized of $2 million attributable to the fair market value of the property he received, plus $100K which represents the net amount of debt relief he benefited from. After all, he had $1 million of debt before the transaction and only $900K after the transaction. Accordingly, his equity in the property was increased from $1 million to $1.1 million on the transaction. In any event, the gain realized will be recognized unless some other section in the Code says otherwise. In this case, § 1031 might apply. In order for § 1031 to apply, a taxpayer must substantiate that he has exchanged property used in a trade or business, or held for the production of income, solely for like-kind property to be used either in a trade or business or for the production of income. If a taxpayer receives something other than like-kind property in an exchange that would have otherwise qualified for § 1031, § 1031(b) states that the gain will be recognized but only to the extent of the fair market value of that other property plus any cash received on the exchange. In this case, Head is trading the yacht, which is either going to be a business yacht or a yacht used for the production of income, for another yacht which we can assume he will also use for the production of income. An exchange of a yacht for a yacht would certainly be a like-kind exchange, but on the exam, I will give you more information about how a taxpayer like Head would intend to use the property he is receiving in an exchange. If he simply planned to use the yacht as a pleasure vehicle, § 1031 would not apply.

Thus, initially, it appears that § 1031 would provide nonrecognition treatment for Head in this transaction. The exchange of liabilities, however, presents a potential problem. The Code states that a taxpayer will be treated as having received cash to the extent that he has relief from liabilities. In this case, if we follow the strict language of the Code, Head would be treated as having received $1 million in cash in this transaction. In that case, since the $1 million would exceed his gain realized, all gain realized would be recognized. The regulations, on the other hand, provide an approach which is much more consistent with the idea of deferring taxes on exchanges in a business or investment situation. The regulations tell us to treat relief of indebtedness as cash only to the extent of net debt relief. In this case, Head started with $1 million of debt and ended up with $900K of debt. Thus, he will have a net debt relief of $100K. This $100K will be treated as cash received by Head, and Head will, in turn, be forced to recognize gain to the extent of that $100K. The rest of his gain realized will not be recognized until he disposes of the property in a transaction which does not qualify for nonrecognition treatment.

Finally, it is important to address Head's basis in the newly acquired property. The Code tells us his basis will be the same as the basis of property he transferred minus any cash and the fair market value of any boot he received, then increased by any gain recognized on the transaction. In essence, in any nonrecognition transaction, the basis in property acquired will always be the same as the basis of property transferred, plus an additional consideration paid on the transaction. In this case, Head would have a $1.5 million basis decreased by $100K, the net decrease in his liabilities, and increased by the $100K of gain he recognized. In other words, Head would keep a $1.5 million basis in his new property. I did not give you the other party's basis in his yacht, but if the other party qualifies for nonrecognition treatment, his basis will be the same as his basis in his original yacht increased by $100K. This is because the other party started with a $900K debt and he increased his debt to $1 million after the exchange. He would be able to increase his basis to the extent of his net increase in liabilities.

One final note—the new yacht received in a tax-free exchange would be treated as the same activity as the old yacht for purposes of §§ 465 and 469. Note that Head's at-risk amount would increase because he has exchanged $1 million of non-recourse debt for $900K of recourse debt.

END

SAMPLE ANSWER TO PRACTICE EXAM #3

Embezzled Funds and Settlement Proceeds. The $100,000 embezzlement proceeds are included in Taxpayer's gross income, as income from illegal activity is taxable despite the recipient's legal obligation to make restitution. (*See James v. United States*, 366 U.S. 213 (1961).) Taxpayer may attempt to characterize the illegal receipts as "loans" to avoid gross income. However, we can assume here, as in most cases, there is no express acknowledgment of an obligation to repay; even if there is, Taxpayer is most likely lying about his intent to repay. If Taxpayer includes the embezzled funds in gross income and subsequently repays his employer, he would be entitled to a deduction in the year of repayment. (*See* Rev. Rul. 65-254, 1965-2 C.B. 50 (holding that repayment of embezzled funds is a loss deductible under § 165).) The $50,000 out-of-court settlement is excludable from gross income. Although it appears to be an accession to wealth, § 104(a)(2) specifically excludes from gross income all damages received (whether by suit or settlement) "on account of" personal, physical injury. The origin of the claim here is a personal physical injury. Thus, the full $50,000—including the payment for lost wages—is excludable.

Sale of X Stock. The first property transaction—the sale of X stock—is a realization event under § 1001. Taxpayer's *adjusted basis* is $25,000 ($25,000 cost basis per § 1012 with no adjustments per § 1016). Taxpayer's *amount realized* is $15,000 (the amount of money received per § 1001(b)). Accordingly, Taxpayer's *loss realized* is $10,000 ($25,000 AB minus $15,000 AB). IRC § 1001(a). The loss is *recognized* because there is no applicable nonrecognition provision. IRC § 1001(c). The next issue is whether the loss is a deductible loss under § 165(a). In the case of individuals, only three types of losses are deductible: business losses, investment losses, and casualty losses. IRC § 165(c)(1)-(3). Taxpayer's loss is a deductible loss, because it is an investment loss under § 165(c)(2). Section 165(f) cautions us, however, that the loss, if characterized as "capital loss," will be subject to the capital loss limitations under §§ 1211 and 1212 and may not be allowed in full in the current year. Therefore, the next issue pertains to the character of the $10,000 loss. A short term capital loss is defined as a "loss from the sale or exchange of a capital asset held for not more than one year" and a long term capital loss is defined as a "loss from the sale or exchange of a capital asset held for more than one year." I.R.C. § 1222(2), (4). The X stock was a capital asset within the meaning of § 1221, because it did not fall within any of the exceptions in § 1221(a)(1)-(8) (*e.g.*, nothing suggests that Taxpayer is a dealer in securities). The X stock was also held for less than a year, because in determining the holding period of an asset we ignore the day of acquisition and include the day of sale. Rev. Rul. 66-7. Accordingly, the $10,000 loss is characterized as a short term capital loss. Before we actually apply the capital loss limitation rules of §§ 1211 and 1212 to see how much of this loss is allowed in the current year, we need to analyze all the property transactions that occur during the year. [The tax consequences of the $1,000 interest payment will be addressed below.]

Sale of Y Stock. The second property transaction—the sale of Y stock—is a realization event under § 1001. What is Taxpayer's adjusted basis in the Y stock? Taxpayer acquired the stock as a gift from Father, excludable from gross income in 2006 per § 102(a) (assuming Father was not Taxpayer's employer and assuming the gift proceeded from Father's detached and disinterested generosity). I.R.C. § 102(a); *Duberstein*. As a result, we must turn to § 1015 to determine Taxpayer's basis in the Y stock. As a general rule, Taxpayer would take Father's adjusted basis at the time of gift ($30,000); however, because Father's adjusted basis at the time of gift ($30,000) exceeded the stock's fair market value at the time of gift ($15,000), Taxpayer's basis is the lower fair market value ($15,000) "for purposes of determining loss." I.R.C. § 1015(a) (*See* "except" language). There are no § 1016 adjustments as dividends do not impact basis. No gift taxes were paid by Father. Accordingly Taxpayer's adjusted basis in the Y stock is $15,000. Taxpayer's amount realized is $10,000, the amount of money received. Accordingly, Taxpayer's loss realized is $5,000. The loss is recognized per § 1001(c). But the important question is whether the loss is "deductible" under § 165? It would appear so, as the § 165(c)(2) limitation is satisfied. However, § 267(a), an overriding Code provision, provides that NO deduction shall be allowed in respect of any loss from the sale of property between persons specified in § 267(b). Under § 267(b), Taxpayer and Sister are "members of a family," as defined in § 267(c)(4). As a result of this disallowance provision, Taxpayer may not deduct the $10,000 loss on the sale of Y stock to Sister. Because no deduction is allowed to Taxpayer, character of the loss is irrelevant. [Note: Although Taxpayer does not get a loss deduction, Sister will reduce the amount of gain recognized on later sale of the stock by the amount of loss disallowed to Taxpayer. More specifically, under § 267(d), Sister's gain realized, if any, on later sale of the stock will be recognized only to the extent it exceeds the loss that was disallowed to Taxpayer. For now, Sister has a § 1012 cost basis in the Y stock of $10,000.] The tax consequences of the dividend will be addressed below.

Sale of Summer Home. The third property transaction—the sale of the summer home—is a Part Sale, Part Gift to Sister, because Sister is paying less than fair market value and Taxpayer is accepting less out of love and respect for her. Under Treas. Reg. § 1.1001-1(e), Taxpayer's gain realized is amount realized minus adjusted basis. [Note that in determining the amount of gain, Taxpayer will be able to recover 100% of his adjusted basis even though Taxpayer's amount realized is less than 100% of the fair market value. This would not be the case if Taxpayer had made a part sale, part gift to a charity. Review I.R.C. § 1011(b).] Taxpayer's amount realized on the sale to Sister is the $80,000—that is, the amount of money received ($30,000) plus the liability assumed by Sister ($50,000).

I.R.C. § 1001(b); *Crane*. What is Taxpayer's adjusted basis in the summer home? Taxpayer acquired the home as a devise from Uncle, excludable from gross income in 2002 per § 102(a). (We're told that Taxpayer did not work for Uncle; hence the exception in § 102(c) does not apply. We can assume that the devise was out of Uncle's detached and disinterested generosity.) As a result, Taxpayer's initial basis in the home was $45,000—fair market value at the time of Uncle's death per § 1014. Were there any basis adjustments by Taxpayer during the time he held the property? Taxpayer made $30,000 of capital improvements in 2007 and must increase basis in that amount per § 1016(a)(1). Taxpayer could not depreciate the summer home (personal property), so there were no downward adjustments per § 1016(a)(2). Taxpayer's adjusted basis, therefore, is $75,000. With an amount realized of $80,000 and an adjusted basis of $75,000, Taxpayer realizes a gain of $5,000 on the sale of the summer home. I.R.C. § 1001(a).

The next issue is whether the gain is recognized. I.R.C. § 1001(c). The only potential exclusion rule is § 121, which excludes gain from the sale of property if the property has been owned and used by the taxpayer as the taxpayer's "principal residence" for two out of the last five years. I.R.C. § 121(a). Is the summer home a "principal residence" within the meaning of § 121? A taxpayer may have more than one residence; but only one will constitute a principal residence for any given year. The regulations provide that whether property is used by the taxpayer as a principal residence depends upon all the facts and circumstances. The property that the taxpayer uses a majority of the time during the year ordinarily will be considered the taxpayer's principal residence. Treas. Reg. § 1.121-1(b). The facts state specifically that the residence is not used as his principal residence. Accordingly § 121 does not apply, and Taxpayer has $5,000 of gain derived from dealing in property included in gross income under § 61(a)(3).

The next issue is the proper character of this recognized gain. Taxpayer would prefer the gain to be characterized as long term capital gain, because such gains are generally taxed at lower rates than ordinary income. A long term capital gain is defined as gain from the sale or exchange of a capital asset held for more than one year. I.R.C. § 1222(3). The summer home is a capital asset because it does not fall within any of the exceptions in § 1221(a)(1)-(8), and it was actually held by Taxpayer for more than one year. Accordingly, the gain is characterized as a long term capital gain under the general capital gain and loss provisions. Special characterization rules, such as §§ 1231 and 1245, are inapplicable here. The rate applicable to this gain will be discussed below after all transactions have been analyzed.

[It should be noted that when Taxpayer borrowed $30,000 from The Money Store in 2007, Taxpayer did not have to include the loan proceeds in gross income. The reason is that there was no accession to wealth; the increase in assets of $30,000 was offset by a corresponding liability to repay that amount. The tax consequences of the home mortgage interest will be considered below.] Sister's basis in the home, determined under Treas. Reg. § 1.1015-4 is $80,000—the greater of the amount Sister paid ($80,000) or Taxpayer's adjusted basis ($75,000).

Sale of Truck. The fourth property transaction—the sale of the truck—is a realization event under § 1001. Taxpayer's amount realized on the sale is $20,000, the amount of money received. I.R.C. § 1001(b). Taxpayer acquired the truck on May 15, 2008, as a gift excludable from gross income. I.R.C. § 102(a), *Duberstein.* Accordingly, Taxpayer's initial basis in the truck was Cousin Leo's adjusted basis at the time of gift. I.R.C. § 1015(a). [Note that the exception in § 1015 does not apply because Cousin's adjusted basis in the truck did not exceed the truck's fair market value at the time of gift.] Cousin's initial cost basis in the truck of $15,000 (§ 1012) was decreased for depreciation allowances (§ 1016). The facts do not tell us what the depreciation deductions were, but we can figure them out. The truck was depreciable property in Cousin's hands, because it was subject to wear and tear and was used in Cousin's trade or business. I.R.C. § 167. The truck had an "applicable recovery period" of five years assuming it was a "light general purpose truck." I.R.C. § 168(a)(2), (c), (e)(3)(B)(i). Because Cousin actually held the truck for longer than the applicable recovery, he fully depreciated the truck claiming a total of $15,000 in depreciation deductions. Therefore, Cousin's adjusted basis in the truck at time of gift to Taxpayer, and, hence, Taxpayer's initial basis in the truck, was $0. After Taxpayer received the truck, he could not take depreciation deductions with respect to the truck even though he used the truck in his trade or business of selling firewood. That is because he had no basis in the truck I.R.C. § 167(c). [Note that even if Taxpayer had a basis in the truck, he would not be able to depreciate the truck, because no depreciation is allowed when property is placed in service and disposed of in the same year. Treas. Reg. § 1.168(d)-1(b)(3)(ii).] In sum, Taxpayer's adjusted basis in the truck at the time of sale was $0. Taxpayer's gain realized on the sale is $20,000 ($20,000 AR minus $0 AB). The gain realized is recognized per § 1001(c).

The next issue is the character of the recognized gain. Taxpayer would like the gain to be characterized as long term capital gain to receive preferential rate treatment. A long term capital gain is defined as *gain* from the *sale or exchange* of a *capital asset* held for *more than one year.* IRC § 1222(3). The truck is not a capital asset within the meaning of § 1221, because it is depreciable property. It appears, then, that the $20,000 gain is characterized as ordinary income. But wait! Section 1231 may add to the characterization issue. Is the gain considered "section 1231 gain"? Section 1231 gain is defined as recognized gain on the sale or exchange of property used in the trade or business. I.R.C. § 1231(a)(3)(A)(i). Is the truck considered "property used in the trade or business" within the meaning of § 1231? The term "property used in the trade or business" means property used in the trade or business (YES!), of a character which is subject to the allowance for depreciation (YES!), held for more than one year (UH OH!). I.R.C. § 1231(b). Taxpayer actually held the truck for only five months, so it would appear at first that § 1231 does not apply. But, because Taxpayer acquired the truck by gift and his basis was determined by reference to Cousin's basis, Taxpayer can "tack" onto his actual holding period Cousin's holding period in the truck. I.R.C. § 1223(2). Therefore, this truck is "section 1231 property," and the gain is section 1231 gain to be placed in the § 1231 principal hotchpot to be netted with other § 1231 gains and losses to determine the gain's ultimate character. Before we actually apply § 1231 and perform any netting, we must turn to § 1245 to see whether it applies. Section 1245 is an overriding provision. IRC § 1245(d). Section 1245 recapture comes into play whenever "section 1245 property" is "disposed of." IRC § 1245(a)(1). The truck is § 1245 property because it is "property which is or has been property of a character subject to allowance for depreciation," and it is disposed of in a sale. IRC § 1245(a)(3). Accordingly, § 1245 will reach into our § 1231 principal hotchpot and pull out part or all of the § 1231 gain and characterize it as ordinary income. The amount treated as ordinary income under § 1245 is the lower of: (1) "recomputed basis" minus adjusted basis; or (2) amount realized minus adjusted basis. IRC § 1245(a)(1). Recomputed basis is simply the property's adjusted basis recomputed by adding back all adjustments reflected in the adjusted basis "on account of deductions . . . allowed or allowable to the taxpayer *or to any other person* for depreciation." IRC § 1245(a)(1)(A). Here, recomputed basis of $15,000 (that is, Taxpayer's adjusted basis of $0K plus depreciation deductions allowed to Cousin of $15,000) exceeds adjusted basis of $0, by $15,000 (the amount of depreciation deductions claimed by Cousin). Amount realized of $20,000 exceeds adjusted basis of $0, by $20,000 (the amount of gain realized by Taxpayer). The lower of the two figures ($15,000) is the amount to be recaptured as ordinary income (the amount attributable to previous depreciation deductions taken with respect to the truck, albeit by Cousin). In conclusion, § 1245 will reach into the § 1231 hotchpot and pull out $15,000 as ordinary income. The remaining $5,000 of gain recognized remains in the principal hotchpot to be netted with all other § 1231 gains and losses during the year. There were no other § 1231 gains or losses. Accordingly, the $5,000 § 1231 gain comes out as long term capital gain, because § 1231 gains for the year of $5,000 exceeded § 1231 losses for the year of $0. I.R.C. § 1231(a)(1). [Note that § 1239 did not apply to characterize this gain as ordinary because the facts state that Taxpayer sold the truck to an unrelated third party.]

Sale of "Cords" of Wood. Taxpayer sold for $5,000 cords of wood for which he paid $2,500. This results in $2,500 of ordinary income (total sales less cost of good sold). I.R.C. § 61(a)(2); Treas. Reg. § 1.61-3. [Note that treating this transaction as gain derived from dealing in property under § 61(a)(3) would produce the same result, as the cords of wood are not capital assets under § 1221 or quasi-capital assets under § 1231(b).]

Receipt of Dividends and Payment of Interest. During the year, Taxpayer received $500 in dividends with respect to Y stock. Taxpayer must include the dividends in gross income per § 61(a)(7).

Taxpayer paid $1,000 in interest on a loan to purchase X stock. Although § 163 allows a deduction for interest paid during the year, § 163(h)(1) disallows any deduction for "personal interest." Excluded from the definition of personal interest is "investment interest" within the meaning of § 163(d). I.R.C. § 163(h)(2)(B). Under § 163(d)(1), the deductibility of investment interest for any year is limited to the net investment income of the taxpayer for the year, which is defined as investment income minus investment expenses. I.R.C. § 163(d)(4)(A). Taxpayer's net investment income for the year is $500 ($500 dividends with respect to Y stock minus $0 investment expenses). Accordingly, Taxpayer may only deduct $500 of his $1,000 investment interest. The remaining $500 is not currently deductible, but will be carried forward to the next tax year and treated as investment interest paid in that year. I.R.C. § 162(d). [Note that "net investment income" does not include net capital gains from dispositions of investment property unless a taxpayer makes an election to take them into account; the cost of making an election is that the taxpayer cannot take advantage of the maximum capital gains rate applicable to such gains. I.R.C. §§ 1(h)(2), 163(d)(4)(b)(iii).]

Taxpayer paid $3,000 mortgage interest on the home equity loan from The Money Store. Excluded from the definition of non-deductible "personal interest" is "qualified residence interest" within the meaning of § 163(h)(3). I.R.C. § 163(h)(2)(D). The $3,000 interest constitutes qualified residence interest if it is interest paid on either acquisition indebtedness or home equity indebtedness with respect to a qualified residence. Although the relevant loan here is called a "home equity loan" by The Money Store, it is actually considered "acquisition indebtedness" by the Code (*i.e.*, indebtedness incurred in acquiring, constructing, or *substantially improving* any *qualified residence* of the taxpayer, and is secured by such residence). The summer home is a qualified residence because a qualified residence includes not only a taxpayer's principal residence (not met here), but also one other residence of the taxpayer which is used by the taxpayer as a residence within the meaning of § 280A(d)(1) (let's assume Taxpayer used the summer home for at least 14 days during the year). I.R.C. § 163(h)(4)(A). Nothing in the facts suggests that Taxpayer has more than $1 million of acquisition indebtedness. I.R.C. § 163(h)(3)(B)(ii). As a result, Taxpayer may fully deduct the $3,000 interest.

Summary of Above. The above transactions produce the following:

Gross Income:

$100,000	Ordinary income	Embezzled proceeds
5,000	LTCG	Summer home
5,000	LTCG	Truck (§ 1231)
15,000	Ordinary income	Truck (§ 1245)
2,500	Ordinary income	Cords of Wood
500	Taxed as cap gains	Dividends

Deductions:

$ 10,000	STCL	X stock
5,000	LTCL	Carry over from last year
500	Ordinary deduction	Investment interest
3,000	Ordinary deduction	Qualified residence interest

We see that Taxpayer has a "net capital loss" for the year—that is, capital losses for the year ($15,000) exceed capital gains for the year ($10,000). I.R.C. § 1222(10). We must therefore apply the capital loss limitation rules of §§ 1211 and 1212. Under § 1211(b), capital losses are allowed to the extent of capital gains, plus (if such losses exceed such gains) the lower of (1) $3,000 or (2) the excess of such losses over such gains ($5,000 here). [Caution: Although the $500 of qualified dividends are taxed as capital gains (15%), they are not treated as capital gains for purposes of the capital loss limitation.] Thus, Taxpayer is allowed to deduct only $13,000 of the $15,000 of capital losses this year. The reaming $2,000 carries over to next year and is treated as a capital loss occurring next year. What is the character of that $2,000 capital loss carryover? In other words . . . Taxpayer had both a STCL and LTCL this year, so which should be used to pay for the $3,000 deduction from ordinary income? We must turn to § 1212(b) for the answer. Any § 1212(b)(1)(A) excess is carried into next year as a short term capital loss. Any § 1212(b)(1)(B) excess is carried into next year as a long term capital loss. Note that § 1212(b)(2) must be read in connection with § 1212(b)(1); it generates a $3,000 constructive short term capital gain for the year. Applying § 1212(b)(2) first and § 1212(b)(1) second, we see that Taxpayer's $2,000 carryover loss will be STCL.

The final issue is whether taxpayer will receive any preferential rate treatment on the above transactions. Taxpayer will receive preferential rate treatment only if Taxpayer has a "net capital gain" for the year. I.R.C. § 1(h). Taxpayer's preliminary net capital gain (ignoring the dividend) is equal to the excess of net long term capital gain over net short term capital loss. I.R.C. § 1222(11). Taxpayer's net long term capital gain is $5,000 ($10,000 LTCG minus $5,000 LTCL). I.R.C. § 1222(7). Taxpayer's net short term capital loss is $10,000 ($10,000 STCL minus $0 STCG). I.R.C. § 1222(6). Taxpayer's preliminary net capital gain, therefore, is $0, because there is no excess. As we see, none of Taxpayer's long term capital gains (*i.e.*, gain from the sale of the summer home and gain from the sale of the truck) will be entitled to preferential rate treatment. That actually makes sense because those gains were already used to allow the capital loss deductions, as discussed above. In other words, the capital losses wiped out all of the capital gains. It should be noted that even though Taxpayer's preliminary net capital gain is $0, we must now add the $500 "qualified dividend" to determine final net capital gain. I.R.C. § 1(h)(11). The $500 qualified dividend will be taxed at a maximum rate of 15%.

END

INDEX

[References are to pages.]

[References are to pages.]

[References are to pages.]

GROSS INCOME—Cont.
Language in Code
    General versus specific . . . 17
    Red flag . . . 21
Problem presented for determining . . . 73

I

INCLUSION PROVISIONS
Generally . . . 4
Defined . . . 109

INCOME
Basis concept (See BASIS)
Gross income (See GROSS INCOME)
Shifting (See SHIFTING OF INCOME)
Unearned income defined . . . 111

INHERITANCE
Date of death basis
    Generally . . . 49
    Problem presented for determining . . . 81
Exclusion from income, problem for determining . . . 74
Insurance proceeds, problem presented for determining taxation of . . . 79
Research, materials for . . . 71

INTERNAL REVENUE CODE (GENERALLY)
Generally . . . 1
Basic tax concepts underlying (See BASIC TAX CONCEPTS)
Economic motivation underlying (See BASIC TAX CONCEPTS)
History of . . . 1
Language in (See LANGUAGE)
Mathematical functions and terminology (See MATHEMATICAL FUNCTIONS)
Mechanics of (See OPERATION OF CODE)
1986, of . . . 109
Operation of (See OPERATION OF CODE)
Organization of (See ORGANIZATION OF CODE)
Structure of (See ORGANIZATION OF CODE)
Vocabulary (See WORDS AND PHRASES)

INTERNAL REVENUE SERVICE (IRS)
Acquiescence to Tax Court opinions . . . 64
Code of (See INTERNAL REVENUE CODE (GENERALLY))
Cumulative Bulletin (See CUMULATIVE BULLETIN)
Delegation orders . . . 65
Determination letters . . . 65
Information letters . . . 65
Nonacquiescence to Tax Court opinions . . . 64
Private Letter Rulings (See PRIVATE LETTER RULINGS)
Publications of
    Generally . . . 65
    Acquiescence/nonacquiescence to Tax Court decisions . . 64
    Cumulative Bulletin (See CUMULATIVE BULLETIN)
    Delegation orders . . . 65
    Determination letters . . . 65
    Information letters . . . 65
    Private Letter Rulings (See PRIVATE LETTER RULINGS)
    Revenue Procedures
        Generally . . . 65
        Defined . . . 111
    Technical advice memoranda . . . 65
Revenue Procedures
    Generally . . . 65
    Defined . . . 111
Tax Court decisions, response to . . . 64
Technical advice memoranda . . . 65

J

JURISDICTION
Generally . . . 57
Appellate Courts, of . . . 59
Trial Courts, of . . . 57

K

"KIDDIE TAX"
Defined . . . 109

L

LANGUAGE
Generally . . . 17; 22
"But does not include" . . . 23
Conjunctives versus disjunctives . . . 18
"Considered" . . . 23
Deductions "allowed" versus "allowable" . . . 24
General versus specific . . . 17
Mandatory versus elective . . . 22
Mathematical functions, indicating (See MATHEMATICAL FUNCTIONS)
Red flag phrase . . . 21
Terminology (See WORDS AND PHRASES)
"Treated as" or "Considered" . . . 23

LAW, SOURCES OF (See SOURCES OF TAX LAW)

LEXIS
Generally . . . 68

LIFE INSURANCE
Problem presented for determining taxation of proceeds . . . 79

LOSSES (See GAINS AND LOSSES)

M

MAINTENANCE PAYMENTS (See ALIMONY)

MATHEMATICAL FUNCTIONS
Generally . . . 11
Addition . . . 11
"Amount which bears the same ratio to...as...bears to ..." . . . 13
Comparative function . . . 15
Lesser/greater function . . . 15
Multiplication . . . 13
Ratios . . . 13
Subtraction . . . 12
"The Excess of...Over" . . . 12
"The Sum of...Plus" . . . 11

MECHANICS OF CODE OPERATION (See OPERATION OF CODE)

N

NONRECOGNITION OF GAIN OR LOSS
Generally . . . 51
Defined . . . 110
Exclusion of gain distinguished . . . 51
Problem presented relating to . . . 90

O

OPERATION OF CODE
Branch block method for following code sections . . . 25

[References are to pages.]